Lecture Notes in Computer Science 2042

Edited by G. Goos, J. Hartmanis, and J. van Leeuwen

Springer
Berlin
Heidelberg
New York
Barcelona
Hong Kong
London
Milan
Paris
Singapore
Tokyo

Kung-Kiu Lau (Ed.)

Logic Based
Program Synthesis
and Transformation

10th International Workshop, LOPSTR 2000
London, UK, July 24-28, 2000
Selected Papers

 Springer

Series Editors

Gerhard Goos, Karlsruhe University, Germany
Juris Hartmanis, Cornell University, NY, USA
Jan van Leeuwen, Utrecht University, The Netherlands

Volume Editor

Kung-Kiu Lau
University of Manchester
Department of Computer Science
Manchester M13 9PL, United Kingdom
E-mail: kung-kiu@cs.man.ac.uk

Cataloging-in-Publication Data applied for

Die Deutsche Bibliothek - CIP-Einheitsaufnahme

Logic based program synthesis and transformation : 10th international
workshop ; selected papers / LOPSTR 2000, London, UK, July 24 - 28,
2000. Kung-Kiu Lau (ed.). - Berlin ; Heidelberg ; New York ; Barcelona ;
Hong Kong ; London ; Milan ; Paris ; Singapore ; Tokyo : Springer, 2001
(Lecture notes in computer science ; Vol. 2042)
  ISBN 3-540-42127-0

CR Subject Classification (1998): F3.1, D.1.1, D.1.6, I.2.2, F.4.1

ISSN 0302-9743
ISBN 3-540-42127-0 Springer-Verlag Berlin Heidelberg New York

Springer-Verlag Berlin Heidelberg New York
a member of BertelsmannSpringer Science+Business Media GmbH

http://www.springer.de

© Springer-Verlag Berlin Heidelberg 2001
Printed in Germany

Typesetting: Camera-ready by author, data conversion by DA-TeX Gerd Blumenstein
Printed on acid-free paper   SPIN 10782531   06/3142   5 4 3 2 1 0

Preface

This volume contains selected papers of LOPSTR 2000, the Tenth International Workshop on Logic-based Program Synthesis and Transformation.[1] In a departure from previous years, LOPSTR 2000 constituted the Program Development stream at CL 2000, the First International Conference on Computational Logic, held at Imperial College, London, on 24-28 July 2000.

This meant that the LOPSTR 2000 Program Committee was also the CL 2000 Program Committee for Program Development, and as such had the responsibility for all Program Development submissions to CL 2000, in addition to the usual LOPSTR abstracts. As a result, there were 18 talks at the workshop, with four papers appearing in the proceedings of CL 2000,[2] and 14 abstracts in the LOPSTR 2000 pre-proceedings.[3] In this volume we have papers based on ten of the abstracts.

So, paradoxically, this volume is slimmer than previous LOPSTR proceedings, whilst this year's Program Committee have had to deal with more submissions and more categories than usual! My heartfelt thanks go to all the members of the Program Committee for their hard and conscientious work in reviewing and selecting the papers at various stages. I would also like to thank all the additional reviewers for their efforts and professionalism.

For organizing CL 2000, I would like to thank the conference chair Marek Sergot, the program chair John Lloyd, and the local organizers Frank Kriwaczek and Francesca Toni. Their efforts were pivotal for the success of CL 2000.

Finally, I would like to thank all the authors who submitted papers and all the workshop attendees. Your continued support is crucial to the future of LOPSTR. The next LOPSTR workshop will be held in Cyprus, with ICLP 2001 and CP 2001. It will mark the tenth anniversary of LOPSTR, so I hope to see many of you there!

March 2001   Kung-Kiu Lau

---

[1] http://www.cs.man.ac.uk/~kung-kiu/lopstr

[2] J.W. Lloyd, V. Dahl, U. Furbach, M. Kerber, K.-K. Lau, C. Palamidessi, L.M. Pereira, Y. Sagiv, P. Stuckey, editors, *Computational Logic — CL 2000, Lecture Notes in Artificial Intelligence* 1861, Springer-Verlag, 2000.

[3] K.-K. Lau, editor, *Pre-Proceedings of the Tenth International Workshop on Logic-based Program Synthesis and Transformation*, Technical Report UMCS-00-6-1, Department of Computer Science, University of Manchester, June 2000. ISSN 1361-6161. (Electronic version at: http://www.cs.man.ac.uk/cstechrep/Abstracts/UMCS-00-6-1.html.)

Program Chair

Kung-Kiu Lau   University of Manchester, UK

Program Committee

David Basin	Albert-Ludwigs-Universität Freiburg, Germany
Annalisa Bossi	Università Ca' Foscari di Venezia, Italy
Antonio Brogi	Università di Pisa, Italy
Maurice Bruynooghe	Katholieke Universiteit Leuven, Belgium
Mireille Ducassé	IRISA/INSA, France
Sandro Etalle	Universiteit Maastricht, The Netherlands
Pierre Flener	Uppsala University, Sweden
Michael Hanus	Christian-Albrechts-Universität zu Kiel, Germany
Ian Hayes	University of Queensland, Australia
Manuel Hermenegildo	Technical University of Madrid, Spain
Patricia Hill	University of Leeds, UK
Baudouin Le Charlier	University of Namur, Belgium
Michael Leuschel	University of Southampton, UK
Michael Lowry	NASA Ames Research Center, USA
Ali Mili	West Virginia University, USA
Torben Mogensen	University of Copenhagen, Denmark
Alberto Pettorossi	University of Rome Tor Vergata, Italy
Don Sannella	University of Edinburgh, UK
Doug Smith	Kestrel Institute, USA
Zoltan Somogyi	University of Melbourne, Australia

Additional Referees

Jamie Andrews	Ian Green	Germán Puebla
Alessandro Avellone	David Hemer	Olivier Ridoux
Yves Bekkers	Brahim Hnich	Dave Robertson
Francisco Bueno	Ed Kazmierczak	Sabina Rossi
Nicoletta Cocco	Zeynep Kızıltan	Salvatore Ruggieri
Robert Colvin	Elvira Pino	Judith Underwood
Mauro Ferrari	Maurizio Proietti	Germán Vidal

Table of Contents

Debugging

A Formal Framework for Synthesis and Verification of Logic Programs

Alessandro Avellone, Mauro Ferrari, and Camillo Fiorentini

Dipartimento di Scienze dell'Informazione, Università degli Studi di Milano
via Comelico 39, 20135 Milano, Italy
{avellone,ferram,fiorenti}@dsi.unimi.it

Abstract. In this paper we present a formal framework, based on the notion of *extraction calculus*, which has been applied to define procedures for extracting information from constructive proofs. Here we apply such a mechanism to give a proof-theoretic account of SLD-derivations. We show how proofs of suitable constructive systems can be used in the context of deductive synthesis of logic programs, and we state a link between constructive and deductive program synthesis.

1 Introduction

It is well known that formal proofs can be used for program synthesis and program verification, and this essentially depends on the availability of an *information extraction mechanism* allowing the capture in an *uniform way* of the implicit algorithmic content of a proof. In this paper we present a formal framework, based on the notion of *extraction calculus*, which has been devised by the authors [4,5,6,7,8] and applied to define procedures for extracting information from proofs of a great variety of logical systems.

Here we apply extraction calculi to give a proof-theoretic account of SLD-derivations. We show how proofs of suitable constructive systems can be used in the context of deductive synthesis of logic programs, and we state a link between constructive and deductive program synthesis (see [3] for a survey on the various approaches to logic program synthesis). We will consider *extended logic programs* constituted by *extended program clauses*, a generalization of usual program clauses where negated atomic formulas are allowed also in the head. Since the choice of the semantics for extended logic programs is problematic in the usual semantical paradigms of Logic Programming, we develop our approach in the setting of *specification frameworks* developed in [9,10]. The intended semantics of specification frameworks is given by *isoinitial models*, a semantics that can be fruitfully combined with a constructive proof theory (see [12] for a comprehensive discussion on isoinitial models, Abstract Data Types Specification and constructive proof-theory).

The main result of our paper concerns the extraction of extended logic programs from proofs in a natural deduction calculus. In particular we prove that the logic programs consisting of the extended program clauses occurring in a

Kung-Kiu Lau (Ed.): LOPSTR 2000, LNCS 2042, pp. 1–17, 2001.

natural deduction proof of a formula $\exists x G(x) \vee \neg \exists x G(x)$, with G atomic, allows us to correctly compute the goal $\leftarrow G(x)$ (i.e., find a term t such that G(t) holds, if such a t exists); here the notion of correctness is the one referred to specification frameworks of [9,10]. This result can be used both to define a synthesis method and to study properties of the deductive synthesis process. Finally we discuss a simple example showing in which sense our framework allows us to treat modularity.

This paper is a first step in the application of extraction calculi to logic program synthesis; we believe that our approach can be further developed and applied to open frameworks and to "disjunctive Logic Programming".

2   Extraction Calculi

In this section we provide a short presentation of our mechanism to extract information from proofs; for a complete discussion see [5,6,7,8]. Our extraction mechanism is based on an abstract definition of the notions of proof and calculus allowing us to treat extraction from Gentzen, Tableau or Hilbert style calculi.

Here we consider first-order languages $\mathcal{L}_\Sigma$ over a set of non logical symbols Σ and the set of logical symbols $\{\wedge, \vee, \rightarrow, \neg, \forall, \exists\}$. A (single-conclusion) *sequent* is an expression $\Gamma \vdash A$, where A is a formula and Γ is a finite set of formulas; we simply write $\vdash A$ to denote a sequent with Γ empty. A *proof* on $\mathcal{L}_\Sigma$ is any finite object π such that:

1. the (finite) set of formulas of $\mathcal{L}_\Sigma$ occurring in π is uniquely determined and nonempty;
2. π proves a sequent $\Gamma \vdash A$, where Γ (possibly empty) is the set of *assumptions* of π, while A is the *consequence* of π.

We use the notation $\pi : \Gamma \vdash A$ to mean that $\Gamma \vdash A$ is the sequent proved by π.

In the following a great care will be devoted to bound the logical complexity (*degree*) of the formulas involved in the information extraction process from a proof. The degree $dg(A)$ of a formula is defined as follows: $dg(A) = 1$ if A is atomic, $dg(\neg A) = dg(A) + 1$; $dg(A) = \max\{dg(B), dg(C)\} + 1$ if A is $B \wedge C$, $B \vee C$ or $B \rightarrow C$; $dg(A) = dg(B) + 1$ if A is either $\exists x B(x)$ or $\forall x B(x)$. The degree $dg(\pi)$ of a proof π is the maximum among the degrees of the formulas occurring in π.

A *calculus* on $\mathcal{L}_\Sigma$ is a pair $(\mathbf{C}, [\cdot])$, where $\mathbf{C}$ is a recursive set of proofs on the language $\mathcal{L}_\Sigma$ and $[\cdot]$ is a recursive map associating with every proof of the calculus the set of its *relevant* subproofs. We require $[\cdot]$ to satisfy the following natural conditions:

1. $\pi \in [\pi]$;
2. for every $\pi' \in [\pi]$, $[\pi'] \subseteq [\pi]$;
3. for every $\pi' \in [\pi]$, $dg(\pi') \le dg(\pi)$.

We remark that any usual single conclusion inference system is a calculus according to our definition. In particular the natural deduction calculi we use in this paper meet this characterization.

Given $\Pi \subseteq \mathbf{C}$, $\mathrm{Seq}(\Pi) = \{\Gamma \vdash A \mid \pi : \Gamma \vdash A \in \Pi\}$ is the set of the *sequents proved in* Π; $\mathrm{Theo}(\Pi) = \{A \mid \ \vdash A \in \mathrm{Seq}(\Pi)\}$ is the set of *theorems proved in* Π, and $[\Pi] = \{\pi' \mid \text{ there exists } \pi \in \Pi \text{ such that } \pi' \in [\pi]\}$ is the *closure under subproofs* of Π in the calculus $\mathbf{C}$. Now, let $\mathcal{R}$ be a set of inference rules of the kind

$$\frac{\Gamma_1 \vdash A_1 \quad \ldots \quad \Gamma_n \vdash A_n}{\Delta \vdash B}\text{R}$$

(where R is the name of the rule). $\mathcal{R}$ is a set of *extraction rules for* $\mathbf{C}$ (*e-rules* for short) if there exists a function $\phi : \mathbf{N} \to \mathbf{N}$ such that, for every $R \in \mathcal{R}$:

1. R can be uniformly simulated in $\mathbf{C}$ w.r.t. ϕ. That is: for every $\pi_1,\ldots,\pi_n$ in $\mathbf{C}$ proving the premises of the rule R, there exists a proof π of the consequence of R such that $\mathrm{dg}(\pi) \leq \max\{\phi(\mathrm{dg}(\pi_1)),\ldots,\phi(\mathrm{dg}(\pi_n))\}$.
2. R is *non-increasing*. That is: the degree of every formula occurring in $\Delta \vdash B$ is bounded by the degree of a formula occurring in $\Gamma_1 \vdash A_1,\ldots,\Gamma_n \vdash A_n$.

Condition (1) says that an extraction rule must be an admissible rule for $\mathbf{C}$, and must be simulated in a uniform way (w.r.t. the degrees) in the calculus $\mathbf{C}$. This means that an extraction rule respects the deductive power of the original calculus in a uniform way. On the other hand Condition (2) says that an extraction rule can coordinate or decompose the information contained in the premises, but it must not create "new" information. Here, Condition (2) accomplishes this by imposing a bound on the degree of the consequence, but more sophisticated conditions using the subformula property or a goal oriented strategy can be used (see [5]).

Examples of e-rules for the natural deduction calculus for Intuitionistic Logic are the *cut rule* and the *substitution rule*

$$\frac{\Gamma \vdash H \quad \Gamma, H \vdash A}{\Gamma \vdash A}\text{CUT}$$

$$\frac{\Gamma \vdash A}{\theta\Gamma \vdash \theta A}\text{SUBST} \qquad \text{with } \theta \text{ a substitution}$$

In our treatment a central role is played by the e-rule SLD^+ introduced in Section 5.

Now, given a set $\mathcal{R}$ of e-rules for $\mathbf{C}$ and $\Pi \subseteq \mathbf{C}$, the *extraction calculus for* Π, denoted by $\mathbb{D}(\mathcal{R}, [\Pi])$, is defined as follows:

1. If $\Gamma \vdash A \in \mathrm{Seq}([\Pi])$, then $\tau \equiv \Gamma \vdash A$ is a proof-tree of $\mathbb{D}(\mathcal{R}, [\Pi])$.
2. If $\tau_1 : \Gamma_1 \vdash A_1,\ldots,\tau_n : \Gamma_n \vdash A_n$ are proof-trees of $\mathbb{D}(\mathcal{R}, [\Pi])$ and

$$\frac{\Gamma_1 \vdash A_1 \quad \ldots \quad \Gamma_n \vdash A_n}{\Delta \vdash B}\text{R}$$

is a rule of $\mathcal{R}$, then the proof-tree

$$\tau \equiv \frac{\tau_1 : \Gamma_1 \vdash A_1 \ \ldots \ \tau_n : \Gamma_n \vdash A_n}{\Delta \vdash B}\text{R}$$

with root $\Delta \vdash B$ belongs to $\mathbb{D}(\mathcal{R}, [\Pi])$.

The following properties follow from the definition of e-rule (see [4,8]):

Theorem 1. *Let $\mathcal{R}$ be a set of e-rules for* **C** *and let Π be a recursive subset of* **C** *with* $\mathrm{dg}(\Pi) \leq c$ *(c $\geq$ 1). Then:*

1. *There exists $h \geq 0$ (which depends on $\mathcal{R}$ and c) such that $\mathrm{dg}(\tau) \leq h$ for every $\tau \in \mathbb{D}(\mathcal{R}, [\Pi])$.*
2. *There exist a subset $\Pi' \subseteq$ **C** and $k \geq 0$ (which depends on $\mathcal{R}$ and c) such that $\mathrm{dg}(\Pi') \leq k$ and $\mathrm{Seq}(\Pi') = \mathrm{Seq}(\mathbb{D}(\mathcal{R}, [\Pi]))$.*

A set of proofs Π is *constructive* if it meets the *disjunction property* (DP):

(DP) $A \vee B \in \mathrm{Theo}(\Pi)$ implies $A \in \mathrm{Theo}(\Pi)$ or $B \in \mathrm{Theo}(\Pi)$;

and the *explicit definability property* (ED):

(ED) $\exists x A(x) \in \mathrm{Theo}(\Pi)$, implies $A(t/x) \in \mathrm{Theo}(\Pi)$ for some ground term t of the language.

Definition 1. *A calculus* **C** *is* uniformly constructive *if there exists a set of e-rules $\mathcal{R}$ for* **C** *such that, for every recursive subset Π of* **C**, $\mathrm{Theo}(\mathbb{D}(\mathcal{R}, [\Pi]))$ *is constructive.*

The properties of a uniformly constructive calculus **C** assure that, if $\pi : \vdash \exists x A(x) \in$ **C**, then we can determine a ground term t such that $A(t)$ is provable in **C** exploiting the information contained in the proof π by means of the calculus $\mathbb{D}(\mathcal{R}, [\pi])$. Moreover, such information can be searched in the calculus $\mathbb{D}(\mathcal{R}, [\pi])$ by means of an enumerative procedure only involving formulas of bounded logical complexity (by Point (1) of Theorem 1). This allows us to define procedures for extracting information from constructive proofs which are of interest in the fields of program synthesis and formal verification [1,6].

In [6,7,8] a wide family of constructive systems (involving theories formalizing Abstract Data Types) is shown to be uniformly constructive, while in [8] an example of a constructive but not uniformly constructive formal system is provided. However, the proofs of uniform constructivity of all the systems discussed in [6,8] rely on extraction rules which are not suitable to get efficient proof search in $\mathbb{D}(\mathcal{R}, [\Pi])$; in particular, all these results involve the cut rule (for a discussion on the complexity of these extraction procedures see [2]). On the other hand, in [5] it is proven that $\mathbb{D}(\mathcal{R}, [\Pi])$ can be characterized as a goal-oriented calculus for suitable proofs involving Hereditary Harrop Formulae (see [13]). In Section 5, we show that the SLD$^+$ rule is sufficient to decide the explicit definability property and the disjunction property for suitable constructive proofs only involving *program clauses* as assumptions; this immediately yields a logic program synthesis method.

3   Specification Frameworks for Logic Programs

Specification frameworks, introduced in [9,10], establish the semantical setting for logic programs. A *framework* $\mathcal{F}$ is a theory in some language $\mathcal{L}_\Sigma$ (namely, a recursively enumerable set of closed formulas of $\mathcal{L}_\Sigma$) and it must define in an unambiguous way the intended semantics of a logic program. In the tradition of Logic Programming [11], the semantics of a program P is determined by P itself; indeed, the *initial* model of P is assumed to be the intended model of P. On the other hand, if we enlarge the language of logic programs some problems arise; for instance, when we introduce negation, it is not clear what the semantics of P should be. We aim to use a generalization of program clauses (we call *extended program clauses*), where negated atomic formulas are allowed also in the head. In this case, the choice of the semantics of P is rather problematic, and even the semantics of completion does not work. To overcome these difficulties, we separate the task of defining the semantics from the task of synthesizing logic programs. Firstly we introduce a framework $\mathcal{F}$ to describe the domain of the problem, exploiting the expressiveness of first-order languages; within the framework we explicitly define the relations to be computed and the goals to be solved by means of a *specification* $\langle D_r, \mathcal{G}_r \rangle$. The link between frameworks and logic programs is settled by natural calculi. We show how the problem of compute a goal G in $\mathcal{F}$ can be reduced to the problem of finding a proof of $\exists x G(x) \vee \neg \exists x G(x)$ in the natural calculus.

In our formalization we aim to exploit the *full* first-order language, without imposing restrictions on the form of the axioms of $\mathcal{F}$; in such a general setting, initial semantics is inadequate, thus, following [9,10], we use the *isoinitial semantics*. We briefly recall some definitions. We say that $\mathfrak{I}$ is an *isoinitial* model of a theory $\mathcal{F}$ if, for every model $\mathfrak{M}$ of $\mathcal{F}$, there exists a unique *isomorphic embedding* (i.e., an homomorphism which preserves relations and their negations) of $\mathfrak{I}$ in $\mathfrak{M}$ (if we take homomorphisms, we obtain the definition of initial models). We stress that an isoinitial model of a theory $\mathcal{F}$ (if it exists) is unique up to isomorphisms, thus it can be considered the intended semantics of $\mathcal{F}$. We recall that a model is *reachable* if every element of its domain is denoted by a ground term of the language; moreover, a theory $\mathcal{F}$ is *atomically complete* if, for every atomic closed formula A of $\mathcal{L}_\Sigma$, either A or $\neg A$ is a logical consequence of $\mathcal{F}$. We can characterize theories which admit isoinitial models as follows:

Theorem 2. *If a theory $\mathcal{F}$ has at least one reachable model, then $\mathcal{F}$ admits an isoinitial model if and only if it is atomically complete.*

This yields the definition of closed framework (see [9,10]):

Definition 2. *A* closed *framework with language $\mathcal{L}_\Sigma$ is a theory $\mathcal{F}$ which satisfies the following properties:*

1. **Reachability.** *There is at least one model of $\mathcal{F}$ reachable by a subset $\mathcal{C}$ of the constant and function symbols of $\mathcal{L}_\Sigma$, called the* construction *symbols. The ground terms containing only construction symbols will be called* constructions.

2. **Freeness.** $\mathcal{F}$ *proves the* freeness axioms *[16] for the construction symbols.*
3. **Atomic completeness.** $\mathcal{F}$ *is atomically complete.*

For instance, Peano Arithmetic $\mathcal{PA}$ is a closed framework: indeed, $\mathcal{PA}$ is atomically complete, the construction symbols are the constant '0' and the unary function symbol 's', the constructions are the ground terms $0, s(0), s(s(0))\dots$. Note that $+$ and $*$ are not construction symbols, since they do not satisfy freeness axioms. Given a closed framework $\mathcal{F}$, we can build a particular isoinitial model $\mathfrak{I}$ of $\mathcal{F}$, we call it the *canonical model* of $\mathcal{F}$, in the following way:

(C1) The domain of $\mathfrak{I}$ is the set of constructions.
(C2) A function f is interpreted in $\mathfrak{I}$ as the function $f_{\mathfrak{I}}$ defined as follows: for every tuple $\underline{t}$ of constructions, the value of $f_{\mathfrak{I}}(\underline{t})$ is the construction s such that $\mathcal{F} \models f(\underline{t}) = s$.
(C3) Every relation symbol r is interpreted in $\mathfrak{I}$ as the relation $r_{\mathfrak{I}}$ such that, for every tuple $\underline{t}$ of constructions, $\underline{t}$ belongs to $r_{\mathfrak{I}}$ if and only if $\mathcal{F} \models r(\underline{t})$.

By atomic completeness, canonical models are representative of any other model as regards the validity of the ground atomic or negated ground atomic formulas; more precisely, for every relation r and every tuple $\underline{t}$, $\mathfrak{I} \models r(\underline{t})$ iff, for every model $\mathfrak{M}$ of $\mathcal{F}$, $\mathfrak{M} \models r(\underline{t})$, iff $\mathcal{F} \models r(\underline{t})$.

Within a framework, a goal is represented by a formula $\exists y\, R(t, y)$, where R is any formula of $\mathcal{L}_{\Sigma}$, to be computationally understood as "find a term s such that $R(t, s)$ is valid in the framework $\mathcal{F}$". Since goals must be handled by logic programs, we need to introduce a new binary relation symbol r which is equivalent in $\mathcal{F}$ to the formula R.

Definition 3. *A specification in a framework $\mathcal{F}$ with language $\mathcal{L}_{\Sigma}$ consists of:*

1. *A definition axiom $D_r \equiv \forall \underline{x} \forall y (r(\underline{x}, y) \leftrightarrow R(\underline{x}, y))$ where $R(\underline{x}, y)$ is a first-order formula in the language $\mathcal{L}_{\Sigma}$;*
2. *A set $\mathcal{G}_r$ of goals of the form $\exists \underline{y}\, r(\underline{t}_0, \underline{y}), \exists \underline{y}\, r(\underline{t}_1, \underline{y}), \dots$, where the $\underline{t}_k$'s are tuples of constructions.*

We can expand in a natural way the canonical model $\mathfrak{I}$ of $\mathcal{F}$ to the language $\mathcal{L}_{\Sigma \cup \{r\}}$ still preserving the semantics of the symbols in $\mathcal{L}_{\Sigma}$. However, it may happen that the expanded model $\mathfrak{I}_r$ is not even a canonical model for $\mathcal{F} \cup \{D_r\}$, since Condition ($C3$) might not hold; therefore the model $\mathfrak{I}_r$ is not representative as regards the relation r. To avoid this, we only consider axioms D_r which define decidable relations, according to the following definition.

Definition 4. *Let $\mathcal{F}$ be a closed framework and let D_r be the definition axiom $\forall \underline{x} \forall \underline{y} (r(\underline{x}, y) \leftrightarrow R(\underline{x}, y))$. We say that D_r completely defines r in $\mathcal{F}$ iff $\mathcal{F} \cup D_r$ satisfies the atomic completeness property.*

If D_r completely defines r in $\mathcal{F}$, then also $\mathcal{F} \cup D_r$ is a closed framework and the model $\mathfrak{I}_r$ which expands $\mathfrak{I}$ is actually the canonical model of $\mathcal{F} \cup D_r$. Clearly, a relation r satisfying Definition 3 may be already in $\mathcal{L}_{\Sigma}$; in this case there is no need of expanding $\mathcal{L}_{\Sigma}$ and $\mathcal{F} \cup D_r$ is trivially atomically complete.

Finally, we introduce extended logic programs. An *extended program clause* is any formula of the kind $A_1 \wedge \ldots \wedge A_n \rightarrow B$, where $n \geq 0$ and $A_1, \ldots, A_n, B$ are atomic formulas or negated atomic formulas; this generalizes the notion of Horn clause (where all formulas are positive) and of program clause (where B must be positive) explained in [11]. An *extended logic program* is a finite set of extended program clauses. As the inference rule, we use the rule SLD^+ defined in Section 5. The notion of *answer substitution* for extended logic programs is the same given for logic programs, that is: given an extended logic program P, a goal $\exists \underline{y} \; r(\underline{t}, \underline{y})$ and a substitution θ, θ is a correct answer substitution for $P \cup \{\leftarrow r(\underline{t}, \underline{y})\}$ if $\theta r(\underline{t}, \underline{y})$ is a logical consequence of P.

The link between specifications and programs is stated by the following definitions.

Definition 5. *Let $\langle D_r, \mathcal{G}_r \rangle$ be a specification in a framework $\mathcal{F}$. A program P is* totally correct *in a model $\mathfrak{M}$ of $\mathcal{F}$ w.r.t. $\langle D_r, \mathcal{G}_r \rangle$ if, for every $\exists \underline{y} \; r(\underline{t}, \underline{y}) \in \mathcal{G}_r$, it holds that:*

1. *If $\exists \underline{y} \; r(\underline{t}, \underline{y})$ is valid in $\mathfrak{M}$, then there is at least a computed answer substitution for $P \cup \{\leftarrow r(\underline{t}, \underline{y})\}$;*
2. *If σ is a computed answer substitution for $P \cup \{\leftarrow r(\underline{t}, \underline{y})\}$, then $\sigma r(\underline{t}, \underline{y})$ is valid in $\mathfrak{M}$.*

In the sequel we consider specifications which completely define new relations, thus total correctness is with respect to the canonical model of $\mathcal{F} \cup D_r$ as stated in the following definition.

Definition 6. *Let $\langle D_r, \mathcal{G}_r \rangle$ be a specification in a closed framework $\mathcal{F}$ and let D_r completely define r in $\mathcal{F}$. A program P is totally correct in $\mathcal{F} \cup D_r$ iff P is totally correct in the canonical model $\mathfrak{I}_r$ of $\mathcal{F} \cup D_r$.*

4 Natural Deduction Calculi for Program Extraction

As a basis of our synthesis process we will use the calculus $\mathcal{ND}_\mathcal{C}(\mathcal{T})$ obtained by adding to the natural calculus $\mathcal{ND}$ of Table 1 the rule $I_\mathcal{T}$ to introduce as axioms the formulas of a theory $\mathcal{T}$, and the induction rule $\text{Ind}^\mathcal{C}$ associated with a finite set $\mathcal{C}$ of constant and function symbols.

We point out that introduction/elimination rules for $\wedge, \vee, \rightarrow, \exists, \forall$ in Table 1 are the usual ones for Minimal Logic (see, e.g., [15]), while we use special rules for negation. In the rules of the caclulus we use square brackets to denote the assumptions discharged by the rule application.

Let $\mathcal{T}$ be a theory; the rule $I_\mathcal{T}$ is as follows:

$$\frac{}{A} I_\mathcal{T} \quad \text{with } A \in \mathcal{T}$$

Let us assume $\mathcal{C}$ to contain the constant and function symbols $s_1, \ldots, s_n$; the *Cover Set Induction Rule* $\text{Ind}^\mathcal{C}$ associated with $\mathcal{C}$ is the rule

Table 1. The calculus $\mathcal{ND}$

$$\frac{\begin{array}{cc}\Gamma_1 & \Gamma_2 \\ \vdots\, \pi_1 & \vdots\, \pi_2 \\ A & B\end{array}}{A \wedge B}\wedge I \qquad \frac{\begin{array}{c}\Gamma \\ \vdots\, \pi \\ A \wedge B\end{array}}{A}\wedge E_l \qquad \frac{\begin{array}{c}\Gamma \\ \vdots\, \pi \\ A \wedge B\end{array}}{B}\wedge E_r$$

$$\frac{\begin{array}{c}\Gamma \\ \vdots\, \pi \\ A\end{array}}{A \vee B}\vee I_l \qquad \frac{\begin{array}{c}\Gamma \\ \vdots\, \pi \\ B\end{array}}{A \vee B}\vee I_r \qquad \frac{\begin{array}{ccc}\Gamma_1 & \Gamma_2,[A] & \Gamma_3,[B] \\ \vdots\, \pi_1 & \vdots\, \pi_2 & \vdots\, \pi_3 \\ A \vee B & C & C\end{array}}{C}\vee E$$

$$\frac{\begin{array}{c}\Gamma,[A] \\ \vdots\, \pi \\ B\end{array}}{A \to B}\to I \qquad \frac{\begin{array}{cc}\Gamma_1 & \Gamma_2 \\ \vdots\, \pi_1 & \vdots\, \pi_2 \\ A & A \to B\end{array}}{B}\to E$$

$$\frac{\begin{array}{c}\Gamma \\ \vdots\, \pi \\ A(p)\end{array}}{\forall x\, A(x)}\forall I \quad \text{where } p \text{ does not occur free in } \Gamma \text{ *} \qquad \frac{\begin{array}{c}\Gamma \\ \vdots\, \pi \\ \forall x\, A(x)\end{array}}{A(t)}\forall E$$

$$\frac{\begin{array}{c}\Gamma \\ \vdots\, \pi \\ A(t)\end{array}}{\exists x\, A(x)}\exists I \qquad \frac{\begin{array}{cc}\Gamma_1 & \Gamma_2,[A(p)] \\ \vdots\, \pi_1 & \vdots\, \pi_2 \\ \exists x\, A(x) & B\end{array}}{B}\exists E \quad \text{where } p \text{ does not occur free in } \Gamma_2, \exists x A(x) \text{ or } B \text{ *}$$

$$\frac{\begin{array}{cc}\Gamma_1 & \Gamma_2 \\ \vdots\, \pi_1 & \vdots\, \pi_2 \\ A & \neg A\end{array}}{B}Contr \qquad \frac{\begin{array}{c}[H_1,\ldots,H_n,A] \\ \vdots\, \pi \\ B \wedge \neg B\end{array}}{H_1 \wedge \ldots \wedge H_n \to \neg A}I\neg \quad \text{with } H_1,\ldots,H_n \text{ atomic or negated formulas. } H_1, \ldots, H_n, A \text{ are the only undischarged assumptions of } \pi.$$

* p is the *proper parameter* of the rule.

$$\frac{\begin{array}{ccc}\Gamma_1,[\Delta_1] & & \Gamma_n,[\Delta_n] \\ \vdots\, \pi_1 & & \vdots\, \pi_n \\ A(t_1) & \cdots & A(t_n)\end{array}}{A(x)}\text{Ind}^{\mathcal{C}}$$

where x is any variable and, for $1 \le j \le n$:

1. If s_j is a constant symbol then Δ_j is empty and t_j coincides with s_j;
2. If s_j is a function symbol of arity k, then $\Delta_j = \{A(y_1),\ldots,A(y_k)\}$ and t_j is the term $s_j(y_1,\ldots,y_k)$.

The formulas in Δ_j are the induction hypotheses, the variables $y_1, \ldots, y_k$ are called *proper parameters* of the Cover Set Induction Rule and must not occur free in $\Gamma_1, \ldots, \Gamma_n, A(x)$; we extend to the rule Ind^C the conditions on proper parameters made in [15,17]. Finally, the induction hypothesis in the Δ_j's are discharged by the rule application.

We say that a proof π of $\mathcal{ND}_C(\mathcal{T})$ proves the sequent $\Gamma \vdash A$ ($\pi : \Gamma \vdash A$) if Γ is the set of the assumptions on which π depends and A is the end-formula of π; a formula A is *provable in* $\mathcal{ND}_C(\mathcal{T})$ if this calculus contains a proof π of the sequent $\vdash A$ (i.e., π has no undischarged assumptions). Finally, we denote with $\mathrm{depth}(\pi)$ the depth of a natural deduction proof, for a formal definition see [17].

5   Program Extraction from Deductive Proofs

In this section we show how proofs of the calculus $\mathcal{ND}_C(\mathcal{T})$ can be used in the context of deductive synthesis of logic programs (for a general discussion on logic program synthesis see [3]).

Definition 7. *Let Π be a finite set of proofs of $\mathcal{ND}_C(\mathcal{T})$. The* (extended logic) *program extracted from Π is the set $\mathcal{P}_\Pi$ of extended program clauses occurring in* $\mathrm{Theo}([\Pi])$.

Accordingly, the program $\mathcal{P}_\Pi$ extracted from Π contains all the extended program clauses H such that the sequent $\vdash H$ is proven in a subproof of some proof in Π. If Π only consists of the proof π, we say that $\mathcal{P}_\Pi$ is the program extracted from π. To study the proof theoretical properties of the program extracted from Π, we use the extraction calculus $\mathbb{D}(\{\mathrm{SLD}^+, \mathrm{SUBST}\}, [\Pi])$ ($\mathbb{D}(\Pi)$ for short), which uses the e-rule SLD^+:

$$\frac{\vdash \theta H_1 \quad \ldots \quad \vdash \theta H_n \quad \overline{\vdash H_1 \wedge \ldots \wedge H_n \to K}}{\vdash \theta K}\ \mathrm{SLD}^+$$

where $H_1 \wedge \ldots \wedge H_n \to K$ is an extended program clause and θ is an arbitrary substitution. If $H_1 \wedge \ldots \wedge H_n \to K$ is a Horn clause, we obtain the usual SLD rule of Logic Programming; thus, SLD^+ is an extension of SLD where negated formulas are treated as atoms and "negation as failure" is not considered. According to this rule, the proof of the goal θK consists in solving the goals $\theta H_1, \ldots, \theta H_n$ obtained by unifying θK with the program clause $H_1 \wedge \ldots \wedge H_n \to K$. We remark that θ is not required to be a *most general unifier*, but this does not affect our treatment because any SLD^+ proof using arbitrary substitutions is an instance of a SLD^+ proof using mgu's. For a deeper discussion about the role of the rule SLD^+ in Logic Programming we refer the reader to [14], where a similar rule is studied.

As for the extraction calculus $\mathbb{D}(\Pi)$, we stress that:

1. the axioms of $\mathbb{D}(\Pi)$ are the sequents of the form $\vdash A$ occurring in the subproofs of Π;
2. the only applied rules are SLD^+ and SUBST.

We point out that $\mathbb{D}(\Pi)$ is a "Logic Programming oriented calculus", since a proof $\tau :\ \vdash G(x)$ in $\mathbb{D}(\Pi)$ can be seen as a refutation of $\mathcal{P}_\Pi \cup \{\leftarrow G(x)\}$, where $\mathcal{P}_\Pi$ is the program extracted from Π. The remarkable point is that, to build the proof τ in $\mathbb{D}(\Pi)$, not all the information contained in the proofs Π is used, but *only* the sequents of $[\Pi]$ of the form $\vdash H$, with H an extended program clause. This means that the program extracted from the proofs in Π contains all the information needed to compute the goal; moreover, the proofs in Π also contain the information needed to guarantee the correctness of the extracted program as we show in Theorem 3 below.

Finally, we point out that, under some conditions, $\mathbb{D}(\Pi)$ is constructive. This fact has a relevant consequence in the relationship between proofs of the natural calculus $\mathcal{ND}_\mathcal{C}(T)$ and the deductive power of the extracted logic programs. Suppose there is a proof $\pi :\ \vdash \exists x G(x)$ in $\mathcal{ND}_\mathcal{C}(T)$ and let us assume that the extraction calculus $\mathbb{D}(\Pi)$ generated by the set $\Pi = \{\pi\}$ is constructive. By definition, $\vdash \exists x G(x)$ is an axiom of $\mathbb{D}(\Pi)$, hence there exists a (trivial) proof of such a sequent in $\mathbb{D}(\Pi)$. By constructivity, $\mathbb{D}(\Pi)$ must also contain a proof τ of the sequent $\vdash \theta G(x)$, for some ground substitution θ. By the above considerations, it follows that the program $\mathcal{P}$ extracted from π is able to compute the answer substitution θ (or a more general one) for the goal $\leftarrow G(x)$.

To better formalize, we introduce the notion of evaluation.

Definition 8 (Evaluation). *Given a set of proofs Π (on $\mathcal{L}_\Sigma$) and a formula A of $\mathcal{L}_\Sigma$, A is evaluated in Π (in symbols $\Pi \triangleright A$) if, for every ground substitution θ, one of the following inductive conditions holds:*

1. *θA is an atomic or a negated formula and $\vdash \theta A \in \mathrm{Seq}(\Pi)$;*
2. *$\theta A \equiv B \wedge C$ and $\Pi \triangleright B$ and $\Pi \triangleright C$;*
3. *$\theta A \equiv B \vee C$ and either $\Pi \triangleright B$ or $\Pi \triangleright C$;*
4. *$\theta A \equiv B \rightarrow C$ and, if $\Pi \triangleright B$ then $\Pi \triangleright C$;*
5. *$\theta A \equiv \forall x B(x)$ and, for every ground term t of $\mathcal{L}_\Sigma$, $\Pi \triangleright B(t)$;*
6. *$\theta A \equiv \exists x B(x)$ and $\Pi \triangleright B(t)$ for some ground term t of $\mathcal{L}_\Sigma$.*

A set Γ of formulas is evaluated in Π ($\Pi \triangleright \Gamma$) if $\Pi \triangleright A$ holds for every $A \in \Gamma$. The following fact can be proved:

Lemma 1. *Let Π be any recursive set of proofs of $\mathcal{ND}_\mathcal{C}(T)$ and let H be an extended program clause. If there exists a proof $\pi :\ \vdash H$ in the closure under substitution of $[\Pi]$, then $\mathbb{D}(\Pi) \triangleright H$.*

Proof. Let $H = A_1 \wedge \ldots \wedge A_n \rightarrow B$ be an extended program clause provable in the closure under substitution of $[\Pi]$, this implies that there exist a sequent $\vdash A_1' \wedge \ldots \wedge A_n' \rightarrow B' \in \mathrm{Seq}([\Pi])$ and a substitution θ' such that $H \equiv \theta'(A_1' \wedge \ldots \wedge A_n' \rightarrow B')$. Now, let us consider an arbitrary ground substitution θ; we must prove that, if $\mathbb{D}(\Pi) \triangleright \{\theta\theta' A_1', \ldots, \theta\theta' A_n'\}$ then $\mathbb{D}(\Pi) \triangleright \theta\theta' B'$. But $\mathbb{D}(\Pi) \triangleright \theta\theta' A_i'$ for every $i = 1, \ldots, n$ implies, by definition of evaluation, that $\mathbb{D}(\Pi)$ contains a proof $\tau_i :\ \vdash \theta\theta' A_i'$ for every $i = 1, \ldots, n$; moreover, $\mathbb{D}(\Pi)$ contains also a proof of $\vdash A'_1 \wedge \ldots \wedge A'_n \rightarrow B'$. We can apply the SLD$^+$-rule

$$
\frac{\tau_1: \ \vdash \theta\theta' A_1 \quad \ldots \quad \tau_n: \ \vdash \theta\theta' A_n \qquad \overline{\vdash A'_1 \wedge \ldots \wedge A'_n \rightarrow B'}}{\vdash \theta\theta' B'} \text{SLD}^+
$$

to get a proof of $\theta\theta' B'$ in $\mathbb{D}(\Pi)$. Since B' is atomic or negated, this implies that $\mathbb{D}(\Pi) \rhd \theta\theta' B'$.

This immediately guarantees that every formula in the extended logic program $\mathcal{P}_\Pi$ extracted from a finite set of proofs $\Pi \subseteq \mathcal{ND}_{\mathcal{C}}(\mathcal{T})$ is evaluated in $\mathbb{D}(\Pi)$.

Lemma 2. *Let Π be a recursive set of proofs of $\mathcal{ND}_{\mathcal{C}}(\mathcal{T})$ over the language $\mathcal{L}_\Sigma$ containing a finite set $\mathcal{C}$ of constant and function symbols, such that $\mathbb{D}(\Pi) \rhd \mathcal{T}$. For every $\pi : \Gamma \vdash A$ belonging to the closure under substitution of $[\Pi]$, if $\mathbb{D}(\Pi) \rhd \Gamma$ then $\mathbb{D}(\Pi) \rhd A$.*

Proof. The proof goes by induction on the depth of π. Suppose $\text{depth}(\pi) = 0$; then either π is a proof of the sequent $A \vdash A$ (i.e., we introduce an assumption A) or π proves the sequent $\vdash A$ with $A \in \mathcal{T}$. In both cases the assertion immediately follows. Now, let us suppose that the assertion holds for any proof $\pi' : \Gamma' \vdash A'$ belonging to the closure under substitution of $[\Pi]$ such that $\text{depth}(\pi') \leq h$, and let us suppose that $\text{depth}(\pi) = h + 1$. The proof goes by cases according to the last rule applied in π. We only see some representative cases.

$\rightarrow$*introduction.* In this case π has the following form:

$$
\pi : \Gamma \vdash A \equiv \quad \begin{array}{c} \Gamma, [B] \\ \vdots \, \pi_1 \\ C \\ \hline B \rightarrow C \end{array} {\rightarrow} I
$$

Let θ be any ground substitution. Since π_1 is a subproof of π, the proof $\theta\pi_1 \equiv \theta\Gamma, \theta B \vdash \theta C$ belongs to the closure under substitution of $[\Pi]$. Suppose that $\mathbb{D}(\Pi) \rhd \theta B$; by applying the induction hypothesis on $\theta\pi_1$ (in fact, $\mathbb{D}(\Pi) \rhd \theta\Gamma$), we get that $\mathbb{D}(\Pi) \rhd \theta C$.

$\forall$*-introduction.* In this case π has the following form:

$$
\pi : \Gamma \vdash A \equiv \quad \begin{array}{c} \Gamma \\ \vdots \, \pi_p \\ B(p) \\ \hline \forall x \, B(x) \end{array} \forall I
$$

Let θ be any ground substitution. Since $\theta\pi_p : \theta\Gamma \vdash \theta B(p)$ belongs to the closure under substitution of $[\Pi]$, the proof $\theta\pi_p[t/p] : \theta\Gamma \vdash \theta B(t)$ belongs to the closure under substitution of $[\Pi]$ for every ground term t of $\mathcal{L}_\Sigma$ (we recall that under the usual assumptions on proper parameters of [15,17], p does not belong to the domain of θ and $\theta\pi_p$ is a correct proof). Hence, by induction hypothesis,

$\mathrm{ID}(\Pi) \triangleright \theta B(t)$ for every ground term t of the language.

$\vee$-*elimination.* In this case π has the following form:

$$
\pi : \Gamma \vdash A \equiv \quad
\begin{array}{ccc}
\Gamma_1 & \Gamma_2, [B] & \Gamma_3, [C] \\
\vdots \pi_1 & \vdots \pi_2 & \vdots \pi_3 \\
B \vee C & A & A
\end{array}
$$
$$\frac{}{A} \vee E$$

Let θ be any ground substitution. Since $\theta\pi_1$ belongs to the closure under substitution of $[\Pi]$, by induction hypothesis either $\mathrm{ID}(\Pi) \triangleright \theta B$ or $\mathrm{ID}(\Pi) \triangleright \theta C$. Therefore we can apply the induction hypothesis either to $\theta\pi_2$ or to $\theta\pi_3$ to deduce that $\mathrm{ID}(\Pi) \triangleright \theta A$.

$\neg$-*introduction.* In this case π has the following form:

$$
\pi : \Gamma \vdash A \equiv \quad
\begin{array}{c}
[H_1, \ldots, H_n, K] \\
\vdots \pi_1 \\
B \wedge \neg B \\
\hline
H_1 \wedge \ldots \wedge H_n \to \neg K
\end{array} I\neg
$$

with $H_1, \ldots, H_n$ atomic or negated formulas. $H_1, \ldots, H_n, K$ are the only undischarged assumptions of π.

Since $H_1 \wedge \ldots \wedge H_n \to \neg K$ is an extended program clause, the assertion immediately follows from Lemma 1.

Cover Set Induction Rule. In this case $\pi : \Gamma \vdash A$ has the following form:

$$
\pi : \Gamma \vdash A \equiv \quad
\begin{array}{ccc}
\Gamma_1, [\Delta_1] & & \Gamma_n, [\Delta_n] \\
\vdots \pi_1 & & \vdots \pi_n \\
B(t_1) & \cdots & B(t_n)
\end{array}
$$
$$\frac{}{B(x)} \mathrm{Ind}^C$$

Let θ be any ground substitution; we have to prove that $\mathrm{ID}(\Pi) \triangleright \theta B(t)$, for every ground term t of $\mathcal{L}_\Sigma$. We proceed by a secondary induction on the structure of t. Let $\mathcal{C}$ consist of the symbols $s_1, \ldots, s_n$; then, either t coincides with some constant symbol s_j or t has the form $s_j(t_1, \ldots, t_k)$, where s_j is a k-ary function symbol of $\mathcal{C}$ and $t_1, \ldots, t_k$ are ground terms. In the former case, there exists a subproof $\pi_j : \Gamma_j \vdash B(t_j)$ of π such that t_j coincides with s_j. Let us consider the proof $\theta\pi_j : \theta\Gamma_j \vdash \theta B(s_j)$; by applying the main induction hypothesis to $\theta\pi_j$ (which belongs to the closure under subproofs of $[\Pi]$), we get $\mathrm{ID}(\Pi) \triangleright \theta B(s_j)$. Otherwise, let us take the subproof $\pi_j : \Gamma_j, B(x_1), \ldots, B(x_k) \vdash B(s_j(x_1, \ldots, x_k))$. The subproof $\pi'_j : \theta\Gamma_j, \theta B(t_1), \ldots, \theta B(t_k) \vdash \theta B(s_j(t_1, \ldots, t_k))$ belongs to the closure under substitution of $[\Pi]$ and, by the secondary induction hypothesis (since $t_1, \ldots, t_k$ are simpler than t), $\mathrm{ID}(\Pi) \triangleright \theta B(t_1), \ldots, \mathrm{ID}(\Pi) \triangleright \theta B(t_k)$. By the main induction hypothesis, we can conclude that $\mathrm{ID}(\Pi) \triangleright \theta B(s_j(t_1, \ldots, t_k))$.

Now we give some conditions about correctness of programs.

Theorem 3. *Let $\langle D_r, \mathcal{G}_r \rangle$ be a specification in a closed framework $\mathcal{F}$ with a finite set of construction symbols $\mathcal{C}$, where D_r completely defines r; let P be* *an extended logic program over the language $\mathcal{L}_{\Sigma \cup \{r\}}$ having $\mathcal{C}$ as constant and function symbols, such that:*

1. *There exists a proof π of the formula $\forall \underline{x}(\exists \underline{y}\ r(\underline{x}, \underline{y}) \vee \neg \exists \underline{y}\ r(\underline{x}, \underline{y}))$ in the calculus $\mathcal{ND}_{\mathcal{C}}(P)$;*
2. *P is valid in the canonical model $\mathfrak{I}_r$ of $\mathcal{F} \cup \{D_r\}$.*

Then, the extended logic program $\mathcal{P}^*$ extracted from π is totally correct in $\mathcal{F} \cup \{D_r\}$.

Proof. Let $\underline{t}$ be a tuple of ground terms of $\mathcal{L}_{\Sigma \cup \{r\}}$. Let us suppose that σ is a computed answer substitution for $\mathcal{P}^* \cup \{\leftarrow r(\underline{t}, \underline{y})\}$. We have $\mathcal{P}^* \models \sigma r(\underline{t}, \underline{y})$; moreover, by the fact that $\mathfrak{I}_r$ is a model of P, we also have that $\mathfrak{I}_r$ is a model of $\mathcal{P}^*$. We can conclude $\mathfrak{I}_r \models \sigma r(\underline{t}, \underline{y})$, and this proves the correctness of $\mathcal{P}^*$. To prove the completeness, let us suppose that $\exists \underline{y}\ r(\underline{t}, \underline{y})$ is valid in the canonical model $\mathfrak{I}_r$. We have to show that, for some tuple $\underline{s}$ of ground terms of $\mathcal{L}_{\Sigma \cup \{r\}}$, $\mathcal{P}^* \cup \{\leftarrow r(\underline{t}, \underline{s})\}$ has a SLD$^+$-refutation. This amounts to showing that $r(\underline{t}, \underline{s})$ is provable in $\mathbb{D}(\Pi)$, where $\Pi = \{\pi\}$. We know, by Lemma 1, that $\mathbb{D}(\Pi) \triangleright P$; we can apply Lemma 2 and state that $\mathbb{D}(\Pi) \triangleright \forall \underline{x}(\exists \underline{y}\ r(\underline{x}, \underline{y}) \vee \neg \exists \underline{y}\ r(\underline{x}, \underline{y}))$, which implies $\mathbb{D}(\Pi) \triangleright \exists \underline{y}\ r(\underline{t}, \underline{y}) \vee \neg \exists \underline{y}\ r(\underline{t}, \underline{y})$, thus either $\mathbb{D}(\Pi) \triangleright \exists \underline{y}\ r(\underline{t}, \underline{y})$ or $\mathbb{D}(\Pi) \triangleright \neg \exists \underline{y}\ r(\underline{t}, \underline{y})$. It follows that either $\mathbb{D}(\Pi) \triangleright r(\underline{t}, \underline{s})$ for some tuple $\underline{s}$ of ground terms of $\mathcal{L}_{\Sigma \cup \{r\}}$ or $\mathbb{D}(\Pi) \triangleright \neg \exists \underline{y}\ r(\underline{t}, \underline{y})$. On the other hand, it is not the case that $\mathbb{D}(\Pi) \triangleright \neg \exists \underline{y}\ r(\underline{t}, \underline{y})$; otherwise, it would follow that $\neg \exists \underline{y}\ r(\underline{t}, \underline{y})$ is valid in $\mathfrak{I}_r$, a contradiction. Thus, we have proven that $\mathbb{D}(\Pi) \triangleright r(\underline{t}, \underline{s})$ for some $\underline{s}$. By definition of evaluation, $\mathbb{D}(\Pi)$ contains a proof τ of $r(\underline{t}, \underline{s})$.

The above proof relies on the fact that formulas are evaluated in a constructive sense in $\mathbb{D}(\Pi)$. To get this the choice of the natural calculus $\mathcal{ND}_{\mathcal{C}}(P)$ is essential; for instance, if we take the classical calculus, then a proof π of $\forall \underline{x}(\exists \underline{y}\ r(\underline{x}, \underline{y}) \vee \neg \exists \underline{y}\ r(\underline{x}, \underline{y}))$ always exists, but in general we have no means to evaluate it in a constructive sense in $\mathbb{D}(\Pi)$. We also remark that there is a close relation between the program $\mathcal{P}^*$ extracted from the proof π and the program P; indeed, $\mathcal{P}^*$ contains the axioms of P which are relevant for the computations of the goals in $\mathcal{G}_r$, moreover it may contain other relevant clauses occurring in the proof π.

If the relation r is total (i.e., for every tuple $\underline{t}$ there is a tuple $\underline{s}$ such that $r(\underline{t}, \underline{s})$ holds), it is preferable to provide a proof of $\forall \underline{x} \exists \underline{y}\ r(\underline{x}, \underline{y})$ in order to apply the previous theorem since this makes easier the reusability of the extracted program.

6   Some Examples

Let us see some examples in the framework $\mathcal{PA}$, having, as canonical model, the standard model $\mathfrak{N}$ of Arithmetic. Suppose we have to solve a decision problem, for instance, to decide whether a number is even. We introduce a new unary relation symbol p together with the definition D_p

$$p(x) \leftrightarrow \exists y(x = y + y)$$

Clearly D_p completely defines p in $\mathcal{PA}$. The set of goals $\mathcal{G}_p$ contains the atoms of
the form $p(0), p(s(0)), p(s(s(0))), \dots$ (we recall that the constructions of $\mathcal{PA}$ are
$0, s(0), \dots$). To synthesize a program P_{even} which is totally correct in $\mathcal{PA} \cup \{D_p\}$,
we have to find an extended logic program P such that P is valid in $\mathfrak{N}$ and a
proof

$$\pi : \ \vdash \forall x (p(x) \vee \neg p(x))$$

exists in the natural calculus $\mathcal{ND}_\mathcal{C}(P)$, where $\mathcal{C} = \{0, s\}$.

We try to get the proof π by applying the Cover Set Induction Rule in-
duced by $\mathcal{C}$; to this end, we need a proof π_1 of $p(0) \vee \neg p(0)$ and a proof π_2 of
$p(s(x)) \vee \neg p(s(x))$ which depends on $p(x) \vee \neg p(x)$. Note that, since $\mathcal{C}$ is a set
of constructions for $\mathcal{PA}$, the induction schema associated with $\mathcal{C}$ is valid in the
model $\mathfrak{N}$, the intended semantics of $\mathcal{PA}$. Thus, we use the Cover Set Induction
Rule as an heuristic to single out the axioms we need to build π. Of course, one
could also strengthen the natural calculus with new rules; on the other hand one
has to revise the previous treatment to guarantee the validity of Theorem 3.

To build the proof π_1, we observe that $p(0)$ is valid in $\mathfrak{N}$. Let us take

$$(E_1) \ p(0) \qquad P := \{(E_1)\}$$

By applying the rule $\vee I_l$ to (E_1), we get a proof of $p(0) \vee \neg p(0)$ in $\mathcal{ND}_\mathcal{C}(P)$. Now
we attempt to build π_2 according to the following schema:

$$\frac{p(x) \vee \neg p(x) \quad \begin{array}{c}[p(x)]\\ \vdots \ \pi_3 \\ p(s(x)) \vee \neg p(s(x))\end{array} \quad \begin{array}{c}[\neg p(x)]\\ \vdots \ \pi_4 \\ p(s(x)) \vee \neg p(s(x))\end{array}}{p(s(x)) \vee \neg p(s(x))} \vee E$$

To complete π_3, we introduce the following axiom valid in $\mathfrak{N}$

$$(E_2) \ p(x) \to \neg p(s(x))$$

which allows us to derive, by applying $\to E$, $\neg p(s(x))$ and then, by $\vee I_r$, $p(s(x)) \vee
\neg p(s(x))$. Thus, adding (E_2) to P, the proof π_3 belongs to $\mathcal{ND}_\mathcal{C}(\mathcal{T})$. The proof
π_4 is symmetric and we have to take

$$(E_3) \ \neg p(x) \to p(s(x)) \qquad P := P \cup \{(E_3)\}$$

At this point, the proof π_1 is completely defined; in virtue of Theorem 3, the
general logic program P_{even} extracted from π is totally correct for $\mathcal{PA} \cup \{D_p\}$
and solves our decision problem; one can easily check that:

$$P_{even} = \{(E_1), (E_2), (E_3)\}$$

Suppose now we have to compute a function, for instance, the function $f(x) =
x + x$. In this case, we have to introduce a binary relation r with the definition D_r:

$$r(x, y) \leftrightarrow y = x + x$$

where D_r completely specifies r and the set $\mathcal{G}_r$ is

$$\mathcal{G}_r = \{\exists y\ r(0,y), \exists y\ r(s(0),y), \exists y\ r(s(s(0)),y), \ldots\}$$

In this case, since the function f is total, we provide a proof

$$\pi:\ \vdash \forall x \exists y\ r(x,y)$$

We build π according to the schema

$$
\cfrac{
\exists y\ (r(0,y)) \qquad\quad
\cfrac{[\exists y\ r(x,y)]}{\begin{array}{c}\vdots\ \pi_3\\ \exists y\ r(s(x),y)\end{array}}
}{\exists y\ r(x,y)}\ \mathrm{Ind}^C
$$

Let us set

$$(F_1)\ r(0,0) \qquad P := \{(F_1)\}$$

It is easy to build π_2 in $\mathcal{ND}_C(P)$. As regards π_3, we observe that the formula

$$(F_2)\ r(x,y) \rightarrow r(s(x), s(s(y)))$$

is valid in $\mathfrak{N}$. We can use (F_2) to derive $\exists y\ r(s(x),y)$ from the assumptions $\exists y\ r(x,y)$; thus, adding (F_2) to P, the proof π_3 belongs to $\mathcal{ND}_C(P)$. Since the proof π has been completed, our synthesis process can be halted and the program extracted from π coincides with P.

We could solve our synthesis process in another way. Let us enrich our specification by a new ternary relation sum with definition D_{sum}

$$sum(x_1, x_2, y) \leftrightarrow y = x_1 + x_2$$

and a goal set

$$\mathcal{G}_{sum} = \{\exists y\ sum(0,0,y), \exists y\ sum(s(0),0,y), \exists y\ sum(0,s(0),y), \ldots\}$$

To find a program for $\mathcal{G}_{sum}$, since sum is a total function, a proof

$$\pi^*:\ \vdash \forall x_1 \forall x_2 \exists y\ sum(x_1, x_2, y)$$

is needed. Suppose that π^* has already been given in some calculus $\mathcal{ND}_C(S)$ so to satisfy the hypothesis of Theorem 3; then a program for $\mathcal{G}_r$ can be easily synthesized. As a matter of fact, let us take

$$(F^*)\ sum(x,x,y) \rightarrow r(x,y) \qquad P := S \cup \{(F^*)\}$$

We can build the following proof in $\mathcal{ND}_C(P)$:

$$
\cfrac{
\cfrac{
\cfrac{\begin{array}{c}\vdots\ \pi^*\\ \forall x_1 \forall x_2 \exists y\ sum(x_1,x_2,y)\end{array}}{\exists y\ sum(x,x,y)}\ \forall E
\qquad
\cfrac{[sum(x,x,z)]\quad \cfrac{}{sum(x,x,z)\rightarrow r(x,z)}\ I_P}{\cfrac{\cfrac{r(x,z)}{\exists y\ r(x,y)}\ \exists I}{}}\ {\rightarrow}E
}{\cfrac{\exists y\ r(x,y)}{\forall x \exists y\ r(x,y)}\ \forall I}\ \exists E
}{}
$$

Since P is valid in $\mathfrak{N}$, by Theorem 3 the program $\mathcal{P}$ extracted from π is totally correct in $\mathcal{PA} \cup D_r \cup D_{sum}$. Note that $\mathcal{P}$ consists of the union of the program S^* extracted from π^* and the axiom (F^*), which is the only extended program clause extracted from the right-hand subproof. Thus, provided that we are able to compute sum, we can compute $r(x, y)$. Now, we can treat apart the task of finding a program for sum. We can proceed as above and we can show that the extended program

$$S = \left\{ \begin{array}{l} sum(0,0,0) \\ sum(x, y, z) \rightarrow sum(s(x), y, s(z)) \end{array} \right\}$$

suffices to build the proof π^* and the extracted program S^* coincides with S. This example shows how one can combine programs computing different functions and reuse them. We can go on with this process considering also the cases where the definition axiom D_r is a complex formula. In this case, to find the appropriate program, it might be necessary many steps of introductions of new relations. This leads to a sequence of of "specifications" $\mathcal{D}_0 \subseteq \mathcal{D}_1 \subseteq \dots$ and of extended logic programs $\mathcal{P}_0 \subseteq \mathcal{P}_1 \subseteq \dots$, where with each $\mathcal{D}_k$ is associated a set of goals $\mathcal{G}_k$. When conditions of Theorem 3 can be applied, this synthesis process can be halted and this provides a halting criterion (see also [10]).

References

1. M. Benini. *Verification and Analysis of Programs in a Constructive Environment.* PhD thesis, Dipartimento di Scienze dell'Informazione, Università di Milano, 1999.
2. S. Buss and G. Mints. The complexity of the disjunction and existential properties in intuitionistic logic. *Annals of Pure and Applied Logic*, 99(3):93–104, 1999.
3. Y. Deville and K. Lau. Logic program synthesis. *Journal of Logic Programming*, 19(20):321–350, 1994.
4. M. Ferrari. *Strongly Constructive Formal Systems.* PhD thesis, Dipartimento di Scienze dell'Informazione, Universitá degli Studi di Milano, Italy, 1997. Available at http://homes.dsi.unimi.it/~ferram.
5. M. Ferrari, C. Fiorentini, and P. Miglioli. Goal oriented information extraction in uniformly constructive calculi. In *Proceedings of WAIT'99: Workshop Argentino de Informática Teórica*, pages 51–63. Sociedad Argentina de Informática e Investigación Operativa, 1999.
6. M. Ferrari, C. Fiorentini, and P. Miglioli. Extracting information from intermediate T-systems. Technical Report 252-00, Dipartimento di Scienze dell'Informazione, Universitá degli Studi di Milano, Italy, 2000. Available at http://homes.dsi.unimi.it/~ferram.
7. M. Ferrari, C. Fiorentini, and P. Miglioli. Extracting information from intermediate semiconstructive HA-systems (extended abstract). *Mathematical Structures in Computer Science*, 11, 2001.
8. M. Ferrari, P. Miglioli, and M. Ornaghi. On uniformly constructive and semiconstructive formal systems. Submitted to *Annals of Pure and Applied Logic*, 1999.
9. K.-K. Lau and M. Ornaghi. On specification frameworks and deductive synthesis of logic programs. In Logic Program Synthesis and Transformation. *Proceedings of LOPSTR'94*. Springer-Verlag, 1994.

10. Kung-Kiu Lau, Mario Ornaghi, and Sten-Åke Tärnlund. The halting problem for deductive synthesis of logic programs. In P. Van Hentenryck, editor, *Logic Programming - Proceedings of the Eleventh International Conference on Logic Programming*, pages 665–683. The MIT Press, 1994.
11. J. W. Lloyd. *Foundations of Logic Programming*. Springer-Verlag, Berlin, 2nd edition, 1987.
12. P. Miglioli, U. Moscato, and M. Ornaghi. Abstract parametric classes and abstract data types defined by classical and constructive logical methods. *Journal of Symbolic Computation*, 18:41–81, 1994.
13. D. Miller, G. Nadathur, F. Pfenning, and A. Scedrov. Uniform proofs as a foundation for logic programming. *Annals of Pure and Applied Logic*, 51:125–157, 1991.
14. A. Momigliano and M. Ornaghi. Regular search spaces as a foundation of logic programming. In R. Dyckhoff, editor, *Proceedings of the 4th International Workshop on Extensions of Logic Programming*, volume 798 of *LNAI*, pages 222–254, Berlin, 1994. Springer.
15. D. Prawitz. *Natural Deduction*. Almquist and Winksell, 1965.
16. J. C. Shepherdson. Negation in logic progamming. In J. Minker, editor, *Found. of Deductive Databases and Logic Programming*, page 19. Morgan Kaufmann, San Mateo, CA, 1988.
17. A. S. Troelstra and H. Schwichtenberg. *Basic Proof Theory*, volume 43 of *Cambridge Tracts in Theoretical Computer Science*. Cambridge University Press, 1996.

Protocols between Programs and Proofs

Iman Poernomo* and John N. Crossley**

School of Computer Science and Software Engineering
Monash University, Clayton, Victoria, Australia 3168
{ihp,jnc}@csse.monash.edu.au

Abstract. In this paper we describe a new protocol that we call the *Curry-Howard protocol* between a theory and the programs extracted from it. This protocol leads to the expansion of the theory and the production of more powerful programs. The methodology we use for automatically extracting "correct" programs from proofs is a development of the well-known Curry-Howard process. Program extraction has been developed by many authors (see, for example, [9], [5] and [12]), but our presentation is ultimately aimed at a practical, usable system and has a number of novel features. These include

1. a very simple and natural mimicking of ordinary mathematical practice and likewise the use of established computer programs when we obtain programs from formal proofs, and
2. a conceptual distinction between *programs* on the one hand, and *proofs of theorems* that yield programs on the other.

An implementation of our methodology is the Fred system.[1] As an example of our protocol we describe a constructive proof of the well-known theorem that every graph of even parity can be decomposed into a list of disjoint cycles. Given such a graph as input, the extracted program produces a list of the (non-trivial) disjoint cycles as promised.

1 Introduction

In constructing new proofs, mathematicians usually use existing proofs and definitions by means of abbreviations, and also by giving names to objects (such as constants or functions) that have already been obtained or perhaps merely proved to exist. These are then incorporated into the (relatively simple) logical steps used for the next stage of the proof. In this paper we mimic this approach by re-using programs that have been guaranteed as "correct"[2] and giving names,

---

* Research partly supported by ARC grant A 49230989.

** The authors are deeply indebted to John S. Jeavons and Bolis Basit who produced the graph-theoretic proof that we use.

[1] The name Fred stands for "Frege-style dynamic [system]". Fred is written in C++ and runs under Windows 95/98/NT only because this is a readily accessible platform. See http://www.csse.monash.edu.au/fred

[2] We write "correct" because the word is open to many interpretations. In this paper the interpretation is that the program meets its specifications.

Kung-Kiu Lau (Ed.): LOPSTR 2000, LNCS 2042, pp. 18–37, 2001.

say f, to any new functions whose programs we extract from proofs of closed formulae of the form $\forall x \exists y A(x,y)$. This is done by the well-known Curry-Howard isomorphism in order to make $A(\bar{n}, f(\bar{n}))$ true, where $\bar{n}$ denotes the numeral (name) for the number n. (See e.g. [11] or [7].) These new functions are therefore also "correct" – provided, of course, that the theory is consistent. The *Curry-Howard protocol* which we introduce is a means of preserving this correctness and seamlessly integrating the functions these programs compute into the logic.

There have been a number of systems exploiting the Curry-Howard notion of formulae-as-types. In particular we mention: Hayashi's system *PX* [9], Constable's *NuPRL* [5], [6] and Coquand and Huet's system *Coq* [12]. The first of these uses a logic different from traditional logics which is not widely known; the last two use a (higher-order) hybrid system of logic and type theory. We discuss their relation to our work in our conclusion in Section 6.

Our protocol works with a logical type theory and a computational type theory. We first describe a fairly general *logical* type theory (LTT) whose types are formulae of a first-order many-sorted calculus and whose terms represent proofs. We next describe our *computational* type theory (CTT) and then the Curry-Howard protocol between elements of the LTT and elements of the CTT. The protocol involves an extraction map between terms of the LTT and programs in the CTT, and a means of representing programs of the CTT in the LTT (including new programs that have been extracted). Our methodology differs from those mentioned above (but see also our conclusion, Section 6) in the following ways. It allows us to

1. first of all, both mimic ordinary mathematical practice in the construction of new mathematics and use established computer programs when we extract programs from formal proofs;
2. use a standard (first-order) many-sorted logic, so that our proofs are easy to follow;
3. establish a conceptual distinction between programs and proofs of theorems about programs; and
4. build a *dynamic* system that is "open" in the sense that new axioms and functions may constantly be added and re-used.

Our division of the labour of proving theorems and running programs between the LTT and the CTT means that

1. when a new function is added to the system, its full implementation details (in the CTT) are usually not available to the LTT,
2. programs that have been proved (say by a separate verification system) to possess a required property may be added to the system and reasoned about in the LTT.

In order to be quite specific, we describe the protocol over ordinary intuitionistic logic (as LTT) and the Caml-light variant of ML (as CTT). However, the protocol can be used over more complex constructive deductive systems and other computational type theories. We briefly describe some examples.

We have built a software system, currently called `Fred`, for "Frege-style dynamic [system]", as an implementation of our system. At present `Fred` produces programs in *ML*. It has a LaTeX output feature, so that we can easily include proofs written in `Fred` in a document such as the present paper.

Remark 1. Of course there always remains the global question (raised at the conference by Alberto Pettorossi) of whether the proofs that we use are correct and whether the software we use preserves correctness. We are almost as vulnerable as any mathematician concerning the correctness of a proof. We say "almost" because our proofs are formalized and therefore checking the steps is a mechanical process. However the extraction process uses software that may be unreliable. We minimize the effects of this because our procedures are simple and simply syntactical. Ideally we would run the process on our own software to check it, but this is, at present, a daunting task.

Example. We demonstrate the system by means of a constructive proof that every even parity graph can be decomposed into a list of disjoint cycles and then extract a program that computes such a list of the non-trivial disjoint cycles from a given graph.

2   The Logical Type Theory and the Computational Type Theory

For definiteness, we take our logic to be a standard intuitionistic natural deduction system. However, the techniques we shall describe apply to other systems of natural deduction, including the labelled deductive systems of [8] and [17]. See Section 5 for further discussion. We work with a many-sorted, first order logic. Many higher-order concepts can be formulated quite adequately in such theories. For example we employ lists which simply comprise a new sort, *List*, with associated functions (for *append*, etc.). We are also able to simulate a limited form of quantification over predicates by using a template rule (see Section 4.1). One can go much further (as Henkin suggests in a footnote in [10]) and, using the protocol outlined here, we are able to reason about modules and structured specifications. (See our paper [8] and section 5 below).

Our reasons for using a many-sorted first order logic rather than higher types (as does, for example, Martin-Löf, [16]) include 1. the fact that we maintain a separation between the *LTT* and the *CTT* whereas others want to create a unified theory and 2. the desire to make our system very user friendly and use the fact that first order logic is familiar to many people.

A theory Th has a collection of sorts generated by a base set of sorts $\mathcal{S}_{Th}$. Its signature $\mathrm{sig}(Th)$ contains names for a set of function symbols (constructors) of the appropriate sorts and for a set of relation symbols. There is a set of Harrop axioms Ax_{Th}, built using only symbols from the signature.

Initial Rules

$$\frac{}{x : A \vdash x : A} \ (\text{Ass I})$$

$$\frac{}{\vdash () : A} \ (\text{Ax I})$$

when $A \in Ax_{Th}$

Introduction Rules

$$\frac{\vdash d : B}{\vdash \lambda x : A.d : (A \to B)} \ (\to \text{I})$$

$$\frac{\vdash d : A \quad \vdash e : B}{\vdash (d,e) : (A \wedge B)} \ (\wedge \text{ I})$$

$$\frac{\vdash d : A}{\vdash (\pi_1, d) : (A \vee B)} \ (\vee_1 \text{ I})$$

$$\frac{\vdash e : B}{\vdash (\pi_2, e) : (A \vee B)} \ (\vee_2 \text{ I})$$

$$\frac{\vdash d : A}{\vdash \lambda x : s.d : \forall x : sA} \ (\forall \text{ I})$$

$$\frac{\vdash d : A[t/x]}{\vdash (t,d) : \exists x : sA} \ (\exists \text{ I})$$

Elimination Rules

$$\frac{\vdash d : (A \to B) \quad \vdash r : A}{\vdash (dr) : B} \ (\to \text{E})$$

$$\frac{\vdash d : (A_1 \wedge A_2)}{\vdash \pi_i(d) : A_i} \ (\wedge \text{ E}_i)$$

$$\frac{\vdash d : \forall x : sA}{\vdash dt : A[t/x]} \ (\forall \text{ E})$$

$$\frac{\vdash d : \perp}{\vdash dA : A} \ (\perp \text{ E})$$

provided A is Harrop

$$\frac{\vdash d : C \quad \vdash e : C \quad \vdash f : (A \vee B)}{\vdash \mathsf{case}(x : A.d : C, y : B.e : C, f : (A \vee B)) : C} \ (\vee \text{ E})$$

$$\frac{d : \exists x : sA \quad \vdash e : C}{\vdash \mathsf{select}(z : s.y : A[z/x].e : C, d : \exists x : sA) : C} \ (\exists \text{ E})$$

Conventions: 1. The usual *eigenvariable* restrictions apply in ($\forall$ I) etc.
2. We assume that all undischarged hypotheses or assumptions are collected and listed to the left of the $\vdash$ sign although we shall usually not display them.

Fig. 1. Logical Rules and Curry-Howard terms. (We omit the types as much as possible for ease of reading.)

Remark 2. Harrop formulae are defined as follows:

1. An atomic formula or $\perp$ is a Harrop formula.
2. If A and B are Harrop, then so is $(A \wedge B)$.
3. If A is Harrop and C is any formula, then $(C \to A)$ is Harrop.
4. If A is a Harrop formula, then $\forall x A$ is Harrop.

The axioms one would normally employ in (constructive) mathematics are Harrop formulae so the restriction is a natural one. It also has a significant effect on reducing the size of our extracted programs (see, e.g. [7]).

Because we are interested in expanding theories as we prove more and more theorems, we view the proof process as the construction of a chain of inclusive *theories*: $Th_1 \subseteq Th_2 \subseteq \ldots$, where we write $Th \subseteq Th'$ when $\mathcal{S}_{Th} \subseteq \mathcal{S}_{Th'}$,

$\mathrm{sig}(Th) \subseteq \mathrm{sig}(Th')$ and $Ax_{Th} \subseteq Ax_{Th'}$. Throughout this paper, we assume that *current* is an integer and $Th_{current}$ is the theory we are using to prove theorems. We shall show how to add an axiom, relation, function or sort to the theory to form a new theory $Th_{current+1} \supseteq Th_{current}$. It is in this sense that our system is dynamic or open.

2.1   The Logical Type Theory

Our logical type theory (*LTT*) is a means of encoding proofs in the natural deduction calculus. The types are many-sorted formulae for a theory and "Curry-Howard terms" (or proof-terms) are essentially terms in a lambda calculus with dependent sum and product types that represent proofs. The rules of our *LTT* are presented in Fig. 1.

Because Curry-Howard terms are terms in a form of lambda calculus, they have *reduction rules* whose application corresponds to proof normalization. (See [7] and [1] for the full list of these reduction rules.)

Note that, unlike other systems for program extraction, terms from a theory that occur within a Curry-Howard term are not reduced by these reduction rules. So, for instance, the normalization chain

$$((\lambda x.(x + x, ())) : \forall x : Nat\ \exists y : Nat\ 2.x = y)3) : \exists y : Nat\ 2.3 = y$$
reduces to $(3 + 3, ()) : \exists y : Nat\ 2.3 = y$

but continues no further – the term $3 + 3$ is treated as a constant. The term $3 + 3$ can only be evaluated when mapped into a programming language – a computational type theory.

In general, a *LTT* is defined as follows.

Definition 1 (*LTT*). *A Logical Type Theory LTT, $\mathsf{L} = \langle L, PT, :, \triangleright \rangle$, consists of*

- *a deductive system $L = \langle Sig_L, \vdash_L \rangle$,*
- *a lambda calculus PT,*
- *a typing relation, written ":", defined between terms of PT and formulae of L, such that*

$$(there\ is\ a\ p \in PT\ such\ that\ \vdash p : A) \Leftrightarrow \vdash_L A$$

- *a normalization relation $\triangleright$, defined over terms of PT, which preserves the type, i.e.*

$$\vdash p : A\ and\ p \triangleright p' \Rightarrow \vdash p' : A.$$

Remark 3. The typing relation and the normalization relation above are assumed to be constructive.

2.2   The Computational Type Theory

To obtain our computational type theory we take any typed programming language that contains the simply typed lambda calculus as a subset (possibly interpreted into it). Any modern functional language (e.g., Scheme, *ML*, Pizza-Java) qualifies. We have chosen (the Caml-light version of) *ML* as our *CTT*.

An important property for the *CTT* for our purposes is the notion of extensional equivalence of programs, written $f \equiv_{ML} g$, which holds when two programs always evaluate to the same value.

In general, a *CTT* should satisfy the following:

Definition 2 *(CTT). A Computational Type Theory CTT,*
  $C = \langle C, :, Sig, \triangleright_C, \equiv_C \rangle$, *is such that*

- *C is a typed programming language.*
- *the typing relation for C, written " : ", is defined over the terms of C and the sorts of Sig.*
- $\triangleright_C$ *is the evaluation relation for* C.
- *the* $\equiv_C$ *relation holds between terms* a, b *of C such that* $a \triangleright_C c$ *and* $b \triangleright_C c$ *implies* $a \equiv_C b$.

We shall, in general use teletype font for actual programs, e.g. f, while the interpretation will be in normal mathematical italics.

3   Protocol between the *CTT* and the *LTT*

The idea here is that, if the Curry-Howard protocol holds between the *CTT* and the *LTT*, then we can extract correct programs from proofs.

We now describe our interpretation of the extraction of correct programs. We define a map Value from programs of the *CTT* to terms of the theory in the *LTT*. This map is used to represent the values of programs in the *LTT*. We say that a program f is an *extended realizer* of a theorem, *A*, when the value of the program Value(f) satisfies the theorem *A*. The definition of extended realizability depends on the choice of *LTT* and *CTT*. For a definition for an intuitionistic *LTT*, see [3] or [8]. The most well-known example of an extended realizer is a program f extracted from a proof of $\forall x \exists y A(x, y)$ such that $A(\bar{n}, \text{Value}(f)(\bar{n}))$ is true.

We also define a map program from terms of the theory to programs of the *CTT*. This map allows us to use functions of the theory in programs of the *CTT*. We define program so that $\text{Value}(\text{program}(c)) = c$.

Correct extraction is then defined *via* a map extract from the *LTT* to the *CTT* which, given a Curry-Howard term $p : A$ gives a program extract(p) which is an extended realizer of *A*. The definition of extract involves a type simplification map ϕ – we require that the type of extract(p) is $\phi(A)$.

The map program is used by extract because Curry-Howard terms involve functions from $Th_{current}$. So any extraction map (from Curry-Howard terms to *CTT* programs) must extend a map (such as program) from $\mathcal{F}_{Th_{current}}$ to the

$$\text{extract}(x : A) = \begin{cases} () & \text{if } \mathfrak{H}(A) \\ \mathbf{x} & \text{otherwise} \end{cases}$$

$$\text{extract}(() : A) = () \qquad \text{extract}(dA : A) = ()$$

$$\text{extract}((\lambda x : A.d) : (A \to B)) = \begin{cases} \text{extract}(d) & \text{if } \mathfrak{H}(A) \\ () & \text{if } \mathfrak{H}(B) \\ \texttt{fun x } - >\text{extract}(d) & \text{otherwise} \end{cases}$$

$$\text{extract}((a, b) : (A \wedge B)) = \begin{cases} \text{extract}(a) & \text{if } \mathfrak{H}(A) \\ & \text{and not } \mathfrak{H}(B) \\ \text{extract}(b) & \text{if } \mathfrak{H}(B) \\ & \text{and not } \mathfrak{H}(A) \\ () & \text{if } \mathfrak{H}((A \wedge B)) \\ (\text{extract}(a), \text{extract}(b)) & \text{otherwise} \end{cases}$$

$$\text{extract}((\lambda x : s.d) : \forall x : SA) = \begin{cases} () & \text{if } \mathfrak{H}(\forall x : S\ A) \\ \texttt{fun x } - >\text{extract}(d) & \text{otherwise} \end{cases}$$

$$\text{extract}((t, d) : \exists x : s\ A) = \begin{cases} \text{program}(t) & \text{if } \mathfrak{H}(A) \\ (\text{program}(t), \text{extract}(d)) & \text{otherwise} \end{cases}$$

$$\text{extract}((\pi_1, d : A_1) : (A_1 \vee A_2)) = \texttt{inl}(\text{extract}(d))$$
$$\text{extract}((\pi_2, d : A_1) : (A_1 \vee A_2)) = \texttt{inr}(\text{extract}(d))$$

$$\text{extract}(\begin{matrix} (d : (A \to B)) \\ (r : A) : B) \end{matrix}) = \begin{cases} \text{extract}(d) & \text{if } \mathfrak{H}(A) \\ () & \text{if } \mathfrak{H}(B) \\ \text{extract}(d)\text{extract}(r) & \text{otherwise} \end{cases}$$

$$\text{extract}(\pi_i(d : (A_1 \wedge A_2)) : A_i) = \begin{cases} () & \text{if } \mathfrak{H}(A_i) \\ \text{extract}(d) & \text{if } \mathfrak{H}(A_j), j \neq i \\ & \text{and not } \mathfrak{H}(A_i) \\ \pi_i(\text{extract}(d)) & \text{otherwise,} \\ & \text{where } \pi_1 \text{ is fst} \\ & \text{and } \pi_2 \text{ is snd} \end{cases}$$

$$\text{extract}((d : \forall x : s\ A(x))(r : s) : A[r/x]) = \begin{cases} () & \text{if } \mathfrak{H}(A[d/x]) \\ \text{extract}(d)r & \text{otherwise} \end{cases}$$

$$\text{extract}(\begin{matrix} \text{case}(x : A.d : C, \\ y : B.e : C, f : (A \vee B)) : C) \end{matrix}) = \begin{cases} () & \text{if } \mathfrak{H}(C) \\ (\texttt{function inl(x) } - >\text{extract}(d) \\ |\texttt{inr(y) } - >\text{extract}(e))\text{extract}(f) & \text{otherwise} \end{cases}$$

$$\text{extract}(\begin{matrix} \text{select}(z : s.y : A[z/x]. \\ e : C, d : \exists x : s.A) : C) \end{matrix}) = \begin{cases} () & \text{if } \mathfrak{H}(C) \\ (\texttt{fun x}- >\text{extract}(e))\text{extract}(d) & \text{if } \mathfrak{H}(A) \\ (\texttt{function z y}- >\text{extract}(e)) & \text{otherwise} \\ \qquad \text{extract}(d) \end{cases}$$

Fig. 2. The definition of extract except we have written $\mathfrak{H}(A)$ for "A is Harrop". The definition of ϕ for our *LTT* and *CTT* is given in Fig. 3

$$\phi(A) = () \qquad \text{if } Harrop(A)$$

$$\phi(A \wedge B) = \begin{cases} \phi(A) & \text{if } Harrop(B) \\ \phi(B) & \text{if } Harrop(A) \\ \phi(A)*\phi(\mathbf{B}) & \text{otherwise} \end{cases}$$

$$\phi(A \vee B) = (\phi(A), \phi(B)) \; \texttt{DisjointUnion}$$

$$\phi(A->B) = \begin{cases} \phi(B) & \text{if } Harrop(A) \\ \phi(A)->\phi(B) & \text{otherwise} \end{cases}$$

$$\phi(\forall x : s \; A) = s->\phi(A)$$

$$\phi(\exists x : s \; A) = \begin{cases} s & \text{if } Harrop(A) \\ s*\phi(\mathbf{A}) & \text{otherwise} \end{cases}$$

where we define

$$\texttt{type('a,'b) DisjointUnion = inl of 'a | inr of 'b ;;}$$

Fig. 3. The definition of the map ϕ for our *LTT* and *CTT* used in defining extract in Fig. 2. (H is the unit type of (). The formula $\bot$ is Harrop so comes under the first clause.)

CTT. The semantic restrictions placed on program ensure that the theorems we prove about functions are actually true of (the results of) their corresponding programs.

The details of the maps for our *LTT* and *CTT* are given in Figs 3 and 2.

The fact that extract produces extended realizers entails that Theorem 1 holds.

Theorem 1. *Given a proof* $p : \forall x : s_1 \exists y : s_2 A(x, y)$ *in the logical type theory, there is a program* extract(f) *of ML type* $s_1 -> s_2$ *in the computational type theory ML such that* $A(x : s_1, \text{Value}(\text{extract}(f))(x) : s_2)$.

The protocol between our *LTT* and *CTT* is generalized in the following way.

Definition 3. *A Curry-Howard protocol holds between the LTT and the CTT when:*

1. *Every sort in the LTT is a type name in the CTT.*
2. *The signature of the CTT is included within that of the logic of the LTT. That is to say:* $Th_{current} \subseteq Sig_C$.
3. *Each term, c, of the CTT, is represented by a term* Value(c), *of the Sig of the LTT.*

4. *There is an extraction map* extract : $LTT \to CTT$ *such that, given a proof*
   $d : A$ *then* extract(d) *is in the* CTT, *is of type* $\phi(A)$ *and is an extended
   realizer for* A.
5. *There is a map* program : $\mathrm{sig}(\mathcal{F}_{Th_{current}}) \to CTT$, *such that if f is a function of $Th_{current}$ and A is its sort, then* program(f) *is a program in the CTT
   with type A.*
6. program *can be extended to an interpretation* program* *of* $\mathrm{sig}(Th_{current})$
   such that every axiom in $Ax_{Th_{current}}$ *is satisfied.*
7. *We suppose that equality between elements of A is represented by* $=: A \times A \in$
   $\mathcal{R}_{Th_{current}}$. *Then the relations* $\equiv_C$ *and* $=$ *are preserved by the interpretations*
   program* *and* Value *in the following way*

$$c_1 \equiv_C c_2 \Leftrightarrow \vdash_L \mathsf{Value}(c_1) = \mathsf{Value}(c_2)$$
$$\mathsf{program}^*(t_1) \equiv_C \mathsf{program}^*(t_2) \Leftrightarrow \vdash_L t_1 = t_2$$

8. *The maps* $\triangleright$ *and* extract *are such that the following diagram commutes:*

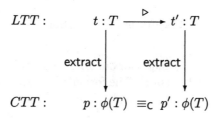

Remark 4. The diagram of *6.* simply states that, if a proof t of T can be simplified to a proof t' of T, then both proofs should yield equivalent programs (in
the sense that they give identical results).

Remark 5. It can be seen that the LTT and CTT we are working with satisfy
this protocol. For example, *6.* is satisfied because we take $\equiv_{ML}$ to be equivalence
of the normal forms of the values of the elements of A in ML.

The Curry-Howard protocol guarantees that there will always be agreement
between the theory's axioms for function terms and the CTT definitions of the
corresponding programs. Note that the CTT programs can be defined in what-
ever way we wish. The user is only required to guarantee that these programs are
correct in the sense of satisfying the Curry-Howard protocol.[3] Thus we retain a
distinction between the *extensional meaning* of functions – given by the axioms
they must satisfy, and their *intensional meaning* – how they are coded in the
computational type theory.

---

[3] This means that the final program is only going to be as correct as the programs
introduced by the user are. Of course the programs extracted from proofs are guaranteed by the existence of the proof to be correct – provided that the axioms are
consistent.

4 Enlarging the Theories

The current logical theory, $Th_{current}$, being used in a proof may be enlarged by adding new function constant symbols or new sorts or even new axioms, provided, of course, that consistency is maintained, to a new theory $Th_{current+1}$.

If, into the CTT, we introduce a new program f, say, that is known to satisfy some property P, then we add a constant f of the same sort and the property $P(f)$ to the theory, $Th_{current}$, in the LTT, yielding a new theory $Th_{current+1}$, and with the map program extended by $program(f) = f$.

For example, the function for determining the length of a list (which gives a number of sort Nat from an element of sort $List(\alpha)$)

$$length_\alpha : List(\alpha) \to Nat$$

is given by the following axioms (where concatenating the element a on the front of the list l is written $\langle a \rangle :: l$ in our LTT)

$$length_\alpha(\epsilon_\alpha) = 0$$
$$length_\alpha(\langle a \rangle :: l) = \overline{1} + length_\alpha(l)$$

These axioms define a function $length_\alpha$ that is total on $List(\alpha)$. If we added them to the current theory of the LTT, then we would have to add some function $length = program(length_\alpha)$ and guarantee that the Curry-Howard protocol is preserved. We might therefore add a corresponding program in the CTT (where concatenating the element a on the front of the list l is written a :: l in our CTT):

```
let rec length = function
                 [ ] -> 0
               | a::l -> 1+length(l)
  ;;
```

and in this way the Curry-Howard protocol would be preserved.

Note that, in larger proofs, when we are anxious to increase efficiency and reduce the size of the program, we may choose to implement the program in a manner different from that suggested by the axiomatization.

4.1 New Predicates and Functions

In ordinary mathematics, we often abbreviate a formula by a predicate. This is a useful way of encapsulating information, aids readability and helps us to identify and use common "proof patterns". In Fred, we extend our logical calculus by means of a meta-rule of predicate abbreviation for a formula F (with zero or more occurrences of the variable x) by:

$$set\ P(x) \equiv F$$

Note that we do not allow predicates over predicates.

We introduce a new function letter f of type F and the following structural meta-rule, *Template*, for any Curry-Howard term $q(x)$ where x is a Curry-Howard term of type P:

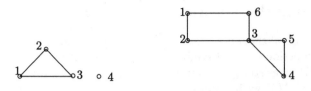

Fig. 4. Two sample graphs

$$\text{If} \qquad set\ P(x) \equiv F, \quad \text{then} \qquad \frac{f : F \quad q(x : P) : Q(P)}{q(f) : Q(F)}$$

That is, if we have formula Q that is dependent on the formula P, then we may substitute the formula F for P in Q. The converse is also a rule. Of course in doing this we must avoid all clashes of variable. *Template* is a means of abstracting a proof over a "formula variable". Defining it as a structural meta-rule is a means of avoiding higher order quantification of formula variables.[4]

Example (*cont.*). **Representing graphs in the formal system.** We consider a standard axiomatization of the theory of graphs, $\mathcal{G}$, in terms of vertices and edges. For the proof of Theorem 2 below, we assume that $Th_{current}$ contains $\mathcal{G}$. The vertices will be represented by positive integers and the graph encoded by a list of (repetition-free) lists of the neighbours of those vertices.(Of course, not all elements of the sort: lists of lists of natural numbers, correspond to graphs.)

Consider the left hand graph with four vertices in Fig. 4. This is represented by the four element list of lists of neighbours $\langle\langle 1,2,3\rangle, \langle 2,1,3\rangle, \langle 3,1,2\rangle, \langle 4\rangle\rangle$ where each element is of sort $List(Nat)$.

These properties are expressible in our formal system $\mathcal{G}$ with the aid of certain extra function symbols. Here is the list of required functions in $\mathcal{F}_{\mathcal{G}}$ and the associated axioms. (We easily arrange that each function is provably total in the formal system by introducing and sometimes using a "default value".) All formulae are considered to be universally closed. We note that appropriate CTT programs must be provided according to the Curry-Howard protocol in definition 3 in section 3.

1. For each sort α, a binary function, $member_{\alpha}$, of two arguments: a natural number n and a list of elements of sort α. The function computes the nth member of the list. The definitions for the cases $\alpha = Nat, List(Nat)$ are given in [13].
2. List successor, S. This function takes a list of natural numbers as argument, adds one to each number in the list and returns the revised list.
3. Position function: $listpos(n, l)$ gives a list of all the *positions* the number n takes in the list l. If the list l does not contain n then the empty list is returned. We take the head position as 0, so position k corresponds to the $k + 1^{st}$ member of the list.

---

[4] As in *Coq*, see [12], this could also be achieved by creating a new sort (for logical formulae), or with a universe hierarchy as in Martin-Löf [16].

4. Initial segment of a list: $initlist(k, l)$ computes the list consisting of the first $k + 1$ elements of the list l; if $k + 1 > length(l)$ then the list l is returned.
5. Tail segment of a list: $tail(l, n)$ takes a list l (of natural numbers) and a number n as arguments and computes the list obtained by deleting the first n members of l.

We now use new predicates and functions to prove our graph-theoretic result. We set a predicate $Graph(l)$ to mean that a list $l : List(List(Nat))$ represents a graph. The formula $Graph(l)$ is defined in Fred by the conjunction of four Harrop formulae (see [13]). A graph has *even parity*, which is represented by the predicate $Evenparity(l)$, if the number of vertices adjacent to each vertex is even.

We next sketch a proof that every even parity graph can be decomposed into a *list of disjoint cycles*. (More details of the proof may be found in [13] and [14].) From this proof we obtain a program that gives a list of the non-trivial disjoint cycles. The theorem to be proved is

Theorem 2.

$$H \vdash \forall l : List(List(Nat))(Evenparity(l) \& start(l) \neq 0$$
$$\rightarrow \exists m : List(List(Nat)) \, (Listcycle(m, l))$$

where l, m are lists (of lists of natural numbers) and $Listcycle(m, l)$ holds if m is a maximal list of the non-trivial disjoint cycles in the graph represented by the list l. The assumption formula H is a conjunction of Harrop formulae that describe the predicate $Listcycle$.

Remark 6. See [13] for details of the function *start* which takes as its argument a list, l, of lists of numbers and returns the head of the first list in l that has length greater than 1. If there is no list in l (with length > 1) then the default 0 is returned.

4.2 Skolemization

We have explained that new programs may be represented in the LTT by enlarging the current theory. Theorem 1 above shows that we can extract a new program that satisfies the Skolemized version of the formula from whose proof we extracted the program. So the Curry-Howard protocol is satisfied if we add a new function symbol (standing for the new program) and a new axiom (for the property satisfied by the new program) to the current theory. From the perspective of the associated Curry-Howard terms, this means that if we have a *proof*, with Curry-Howard term t, of $\forall x \exists y A(x, y)$, then (the universal closure of) $A(x, f_A(x))$ can be treated as a new *axiom*, with f_A a constant identified with a program in the CTT representing extract(t). Formally, we introduce the following structural meta-rule, *Skolemization*, to allow us to introduce new functions.

If $A(x, y)$ is a Harrop formula and t is a Curry-Howard term of type $\forall x \exists y A(x, y)$, then

$$\frac{Th_{current} \vdash t : \forall x \exists y A(x, y)}{Th_{current+1} \vdash () : \forall x A(x, f_A(x))}$$

where f_A is a new function constant, $Th_{current+1}$ is $Th_{current}$ extended by the function letter f_A and the axiom $\forall x A(x, f_A(x))$, and program is extended by setting $\mathsf{program}(f_A) = \mathsf{extract}(t)$.

The importance of the *Skolemization* rule to our system is that it makes the proof process much more like the ordinary practice of (constructive) mathematics. While it is possible to use a formula, $\forall x \exists y A(x, y)$, in a proof, it is more natural to give the y a name $f_A(x)$ by using a new function letter, f_A, and provide, either from the proof or otherwise, an associated program, $\mathsf{f} = \mathsf{program}(f_A)$ in the CTT, and then use $P(f_A(x))$ in further proofs. Notice that the sort of f_A corresponds to a higher type object in the CTT but is still a first order element in our LTT. See the end of our example in section 5 for a good illustration.

In [13] we showed how to extract a program, from a Curry-Howard term t, for finding a cycle (represented by the predicate $Cycle$) in an even parity graph (represented by the predicate $Evenparity$):

$$t : \forall x : List(List(Nat)) \, \exists y : List(Nat)(Graph(x) \wedge Evenparity(x) \rightarrow Cycle(y, x))$$

Once this has been done, we can use the *Skolemization* meta-rule to add a new function symbol $F : List(List(Nat)) \rightarrow List(Nat)$ to our current theory, together with the new (Harrop) axiom

$$() : \forall x : List(List(Nat)) \, (Evenparity(x) \rightarrow Cycle(F(x), x))$$

The Curry-Howard protocol is preserved by adding $\mathsf{program}(F) = \mathsf{extract}(t)$, the extracted program in the CTT. As will be seen, the function F is pivotal in our proof.

4.3 New Induction Rules

Adding a sort s with constructors often gives rise to a structural induction rule in the usual manner.[5] This requires introducing a new recursion operator rec and a new kind of Curry-Howard term. However, unlike other systems, we do not provide a reduction rule for this operator (apart from reducing subterms). Instead, we ensure that our extraction map, extract, maps occurrences of this operator to a recursion in the CTT so that the extraction theorem still holds. We give two examples.

A definition of the sort Nat (natural numbers) will give rise to the induction rule

$$\frac{a : A(0) \quad R : \forall x : Nat \, (A(x) \rightarrow A(s(x)))}{\mathsf{rec}(y : Nat, a, R) : \forall y : Nat \, A(y : Nat)}$$

(Induction rule generated for natural numbers)

and the program $\mathsf{extract}(\mathsf{rec}(x : Nat, a, R))$:

---

[5] Hayashi [9] has a very general rule for inductive definitions but we do not need such power for our present purposes.

```
let rec rho (y,a,R) =
begin match y with
0        ->     a
|_       -> R (y-1) (rho ((y-1),a,R))
```

Note that this applies in reverse as well. Given a form of recursion in the *CTT* (for example, in Fig. 5: rho_ChaininductionLList) we may generate a corresponding induction rule and recursion term in the *LTT*. Of course this means that we are expanding the *LTT* and therefore, in the same way as when we add any axiom or deduction rule to a logical theory, we have to be careful to ensure that consistency is preserved. The case of the recursion in Fig. 5 corresponds to an example of descending chain induction over lists:

$$\frac{A(l_0),\dots,A(l_r) \quad \forall l \,((A(g(l)) \to A(l))}{\forall l\ A(l)}$$

(Modified List Induction)

where g is some function giving a list $g(l)$ that is a "simpler" list than l, or else a base case list among $l_0,\dots,l_r$.

Example (*cont.*). The idea behind the proof of the main theorem is as follows. We start with an even parity graph l and apply the function F obtained by *Skolemization*. this yields a cycle. By deleting the edges of this cycle from L we are left with another graph, $g(l)$ that is again of even parity. We then repeat the process, starting with $g(l)$ to form $g(g(l))$, etc., until we are left with an empty graph. The list of non-trivial disjoint cycles of l is then given by $\langle F(l), F(g(l)), F(g(g(l))),\dots\rangle$. The base case for a list l occurs when the l has been obtained by deleting all the edges. Because $g(l)$ either gives a "simpler" list than l or else a base case list, we can achieve this proof by using the modified list induction mentioned above. We therefore add g to the current theory and a set of axioms describing its properties (and, as usual, the corresponding program in the *CTT*).

The *ML* program extracted is displayed in Fig. 5 where Cgrmain is a program corresponding to other lemmas in the proof of the theorem and g and F are the pre-programmed functions that satisfy the Curry-Howard protocol.

We present some practical results. Here is the result for the graph with four vertices in Fig. 4 (section 4) returned as a list of lists (llist). (The graph has one non-trivial and one trivial cycle.)

```
#main [[1;2;3];[2;1;3];[3;1;2];[4]];;
- :  int list list  = [[1;3;2;1]]
```

Next we consider the even parity graph on the right in Fig. 4 (Section 4) with vertices $1,\dots,6$ and extract the list of non-trivial disjoint cycles in it.

```
#main [[1;2;6];[2;1;3];[3;2;4;5;6];[4;3;5];[5;4;3];[6;1;3]];;
- :  int list list = [[1;6;3;2;1];[3;5;4;3]]
```

and return values of imperative programs. The underlying calculus is similar to Hoare Logic, but with a constructive, natural deduction presentation. We develop new Curry-Howard terms for representing proofs in this calculus: these terms extend those given here in order to deal with rules that are specific to reasoning about imperative programs. Again, the normalization relation is defined so as to preserve the protocol. We then define an extract map from the *LTT* to an imperative *CTT*, which preserves the protocol, and allows us to extract imperative programs from proofs of specifications.

The *LTT/CTT* demarcation is particularly natural in this context. The *CTT* (like most imperative languages, such as C++ or Java) obeys a particular (call-by-value) evaluation strategy. On the other hand, it is most natural for the *LTT* to be indifferent to the order in which Curry-Howard terms are normalized. This is because we chose an *LTT* with a familiar underlying logic where simplifications of logical proofs can be carried out independent of order.

In contrast, a unified approach to representing imperative programs, and reasoning about programs, with a single type theory representing both proofs and programs, would require that the call-by-value evaluation strategy be imposed on logical proofs as well as programs. This would require an underlying logic with which most users would be unfamiliar. Such a naïve approach to adapting Curry-Howard methods to imperative program synthesis would not be simple to devise, and would be difficult to use. Thus the Curry-Howard protocol appears to be necessary in order to define a simple approach to adapting Curry-Howard methods to imperative program synthesis.

6   Related Work and Conclusions

The advantages of the Curry-Howard protocol are practical. We have chosen to use a *LTT* based on a first-order, many-sorted logic, because this is an easy type of deductive system to use. Additionally, adopting a loose coupling between terms and sorts of the *LTT* and programs and types of the *CTT* promotes a natural conceptual distinction: the logic is used for reasoning about programs, while the *CTT* is used for representing programs.

In some cases the protocol, or something like it, appears to be necessary in order to be able to define a simple Curry-Howard style extraction mechanism for more complicated logical systems. For example, without the protocol, Curry-Howard style synthesis would be difficult to achieve over the proof system for reasoning about algebraic specifications.

Martin-Löf [16] makes the point that his type theory is *open* in the sense that new terms and new types may be added (*via* a computational definition) at any point in time. Because logic and computational types have the same status, any axioms concerning a new term or elements of a new type have to be proved from such a computational definition. On the other hand, the introduction of a new function symbol or sort is accompanied by a set of axioms that are *taken as* true (just as in ordinary mathematics). Our Curry-Howard protocol demands that a suitable new function or type has been correspondingly introduced in the *CTT* so that our extraction theorem still holds. While it is true that Martin-Löf's and Constable's systems can re-use programs, those programs have to be encoded into the standard syntax. With ours they remain in the *CTT* and do not need rewriting.

In the area of type theory, Zhaohui Luo's *Extended Calculus of Constructions* (*ECC*, [15]) is similar in motivation to our framework. The *ECC* provides a predicative universe *Prop* to represent logical propositions and a Martin-Löf-style impredicative universe hierarchy to represent programs. As in Martin-Löf, the impredicative universes are open, so the same comparison holds. Like our system, the *ECC* has a similar division of labour between proving properties of programs (in *Prop*) and creating new programs and types (in the universe hierarchy). The *ECC* was designed to provide a unified framework for the two (recognised) separate tasks of logical reasoning and program development but not with program synthesis in mind. This means that in the *ECC* there is no notion of a simplifying extraction map between terms that represent proofs and program terms – they are identified. Consequently it would not make sense to add to it a rule such as our *Skolemization*.

We have presented the Curry-Howard protocol in an informal metalogic. Anderson [2] used the Edinburgh Logical Framework to provide a similar relationship between proofs in a logical type theory and programs in a computational type theory. That work was primarily concerned with defining that relationship so as to obtain optimized programs. However, representations of optimized programs are not added to the logical type theory. Our metalogical results might benefit from a similar formal representation.

Constable's *NuPRL* system [6] contains an untyped lambda calculus for program definitions. Untyped lambda programs may then be reasoned about at the type level. (One of the main purposes of *NuPRL* is to do verification proofs of programs in this manner). In [4], it was shown how to use *NuPRL*'s set type to view such verifications as a kind of program extraction. Similarly, Coquand and Huet's *Coq* [12] is able to define *ML* programs directly and prove properties of them. However, it seems that little work has been done on the possibility of integrating this type of verification with program extraction along the lines we have described: rather, they are treated as separate applications of the system.

There are several extensions that could be made to our system and its implementation `Fred`:

- Currently, `Fred` is a purely interactive theorem prover. However the underlying logic is very standard, so it should be easy to integrate a theorem prover for many-sorted logic automatic as a front-end to `Fred`.
- Clearly it is better to have more structure in the theory being used by the *LTT*. As it gets larger, it might contain many different sorts, functions and axioms. This paper is really a "prequel" to our paper [8], where we defined how a *LTT* could be given with respect to a set of structured algebraic specifications in the language *CASL*. The results presented there obey the protocol we have outlined here and demonstrate its utility.

When we import a program from the *CTT* as a constant in the *LTT* (with appropriate axioms), we assume that the program satisfies the axioms and that these axioms are consistent. It is up to the programmer to guarantee this. We assume that the programmer has used some means of guaranteeing this (for example by using Hoare logic or *Coq*). Both *NuPRL* and *Coq* allow for this guarantee to be constructed within the logic itself. We *could* create a theory of *CTT* programs for use in the *LTT* for the purposes of such verification but our present approach admits all sorts of different verification procedures. In particular, although we have not dealt with the issue here, we are able to use certain *classically* proved results.[6]

However, with the rise of component-based software development and the acceptance of many different verification/synthesis methodologies, it seems that, in the future, any component-based synthesis/development will be done in a situation where the prover does *not* have access to source code enabling his/her own verification and will have to rely on the supplier for a guarantee. In this case interoperability will demand that this is (or can be) expressed in a standard logical language. Viewed in this light, methodologies such as the one we have outlined may be a sensible and practical means of integrating Curry-Howard-style program synthesis with other techniques.

References

1. David Albrecht and John N. Crossley. Program extraction, simplified proof-terms and realizability. Technical Report 96/275, Department of Computer Science, Monash University, 1996.
2. Penny Anderson. *Program Derivation by Proof Transformation*. PhD thesis, Carnegie Mellon University, 1993.
3. Ulrich Berger and Helmut Schwichtenberg, Program development by Proof Transformation. Pp. 1–45 in *Proceedings of the NATO Advanced Study Institute on Proof and Computation*, Marktoberdorf, Germany, 1993, published in cooperation with the NATO Scientific Affairs Division.
4. James L. Caldwell. Moving Proofs-As-Programs into Practice. Pp. 10–17 in *Proceedings 12th IEEE International Conference Automated Software Engineering*, IEEE Computer Society, 1998.
5. Robert L. Constable. The structure of Nuprl's type theory. Pp. 123–155 in H. Schwichtenberg, editor, *Logic of computation (Marktoberdorf, 1995)*, NATO Adv. Sci. Inst. Ser. F Comput. Systems Sci., **157**, Springer, Berlin, 1997.
6. Robert L. Constable, S. F. Allen, H. M. Bromley, W. R. Cleaveland, J. F. Cremer, R. Harper, D. J. Howe, T. B. Knoblock, N. P. Panangaden, J. T. Sasaki, and S. F. Smith. *Implementing Mathematics with the Nuprl Development System*. Prentice-Hall, Englewood Cliffs, New Jersey, 1986.
7. John N. Crossley and John C. Shepherdson. Extracting programs from proofs by an extension of the Curry-Howard process. Pp. 222–288 in John N. Crossley, J. B. Remmel, R. Shore, and M. Sweedler, editors. *Logical Methods: Essays in honor of A. Nerode*. Birkhäuser, Boston, Mass., 1993.

---

[6] This includes some results requiring the law of the excluded middle.

8. John N. Crossley, Iman Poernomo and M. Wirsing. Extraction of Structured Programs from Specification Proofs. Pp. 419-437 in D. Bert, C. Choppy and P. Mosses (eds), *Recent Trends in Algebraic Development Techniques (WADT'99)*, Lecture Notes in Computer Science, **1827**, Berlin: Springer, 2000.

9. Susumu Hayashi and Hiroshi Nakano. *PX, a computational logic*. MIT Press, Cambridge, Mass., 1988.

10. Leon Henkin. Completeness in the Theory of Types. *Journal of Symbolic Logic*, **15** (1950) 81–91.

11. William A. Howard. The formulae-as-types notion of construction. Pp. 479–490 in John R. Seldin and R. J. Hindley, editors, *To H.B. Curry : essays on combinatory logic, lambda calculus, and formalism*. Academic Press, London, New York, 1980.

12. Gerard Huet, G. Kahn, and C. Paulin-Mohring. *The Coq Proof assistant Reference Manual: Version 6.1.* Coq project research report RT-0203, Inria, 1997.

13. John S. Jeavons, I. Poernomo , B. Basit and J. N. Crossley. A layered approach to extracting programs from proofs with an application in Graph Theory. Paper presented at the Seventh Asian Logic Conference, Hsi-Tou, Taiwan, June 1999. Available as T. R. 2000/55, School of Computer Science and Software Engineering, Monash University, Melbourne, Australia.

14. John S. Jeavons, I. Poernomo, J. N. Crossley and B. Basit. **Fred**: An implementation of a layered approach to extracting programs from proofs. Part I: an application in Graph Theory. *AWCL (Australian Workshop on Computational Logic)*, *Proceedings*, Canberra, Australia, February 2000, pp. 57–66.

15. Zhaohui Luo. *Computation and Reasoning: A Type Theory for Computer Science*. Oxford University Press, 1994.

16. Per Martin-Löf. *Intuitionistic Type Theory*. Bibliopolis, 1984.

17. Iman Poernomo. PhD thesis, School of Computer Science and Software Engineering, Monash University, in preparation.

A Technique for
Modular Logic Program Refinement

Robert Colvin, Ian Hayes, and Paul Strooper

Software Verification Research Centre and School of Computer Science and Electrical
Engineering
University of Queensland, Brisbane, Australia
{robert,ianh,pstroop}@csee.uq.edu.au

Abstract. A refinement calculus provides a method for transforming
specifications to executable code, maintaining the correctness of the code
with respect to its specification. In this paper we introduce modules into
a logic programming refinement calculus. Modules allow data types to
be grouped together with sets of procedures that manipulate the data
types. By placing restrictions on the way a program uses a module, we
develop a technique for refining the module so that it uses a more efficient
representation of the data type.

1 Introduction

The logic programming refinement calculus [6] provides a method for systematically deriving logic programs from formal specifications. It is based on: a *wide-
spectrum language* that can express both specifications and executable programs;
a *refinement relation* that models the notion of correct implementation; and a
collection of *refinement laws* providing the means to refine specifications to code
in a stepwise fashion.

The wide-spectrum language includes assumptions and general predicates
(specification constructs), as well as a subset that corresponds to Horn clauses
(code). The refinement relation is defined so that an implementation must produce the same set of solutions as the specification it refines, but it need do so
only when the assumptions hold. There are refinement laws for manipulating
assumptions and predicates, and for introducing code constructs.

Data refinement [12] is the process of changing the representation of a type in
a program. This may be done to replace a specification type with an implementation type, or to use a more efficient representation of the type. The original,
or *abstract*, type, is related to the new, or *concrete*, type, via a predicate called
the *coupling invariant*. In earlier work [2], a framework for performing data
refinement on logic programs on a procedure-by-procedure basis was developed.
In this paper we consider data refinement of *modules*, which are collections of
procedures that operate on an associated data type. For example, a module *Set*,
using the set data type, might include procedures to add an element to a set
and to check set membership.

Kung-Kiu Lau (Ed.): LOPSTR 2000, LNCS 2042, pp. 38–56, 2001.
© Springer-Verlag Berlin Heidelberg 2001

A program that uses the *Set* module is not directly implementable because the set data type is not supported by logic programming languages such as Prolog. We would like to be able to replace the calls to the *Set* module with calls to a module that implements the same operations, except on an implemented type, e.g., Prolog lists. To reason about such situations, we introduce a notion of module refinement, which characterises the conditions under which procedure calls to one module may be systematically replaced by the corresponding procedure calls to another.

Sect. 2 presents an overview of the wide-spectrum language, and the semantics of the logic programming refinement calculus. Sect. 3 introduces modules into the wide-spectrum language, and explains how they may be used. In Sect. 4 we describe a set of conditions that allow one module to be used in place of another, resulting in a refinement of the calling program. As an example we show how a set can be represented using a list. Sect. 5 presents the refinement of a simple calculator module, similar to one presented by Morgan [12].

2 Refinement Calculus for Logic Programs

2.1 Wide-Spectrum Language

In our wide-spectrum language we can write both specifications as well as executable programs. This has the benefit of allowing stepwise refinement within a single notational framework. A summary of the language is shown in Fig. 1.

$\langle P \rangle$ - specification	(S, T) - sequential conjunction
$\{A\}$ - assumption	$(\exists X \bullet S)$ - existential quantification
$(S \vee T)$ - disjunction	$(\forall X \bullet S)$ - universal quantification
$(S \Leftrightarrow T)$ - parallel conjunction	$pc(K)$ - procedure call

Fig. 1. Summary of wide-spectrum language

Specifications and assumptions. A specification $\langle P \rangle$, where P is a predicate, represents a set of instantiations of the free variables of the program that satisfy P. For example, the specification $\langle X = 5 \vee X = 6 \rangle$ represents the set of instantiations $\{5, 6\}$ for X. An assumption $\{A\}$, where A is a predicate, allows us to state formally what a program fragment assumes about the context in which it is used. For example, some programs may require that an integer parameter be non-zero, expressed as $\{X \neq 0\}$.

Program Operators. The disjunction of two programs $(S \vee T)$ computes the union of the results of the two programs. There are two forms of conjunction: a parallel version $(S \Leftrightarrow T)$, where S and T are evaluated independently and the intersection of their respective results is formed on completion; and a sequential form (S, T), where S is evaluated before T. In the sequential case, T may assume the context established by S.

Quantifiers. The existential quantifier $(\exists X \bullet S)$ generalises disjunction, computing the union of the results of S for all possible values of X. Similarly, the universal quantifier $(\forall X \bullet S)$ computes the intersection of the results of S for all possible values of X.

Procedures. A procedure definition has the form $pc(F) \stackrel{\wedge}{=} S$, where S is a wide-spectrum program. It defines the procedure called pc with a list of formal parameter names F and body S. A call on the procedure pc is of the form $pc(K)$, where K is a list of actual parameters.

Types and modes. To specify data types we assume that our underlying first-order predicate language contains a rich set of data type constructors, such as those provided by the Z specification notation [15]. The type of a variable can be declared either within a specification construct, e.g., if listnat is the set of all lists of natural numbers, $\langle L \in$ listnat$\rangle$; or within an assumption, e.g., $\{L \in$ listnat$\}$. The former establishes the type within a program, while the latter acts as a precondition to a program. A type assumption such as above is similar to the condition that a variable be input, i.e., have the mode "ground". This information may help in the refinement process, as well as constrain the way a calling program can use the procedure (it must ensure that the assumptions are satisfied). A more detailed examination of types in the refinement calculus for logic programs is presented in [3].

2.2 Semantics

To define the semantics of the extended language we consider the effect of a program if assumptions are ignored, and the conditions under which programs are guaranteed not to abort. We give a declarative semantics in terms of predicates that characterise sets of answers. Because the semantics deal with sets of answers, it cannot distinguish a program that returns an answer once from a program that returns the same answer multiple times, or even an infinite number of times. Hence we do not deal directly with termination in our specification language. We leave concerns such as clause ordering as a task for the actual translation of programs in the wide-spectrum language to Prolog (or any chosen logic programming language). Such translations may use already well-developed techniques for logic program transformation. A more detailed semantics for the wide-spectrum language is presented in [7]. For brevity we present a simplified version here.

   The function ef gives the effect of a program as a characteristic predicate of the results computed by the program. The effect function for the basic constructs in our language is detailed in Fig. 2(a). The function ok defines the circumstances under which a program is guaranteed not to abort. The details of ok for basic constructs are given in Fig. 2(b). To define the semantics of a procedure call $pc(K)$, we assume the existence of the procedure definition $pc(F) \stackrel{\wedge}{=} S$. We then define ok and ef by substituting actual parameters K for formal parameters F in the body S (notationally, $S\left[\frac{K}{F}\right]$).

In the following, P and A are predicates, S and T are commands, X is a variable, F is a list of formal parameter variables, K is a list of actual parameter expressions, and pc is a procedure defined as $pc(F) \stackrel{\wedge}{=} S$.

$$ef.\langle P \rangle \stackrel{\wedge}{=} P \qquad\qquad ok.\langle P \rangle \stackrel{\wedge}{=} true$$
$$ef.\{A\} \stackrel{\wedge}{=} true \qquad\qquad ok.\{A\} \stackrel{\wedge}{=} A$$
$$ef.(S \vee T) \stackrel{\wedge}{=} ef.S \vee ef.T \qquad ok.(S \vee T) \stackrel{\wedge}{=} ok.S \Leftrightarrow ok.T$$
$$ef.(S \Leftrightarrow T) \stackrel{\wedge}{=} ef.S \Leftrightarrow ef.T \qquad ok.(S \Leftrightarrow T) \stackrel{\wedge}{=} ok.S \Leftrightarrow ok.T$$
$$ef.(S,T) \stackrel{\wedge}{=} ef.S \Leftrightarrow ef.T \qquad ok.(S,T) \stackrel{\wedge}{=} ok.S \Leftrightarrow (ef.S \implies ok.T)$$
$$ef.(\exists X \bullet S) \stackrel{\wedge}{=} (\exists X \bullet ef.S) \qquad ok.(\exists X \bullet S) \stackrel{\wedge}{=} (\forall X \bullet ok.S)$$
$$ef.(\forall X \bullet S) \stackrel{\wedge}{=} (\forall X \bullet ef.S) \qquad ok.(\forall X \bullet S) \stackrel{\wedge}{=} (\forall X \bullet ok.S)$$
$$ef.pc(K) \stackrel{\wedge}{=} ef.(S\left[\tfrac{K}{F}\right]) \qquad ok.pc(K) \stackrel{\wedge}{=} ok.(S\left[\tfrac{K}{F}\right])$$

(a) The effect of program constructs

(b) Non aborting conditions of program constructs

Fig. 2. Semantics

Refinement between programs is defined by reducing the circumstances under which abortion is possible — that is, by weakening ok — while maintaining the effect in those cases where abortion is not possible. Hence refinement of program S by program T, written $S \sqsubseteq T$, is defined by

$$S \sqsubseteq T \;==\; ok.S \Rightarrow (ok.T \Leftrightarrow (ef.S \iff ef.T)) \tag{1}$$

For example, assuming X and Y are integers,

$$\{X \geqslant 0\}, \langle Y = abs(X)\rangle \sqsubseteq \langle Y = X \rangle$$

because $X \geqslant 0 \Rightarrow (true \Leftrightarrow (Y = abs(X) \iff Y = X))$.

Program equivalence ($\sqsupseteq\!\sqsubseteq$) is defined as refinement in both directions.

$$S \sqsupseteq\!\sqsubseteq T \;==\; (S \sqsubseteq T \Leftrightarrow T \sqsubseteq S)$$

Our definition of refinement does not allow the reduction of non-determinism that imperative refinement allows; in logic programming we are interested in *all* possible solutions, and hence any refinement must also return all of those solutions. The equivalent of imperative non-determinism in the logic programming context is for a specification to allow any one of a set of sets of solutions to be returned by an implementation. Our approach does not handle such non-determinism.

2.3 Refinement Laws

Using the definition of refinement and the definitions in Fig. 2, we may prove general refinement laws to allow program derivations. For example,

Law 1   **Law 2**   **Law 3**

$$\frac{S \sqsubseteq S'; (\{ok.S \Leftrightarrow ef.S\}, T \sqsubseteq T')}{S, T \sqsubseteq S', T'} \qquad \frac{A \Rightarrow B}{\{A\} \sqsubseteq \{B\}} \qquad \frac{P \iff Q}{\langle P \rangle \sqsupseteq \langle Q \rangle}$$

The hypotheses above the line must be satisfied before the transformation below the line can be employed. Law 1 is a monotonicity law; it states that if a) S refines to S', and b) T refines to T' in the context established by S, then the sequential conjunction (S, T) refines to (S', T'). Monotonicity holds for all the operators and both quantifiers in the wide-spectrum language. Law 2 demonstrates how assumptions may be weakened. Law 3 states that a specification statement $\langle P \rangle$ is equivalent to $\langle Q \rangle$ if $P \iff Q$. This corresponds to maintaining ef in the refinement relation.

The semantics for the refinement calculus have been incorporated into a prototype tool [8]. This has been used to prove laws such as the above, and to perform refinements.

2.4   Comparison to Logic Program Synthesis

In this section we make comparisons between the refinement calculus approach and logic program synthesis (a comprehensive survey of which is presented in [4]). Both are frameworks for deriving logic programs from specifications. In Sect. 6 we compare our framework for module refinement to other module-based logic program derivation frameworks.

The technique of stepwise refinement is similar to deductive synthesis [9], in which a specification is successively transformed using synthesis laws proven in an underlying framework (typically first-order logic). A significant difference between the two approaches is the specification language that they use. In the refinement calculus, formulae can be used both as assumptions and as program fragments (in specification constructs). This separation allows the refinement steps to take place with respect to a context, which may contain the types of variables or any arbitrary predicate. Lau and Ornaghi [10] describe a *conditional* specification, which may include contextual information. For instance, the specification of a procedure p with an input condition IC on parameter Y, and output condition OC on parameter X, and defining relation $R(X, Y)$, would be defined as follows.

$$IC(Y) \Rightarrow (p(X, Y) \iff R(X, Y) \Leftrightarrow OC(X))$$

This is similar to the following definition in the wide-spectrum language:

$$p(X, Y) \mathrel{\hat{=}} \{IC(Y)\}, \langle R(X, Y) \Leftrightarrow OC(X) \rangle$$

The refinement calculus approach is slightly more general, since it allows any subcomponent of a program to have an associated assumption component. The refinement calculus also allows the refinement of program fragments with respect to a context, rather than the procedure as a whole.

Another difference is that unlike many deductive synthesis schemes, the refinement calculus does not prove correctness with respect to the SLD computation rule. The final translation from a wide-spectrum program to executable logic program code is a separate exercise (cf. Deville's transformation of a logic description to code [5]). Target languages other than Prolog may be considered. For instance, Mercury [14] has sophisticated techniques for performing clause and goal ordering automatically, in order to satisfy mode and determinism constraints, and to ensure termination.

3   Modules

In this section we introduce modules in the wide-spectrum language and explain how they may be used. Our module specifications define an opaque data type, and provide the type name and procedures that operate on the data type. (In this paper we only consider modules that provide a single opaque type, however it is straightforward to generalise this to multiple types.) We focus on programs that respect the intended modes of the procedures, and only manipulate opaque type parameters via the procedures of the module. Our intention is to allow efficient implementations of modules using alternative representations of the data type.

3.1   Module Specifications

In logic programming languages such as Prolog there is no notion of a 'hidden' or 'local' state. The current value of the data type in question must always be passed as a parameter to a procedure in the module, but the actual representation of the data type in the implementation is hidden making the data type *opaque*. To allow more powerful refinement rules we split opaque parameters into two categories, *input* and *output*, which correspond with the logic programming *modes* "ground" and "var" (unbound), respectively. Upon a procedure call, opaque inputs have already been instantiated to the module type and opaque outputs must be uninstantiated.

In addition, procedures have a possibly empty set of regular parameters, which are not of the declared module type. These parameters may be used to supply information to procedures that construct opaque values, or to extract information from opaque parameters. That is, they act as the top-level interaction with the rest of the program, and are manipulated by programs that use the module. The general case of module refinement presented later treats regular inputs and outputs the same, and thus we do not distinguish between them at this level.

Fig. 3 is an example module that defines operations on a set of natural numbers, described by $\mathbb{FN}$ (the set of all finite subsets of natural numbers). For clarity, the type signature of each procedure in the module is declared. We do not include a signature for individual procedures in general, however, the signature helps to indicate the way in which modules are to be used. The type of opaque inputs and outputs are subscripted with i and o, respectively. In the body of each procedure, opaque inputs have an assumption about their type, that is, their intended mode is "ground". The specification of each procedure guarantees that the opaque outputs are of the opaque type. Procedures *add* and *mem* also make use of a regular parameter, E.

Module*Set*
  Type setnat == $\mathbb{FN}$
  $init(S': \textbf{setnat}_o)$
  $add(E:\mathbb{N}, S: \textbf{setnat}_i, S': \textbf{setnat}_o)$
  $mem(E:\mathbb{N}, S: \textbf{setnat}_i)$

  $init(S') \stackrel{\wedge}{=} \langle S' = \{\}\rangle$
  $add(E, S, S') \stackrel{\wedge}{=} \{S \in \textbf{setnat} \Leftrightarrow E \in \mathbb{N} \Leftrightarrow E \notin S\}, \langle S' = S \cup \{E\}\rangle$
  $mem(E, S) \stackrel{\wedge}{=} \{S \in \textbf{setnat}\}, \langle E \in S\rangle$
End

Fig. 3. Abstract set module

Aside: One could abbreviate the specifications in Fig. 3 by omitting the explicit assumptions about the types of the opaque inputs and using the convention that an opaque input implicitly has its type assumption associated with it. For example, *add* would be abbreviated to $\{E \in \mathbb{N} \Leftrightarrow E \notin S\}, \langle S' = S \cup \{E\}\rangle$. For clarity we avoid such abbreviations in this paper.

A module procedure falls into one of several categories, based on whether the procedure has an opaque input, an opaque output, or both. (The framework can be easily extended to work with multiple input, output, and regular parameters, but for simplicity of presentation we do not consider such cases in this paper.) Following the terminology of Liskov and Guttag [11], a procedure without an opaque input is referred to as an *initialisation* procedure, e.g., *init*, which instantiates S' to the empty set. A procedure without an opaque output is referred to as an *observer*. It typically provides information about the value of the opaque input, e.g., *mem* is an observer that determines whether the regular parameter E is in the opaque input set S, or instantiates E to each member of S. A procedure with both an opaque input and output is called a *constructor*. It can be likened to updating the state in an imperative module. For instance, the procedure *add* has an opaque output S', which is equal to the union of the opaque input S and the singleton set $\{E\}$, provided E is not in the input set S. In order for the assumption $E \in \mathbb{N} \Leftrightarrow E \notin S$ to hold, the actual parameter supplied for E must be ground. Note that *init* and *add* both guarantee that their opaque output is an element of **setnat**. This is required so that the type assumptions of subsequent calls using S' as an input are satisfied.

3.2   Using Modules

Our intuition is that a module is to be used in the construction and maintenance of some data structure throughout multiple procedure calls. We therefore consider programs whose procedure calls are ordered so that the intended modes of the opaque inputs and outputs are satisfied, and the variables used as opaque inputs and outputs are local to the program. For illustrative purposes, consider a program that checks whether the value of the regular (non-opaque) parameter X is either 1 or 2, using the *Set* module.

$$(\exists S \bullet init(S), (\exists S' \bullet add(1, S, S'), (\exists S'' \bullet add(2, S', S''), mem(X, S'')))) \quad (2)$$

The use of sequential conjunction reflects the notion of the changing state and also allows us to satisfy the assumptions of the later calls. Initially, S is instantiated to the empty set. The two calls to *add* update S to S' and then to S''. Overall, the only variable we are interested in is X – the opaque parameters are local because they are existentially quantified when they are used as an output.

For programs using a module, we consider only those that correspond to code, that is, they use only disjunction, sequential conjunction, existential quantification and calls to defined procedures. All actual opaque parameters used in the program must be existentially quantified (they are local to the program), while regular parameters may be either local or free. We therefore allow the following structural cases, where $\mathcal{C}$, $\mathcal{C}_1$ and $\mathcal{C}_2$ are subcomponents of the same structural form.

1. a null command, $\langle true \rangle$;
2. the disjunction of two components, $(\mathcal{C}_1 \vee \mathcal{C}_2)$;
3. the sequential conjunction of a non-module procedure call and a component, $(f, \mathcal{C})$;
4. a component existentially quantified by a regular variable, $(\exists V \bullet \mathcal{C})$; and
5. a sequential conjunction of a module procedure call and a component, with the opaque output of the procedure, if there is one, existentially quantified.
   $(\exists O \bullet p(V, I, O), \mathcal{C})$
   V, I, and O are the regular, opaque input, and opaque output parameters respectively.

Each subcomponent may contain references to opaque inputs that have been used previously as opaque outputs. These variables have been quantified at an outer level (via form 5), but not in the component itself. In the example (2), the call to *mem* has the variables S, S' and S'' in scope, although only S'' is used. We refer to the set of opaque variables, which may be used as opaque inputs, as IV. In form 5, the opaque input, I, must be a member of IV, and the subcomponent, $\mathcal{C}$, includes the opaque output, O, of p as an element of the set of the variables that it may use as opaque inputs, along with the variables inherited from IV. For instance, in (2), the program fragment $(\exists S'' \bullet add(2, S', S''), mem(X, S''))$, which is an instance of form 5, has S and S' as possible opaque inputs, while the subcomponent $mem(X, S'')$ has, in addition to these, S''.

The only procedures that may manipulate opaque-type variables are those provided by the module, although opaque parameters may be passed via intermediate procedures, provided they are not manipulated along the way. In particular, we disallow equality between opaque-type variables within the program because, for example, two abstract sets, S and S', may have the same set value, but the concrete representations of the two variables as lists, L and L', can be different lists, although they contain the same elements (in different orders). If an equality operation is required on sets, it should be provided explicitly via a module procedure, which in the concrete list implementation must check whether the two lists contain the same elements (or make use of a unique ordered list to represent the set and use equality on lists).

Related to the issue of equality, each actual opaque output parameter must be a distinct uninstantiated variable, that is, a variable may only be used as an output parameter once. This is because the use of an instantiated variable as an output encodes an equality, e.g., if S is instantiated then $p(S)$ is equivalent to $(\exists S' \bullet p(S'), \langle S' = S \rangle)$. For example, consider the following sequence of operations using the set module.

$$\exists\, S \bullet init(S), \exists S' \bullet add(1, S, S'), \exists S'' \bullet add(2, S', S''),$$
$$\exists\, T \bullet init(T), \exists T' \bullet add(2, T, T'), add(1, T', S'')$$

Note that the last parameter of the last call to add, S'', is the same as the last parameter of the second call to add. If we interpret this program as operations on sets, we expect it to succeed, but an implementation using lists may fail because, although the lists [1,2] and [2,1] have the same sets of elements, they are different lists. One could remove the restriction that outputs should be uninstantiated by insisting on a unique concrete representation of each abstract value, however, the restriction on outputs allows a wider range of implementations of modules. The restriction may always be avoided by explicit use of a set equality procedure provided by the module, e.g., the call $add(1, T', S'')$ above would be replaced by

$$(\exists T'' \bullet add(1, T', T''), equals(S'', T''))$$

assuming that the procedure $equals$ models set equality.

The structural form and the restrictions defined above are amenable to checking by purely syntactic means.

4   Module Refinement

In general, we say a module $\mathcal{A}$ is refined by a module $\mathcal{B}$ if for all possible programs p using calls to module $\mathcal{A}$, p is refined by the program p' obtained by replacing all calls to $\mathcal{A}$ by corresponding calls to $\mathcal{B}$. However, within this paper we place restrictions on the form of the program p as discussed in Sect. 3.2. The motivation for this is to allow more efficient representations of the data types to be used.

Consider the Set module defined in Fig. 3. A program that uses it, e.g., (2), is not directly implementable, since the Set module uses the abstract type **setnat**. We would like to be able to replace the calls to $init$, add, and mem from the Set module with corresponding calls on a module that implements the operations on an implementation data type, e.g., a Prolog list. Of course, replacing the

Module Set^+
   Type listnat $== \{L\!: list | \text{ran } L \in \mathbb{FN}\}$
   $init^+(L'\!: \text{listnat}_o)$
   $add^+(E\!: \mathbb{N}, L\!: \text{listnat}_i, L'\!: \text{listnat}_o)$
   $mem^+(E\!: \mathbb{N}, L\!: \text{listnat}_i)$

   $init^+(L') \overset{\wedge}{=} \langle L' = [\,] \rangle$
   $add^+(E, L, L') \overset{\wedge}{=} \{L \in \text{listnat} \Leftrightarrow E \in \mathbb{N} \Leftrightarrow E \notin \text{ran } L\}, \langle L' = [E|L] \rangle$
   $mem^+(E, L) \overset{\wedge}{=} \{L \in \text{listnat}\}, \langle E \in \text{ran } L \rangle$
End

Fig. 4. Concrete set module

references to the *Set* module with references to the list module must result in a refinement of the program in question. We refer to the module with an abstract type as the abstract module, and the implementation module as the concrete module.

Following the imperative refinement calculus, we use a *coupling invariant* to relate the abstract and concrete types (cf. [12,2]). However, for our modules the coupling invariant is used to relate the opaque parameters, rather than the single occurrence of the local state of Morgan-style modules [12]. In the *Set* example we may represent the set opaque type by a list. If S is a set and L is a list, a suitable coupling invariant is $S = \text{ran } L \Leftrightarrow L \in \text{listnat}$, where 'ran ' returns the set of elements in a list and listnat is the type representing a list of natural numbers. Fig. 4 gives an implementation of the set module using the type listnat. We use the convention that the names of concrete modules, procedures and variables are superscripted with '+'.

In general, procedures of an implementation module are not refinements (as defined by (1)) of the corresponding abstract procedures. Rather they are *data refinements*. For example, although module Set^+ is intuitively an implementation of Set given the chosen coupling invariant, it is not the case that $add(E, S, S')$ refines to $add^+(E, L, L')$. Even assuming the corresponding opaque inputs and outputs are related via the coupling invariant, applying the definition of refinement to $add(E, S, S') \sqsubseteq add^+(E, L, L')$ requires the following to hold:

$$(S = \text{ran } L \Leftrightarrow L \in \text{listnat} \Leftrightarrow S' = \text{ran } L' \Leftrightarrow L' \in \text{listnat}) \Rightarrow$$
$$(S \in \textbf{setnat} \Leftrightarrow E \in \mathbb{N} \Leftrightarrow E \notin S) \Rightarrow$$
$$(L \in \text{listnat} \Leftrightarrow E \in \mathbb{N} \Leftrightarrow E \notin \text{ran } L) \Leftrightarrow$$
$$(S' = S \cup \{E\} \iff L' = [E|L])$$

The equivalence on the bottom line does not hold – it holds only in the '$\Leftarrow$' direction. There are many list representations for any non-empty set: any permutation of a list that contains all the elements of the set, possibly with some elements of the set appearing multiple times in the list. To establish an equivalence in the bottom line above, we would need to replace $L' = [E|L]$ by $\text{ran } L' = \{E\} \cup \text{ran } L$. This has the effect in the implementation of (trying to) generate all such list representations. However, just one representation is sufficient because we are not directly interested in the representations of intermediate lists; we are only interested in the sets they represent.

If the *Set* module is only ever used by programs that are in the form defined in Sect. 3.2, we may use the more efficient representation. To prove this in general we inductively show that all programs C that use the abstract module and respect the structural form outlined in Sect. 3.2, refine to the equivalent program C^+, which uses the concrete module. We assume that the coupling invariant holds between all corresponding pairs of abstract and concrete opaque inputs to the component. To represent this succinctly, we use the notation $CI(IV, IV^+)$, where IV (IV^+) is the set of possible abstract (concrete) opaque inputs for component C (C^+).

$$\{CI(IV, IV^+)\}, C \sqsubseteq C^+ \tag{3}$$

We use this as our inductive assumption for all subcomponents. The hypothesis is trivially established initially because all opaque-type variables are local to the components, and hence there are no opaque inputs to the components as a whole.

We now prove (3) for each of the structural cases defined in Sect. 3.2. The first case is the base case, the null command, which is trivially refined by itself. For case 2, we must show:

$$\{CI(IV, IV^+)\}, C_1 \lor C_2 \sqsubseteq C_1^+ \lor C_2^+$$

This is straightforward: using the inductive hypothesis (3) each of the abstract components is refined by its concrete counterpart, and hence (by monotonicity) the consequence holds. Cases 3 and 4 may be shown in a similar fashion. The final case is the interesting one. To prove this, we show for all corresponding abstract and concrete procedures $p(V, I, O)$ and $p^+(V, I^+, O^+)$, and for all subcomponents C and C^+ that satisfy the inductive hypothesis,

$$\{CI(IV, IV^+)\}, (\exists O \bullet p(V, I, O), C) \sqsubseteq (\exists O^+ \bullet p^+(V, I^+, O^+), C^+) \tag{4}$$

We outline a proof of (4) in Fig. 5. The assumption $\{CI(IV, IV^+)\}$ is left as an implicit context to simplify the presentation of the figure. Note that the opaque inputs to the subcomponent C, may include the opaque output, O, of p, as well as inputs from IV, and similarly for C^+. We explain the proof obligations for each step, as well as illustrating them using the procedures *add* and add^+. In the general formulae, we use the abbreviations p for $p(V, I, O)$ and p^+ for $p^+(V, I^+, O^+)$.

Before progressing we note that the opaque output parameters O and O^+ must not occur free in (nfi) the assumptions of p and p^+ respectively. This is because any assumptions made about an uninstantiated variable may result in abortion.

$$(O \text{ nfi } ok.p) \Leftrightarrow (O^+ \text{ nfi } ok.p^+) \tag{5}$$

These two conditions allow us to simplify the proof obligations for steps 5 and 1, respectively. For the set example, note that S' does not appear in the assumption of *add*, and L' does not appear in the assumption of add^+.

$$\exists O \bullet p(V, I, O), \mathcal{C}$$
$\sqsubseteq$ Step 1. augment with concrete representation
$$\exists O \bullet (p(V, I, O) \Leftrightarrow (\exists O^+ \bullet p^+(V, I^+, O^+))), \mathcal{C}$$
$\sqsubseteq$ Step 2. extend scope of O^+
$$\exists O, O^+ \bullet (p(V, I, O) \Leftrightarrow p^+(V, I^+, O^+)), \mathcal{C}$$
$\sqsubseteq$ Step 3. apply inductive hypothesis (3)
$$\exists O, O^+ \bullet (p(V, I, O) \Leftrightarrow p^+(V, I^+, O^+)), \mathcal{C}^+$$
$\sqsubseteq$ Step 4. reduce scope of O
$$\exists O^+ \bullet (p^+(V, I^+, O^+) \Leftrightarrow (\exists O \bullet p(V, I, O))), \mathcal{C}^+$$
$\sqsubseteq$ Step 5. diminish abstract representation
$$\exists O^+ \bullet p^+(V, I^+, O^+), \mathcal{C}^+$$

Fig. 5. Inductive proof of (4)

Step 1. Starting with the abstract program $(\exists O \bullet p(V, I, O), \mathcal{C})$, we introduce the concrete procedure p^+, with the concrete opaque output, if there is one, existentially quantified. This step is valid provided $p(V, I, O)$ is refined by $p(V, I, O) \Leftrightarrow (\exists O^+ \bullet p^+(V, I^+, O^+))$ in a context that guarantees the coupling invariant holds between the opaque inputs, I and I^+ (because I is a member of IV and I^+ is the corresponding member of IV^+). The refinement holds provided whenever p does not abort, p^+ does not abort and the overall effects of the two program are equivalent, i.e., $ef.p \Longleftrightarrow (ef.p \Leftrightarrow (\exists O^+ \bullet ef.p^+))$. Using the equivalence $(P \Longleftrightarrow (P \Leftrightarrow Q)) \Longleftrightarrow (P \Longrightarrow Q)$, this last condition can be rewritten as an implication.

$$CI(I, I^+) \Leftrightarrow ok.p \Rightarrow ok.p^+ \Leftrightarrow (ef.p \Rightarrow (\exists O^+ \bullet ef.p^+))$$

Instantiating this condition for add and add^+ gives the following condition.

$$S = \mathrm{ran}\, L \Leftrightarrow L \in \mathsf{listnat} \Leftrightarrow S \in \mathbf{setnat} \Leftrightarrow E \in \mathbb{N} \Leftrightarrow E \notin S \Rightarrow$$
$$L \in \mathsf{listnat} \Leftrightarrow E \in \mathbb{N} \Leftrightarrow E \notin \mathrm{ran}\, L \Leftrightarrow$$
$$(S' = \{E\} \cup S \Rightarrow (\exists L' \bullet L' = [E|L]))$$

Step 2. We extend the scope of O^+ to be the same as that of O. The concrete opaque output, O^+, is assumed not to occur free in $p(V, I, O)$ or in $\mathcal{C}$. Hence this step is straightforward. The proof obligation is O^+ nfi $p, \mathcal{C}$.

Step 3. We apply the inductive hypothesis (3) to refine $\mathcal{C}$ to $\mathcal{C}^+$. To apply (3), we must establish $CI(O, O^+)$ in the context of $\mathcal{C}$, that is, the coupling invariant is established for the opaque outputs of p and p^+ given that it holds for the opaque inputs. We require that the combination of the effects of p and p^+ establish $CI(O, O^+)$.

$$CI(I, I^+) \Leftrightarrow ok.p \Rightarrow ((ef.p \Leftrightarrow ef.p^+) \Rightarrow CI(O, O^+))$$

Instantiating this condition for add and add^+ gives:

$$S = \operatorname{ran} L \Leftrightarrow L \in \mathsf{listnat} \Leftrightarrow S \in \mathsf{setnat} \Leftrightarrow E \in \mathbb{N} \Leftrightarrow E \notin S \Rightarrow$$
$$((S' = \{E\} \cup S \Leftrightarrow L' = [E|L]) \Rightarrow (S' = \operatorname{ran} L' \Leftrightarrow L' \in \mathsf{listnat}))$$

The expression $S' = \operatorname{ran} L'$ may be simplified to $\{E\} \cup S = \operatorname{ran} [E|L]$, which holds because $S = \operatorname{ran} L$. We also satisfy $L' \in \mathsf{listnat}$ by noting that $L \in \mathsf{listnat}$ and $E \in \mathbb{N}$.

Step 4. Now the abstract variable O only appears in the call to p. We may reduce the scope of O. As above, this is satisfied by careful choice of variable names. The proof obligation is O nfi p^+, C^+.

Step 5. We can eliminate the abstract procedure call if, similar to the first step, we prove that the execution of p^+ guarantees that there exists an abstract opaque output parameter for p that does not affect the constraints on the regular parameters.

$$CI(I, I^+) \Leftrightarrow ok.p \Rightarrow (ef.p^+ \Rightarrow (\exists O \bullet ef.p))$$

In simplifying to this condition we have assumed the condition from Step 1 holds. Instantiating this condition for *add* and *add^+* gives the following condition.

$$S = \operatorname{ran} L \Leftrightarrow L \in \mathsf{listnat} \Leftrightarrow S \in \mathsf{setnat} \Leftrightarrow E \in \mathbb{N} \Leftrightarrow E \notin S \Rightarrow$$
$$(L' = [E|L] \Rightarrow (\exists S' \bullet S' = \{E\} \cup S))$$

This completes the proof that any program of the correct form using an abstract module is refined by the equivalent program using the concrete module, provided the conditions specified in Steps 1 through 5 hold for all pairs of corresponding procedures in the modules. We summarise these conditions as Condition A and Condition B below. obligations for steps 1, 3 and 5.

Condition A

$$CI(I, I^+) \Leftrightarrow ok.p \Rightarrow \tag{6}$$
$$ok.p^+ \Leftrightarrow \tag{7}$$
$$(ef.p \Rightarrow (\exists O^+ \bullet ef.p^+)) \Leftrightarrow \tag{8}$$
$$(ef.p^+ \Rightarrow (\exists O \bullet ef.p)) \Leftrightarrow \tag{9}$$
$$(ef.p \Leftrightarrow ef.p^+ \Rightarrow CI(O, O^+)) \tag{10}$$

The full instantiation of Condition A for *add* and *add+* is:

$$S = \operatorname{ran} L \Leftrightarrow L \in \mathsf{listnat} \Leftrightarrow S \in \mathsf{setnat} \Leftrightarrow E \in \mathbb{N} \Leftrightarrow E \notin S \Rightarrow$$
$$L \in \mathsf{listnat} \Leftrightarrow E \in \mathbb{N} \Leftrightarrow E \notin \operatorname{ran} L \Leftrightarrow$$
$$(S' = \{E\} \cup S \Rightarrow (\exists L' \bullet L' = [E|L])) \Leftrightarrow$$
$$(L' = [E|L] \Rightarrow (\exists S' \bullet S' = \{E\} \cup S)) \Leftrightarrow$$
$$((S' = \{E\} \cup S \Leftrightarrow L' = [E|L]) \Rightarrow (S' = \operatorname{ran} L' \Leftrightarrow L' \in \mathsf{listnat}))$$

Condition B is a combination of (5) and the proof obligations for steps 2 and 4.

Condition B

$$O \text{ nfi } ok.p, p^+, C^+ \Leftrightarrow O^+ \text{ nfi } ok.p^+, p, C \tag{11}$$

This condition may be satisfied by each program that uses the module by careful choice of variable names.

Condition A for an initialisation procedure is slightly simpler, as it does not have an opaque input. Therefore, in the premiss on line (6) of Condition A, only $ok.p$ may be assumed. For example, consider the *init* procedure for the set module. Because there are no opaque inputs, and for both *init* and $init^+$ the ok condition is just *true*, the instantiated Condition A for *init* and $init^+$ is the following easily validated condition.

$$(S = \{\} \Rightarrow (\exists L \bullet L = [\,])) \Leftrightarrow$$
$$(L = [\,] \Rightarrow (\exists S \bullet S = \{\})) \Leftrightarrow$$
$$((S = \{\} \Leftrightarrow L = [\,]) \Rightarrow S = \text{ran } L \Leftrightarrow L \in \text{listnat})$$

Observers do not have an opaque output, so the coupling invariant need not be established as in (10). Also, the quantifications over O and O^+ are empty and may be eliminated. This simplifies Condition A for an observer to

$$\{CI(I, I^+)\}, p(V, I) \sqsubseteq p^+(V, I^+) \tag{12}$$

For the *mem* procedure of the set module, instantiating (12) gives:

$$\{S = \text{ran } L \Leftrightarrow L \in \text{listnat}\}, \{S \in \mathbf{setnat}\}, \langle E \in S \rangle \sqsubseteq \{L \in \text{listnat}\}, \langle E \in \text{ran } L \rangle$$

This holds from Laws 1 - 3.

We have shown that all three procedures of *Set* and Set^+ are related to their counterparts via the coupling invariant $S = \text{ran } L \Leftrightarrow L \in \text{listnat}$ and Condition A. Hence the module *Set* may be replaced by Set^+ for use in any program of the form that respects Condition B.

5   Example: Calculator Module

Consider the abstract specification of a simple calculator given in Fig. 6. It keeps track of a list of numbers and can return the integer part of the average of the list. Procedure *init* is an initialisation procedure which sets its opaque output to the empty list. Procedure *add* is a constructor that places the regular (input) parameter E at the head of the list. The observer *mean* can be used to generate or test that a number M is the integer part of the average of the input parameter. Note that *mean* includes an assumption that L is not empty. This module is similar to an example presented by Morgan [12].

The calculator may be more efficiently represented using two numbers instead of a list. One number, T, keeps track of the sum (total) of elements in the list,

Module *Calculator*

> **Type** listnat $== \{L: list | \text{ran } L \in \mathbb{FN}\}$
> $init(L': \text{listnat}_o)$
> $add(E: \mathbb{N}, L: \text{listnat}_i, L': \text{listnat}_o)$
> $mean(M: \mathbb{N}, L: \text{listnat}_i)$

> $init(L) \stackrel{\wedge}{=} \langle L = [\,] \rangle$
> $add(E, L, L') \stackrel{\wedge}{=} \{L \in \text{listnat} \Leftrightarrow E \in \mathbb{N}\}, \langle L' = [E|L] \rangle$
> $mean(L, M) \stackrel{\wedge}{=} \{L \in \text{listnat} \Leftrightarrow L \neq [\,]\}, \langle (\sum L)/\#L = M \rangle$

End

Fig. 6. Abstract calculator module

and the other C, maintains a count of the number of elements in the list. The coupling invariant is thus

$$CI(L, (T, C)) == (T = \textstyle\sum L \Leftrightarrow C = \#L \Leftrightarrow T \in \mathbb{N} \Leftrightarrow C \in \mathbb{N})$$

Note that this coupling invariant is different to the set example in that there is a unique concrete representation for each abstract representation.

We derive a concrete implementation of this module, using Condition A as a guide. Each procedure p of *Calculator* is of the form $\{A\}, \langle P \rangle$. We derive the corresponding concrete procedure p^+ in a similar form, i.e., $\{A^+\}, \langle P^+ \rangle$.

Our first step is to derive A^+ such that (6) implies (7), i.e., $CI(I, I^+) \Leftrightarrow A \Rightarrow A^+$. Note that the value *true* for A^+ always satisfies this, but to allow the most flexibility in the implementation we prefer to choose the strongest A^+ that does not involve the abstract variable. For example, consider the concrete version of *add*. To derive the assumption, we choose an A^+ such that

$$T = \textstyle\sum L \Leftrightarrow C = \#L \Leftrightarrow T \in \mathbb{N} \Leftrightarrow C \in \mathbb{N} \Leftrightarrow L \in \text{listnat} \Leftrightarrow E \in \mathbb{N} \Rightarrow A^+$$

We satisfy this by choosing A^+ to be the type constraint on the concrete opaque inputs and regular parameters, i.e., $T \in \mathbb{N} \Leftrightarrow C \in \mathbb{N} \Leftrightarrow E \in \mathbb{N}$.

The next step is to derive the predicate P^+ such that (6) implies (10), i.e.,

$$CI(I, I^+) \Leftrightarrow A \Rightarrow (P \Leftrightarrow P^+ \Rightarrow CI(O, O^+))$$

For instance, to derive the specification of *add*, we choose a P^+ such that

$$T = \textstyle\sum L \Leftrightarrow C = \#L \Leftrightarrow T \in \mathbb{N} \Leftrightarrow C \in \mathbb{N} \Leftrightarrow L \in \text{listnat} \Leftrightarrow E \in \mathbb{N} \Rightarrow$$
$$(L' = [E|L] \Leftrightarrow P^+ \Rightarrow T' = \textstyle\sum L' \Leftrightarrow C' = \#L' \Leftrightarrow T' \in \mathbb{N} \Leftrightarrow C' \in \mathbb{N})$$

The coupling invariant on the opaque outputs may be simplified to the following by using the coupling invariants on the opaque inputs and $L' = [E|L]$.

$$T' = E + T \Leftrightarrow C' = C + 1$$

We choose this as P^+, as it satisfies (10).

Module $Calculator^+$
  Type calc $==$ N $\times$ N
  $init((T,C)\colon \mathsf{calc}_o)$
  $add(E\colon\mathrm{N}, (T,C)\colon\mathsf{calc}_i, (T',C')\colon\mathsf{calc}_o)$
  $mean(M\colon\mathrm{N}, (T,C)\colon\mathsf{calc}_i)$

  $init^+((T,C)) \stackrel{\wedge}{=} \langle T = 0 \Leftrightarrow C = 0\rangle$
  $add^+(E,(T,C),(T',C')) \stackrel{\wedge}{=}$
    $\{(T,C) \in \mathsf{calc} \Leftrightarrow E \in \mathrm{N}\}, \langle (T',C') = (E+T, 1+C)\rangle$
  $mean^+((T,C),M) \stackrel{\wedge}{=} \{(T,C) \in \mathsf{calc} \Leftrightarrow C \neq 0\}, \langle T/C = M\rangle$
End

Fig. 7. Concrete calculator module

The final step is to check that P^+ satisfies (8) and (9). For the concrete version of *add*, this holds from the one-point rule.

We therefore define add^+ as

$$\{T \in \mathrm{N} \Leftrightarrow C \in \mathrm{N} \Leftrightarrow E \in \mathrm{N}\}, \langle T' = E + T \Leftrightarrow C' = C + 1\rangle$$

We may use a similar process to derive the concrete representation of *init*. We derive the concrete implementation of *mem* by using (12), that is, we refine the abstract implementation with the coupling invariant in context. The full concrete module is shown in Fig. 7.

6   Related Work

Specifications of procedures and modules in our wide-spectrum language, incorporating specification devices such as assumptions, are similar to Morgan's model-based module specifications [12], though in his case the modules provide a "hidden" state that is not possible in traditional logic programs. However Bancroft and Hayes [1] have extended the imperative calculus to include opaque module specifications similar to ours. Our terminology is based on that of Liskov and Guttag [11], where a module presents an interface of operations that can be performed on an opaque data type. Our module specifications are similar to the module declarations of languages such as Mercury [14].

There are many other existing logic programming frameworks for modules or module-like encapsulation, e.g., [16,14]. Many of these define modules by the algebraic specification of abstract data types (ADTs) [17]. The behaviour of a module is defined in terms of the behaviour of its operations. An implementation may be derived by ensuring it maintains the behaviour of the module. Read and Kazmierczak [13] present a particular method of developing modular Prolog programs from axiomatic specifications. They write their programs in a module system based on that of extended ML. The specification of a module is written in the form of a set of axioms stating the required properties of the procedures of the module. To define the semantics of refinement, Prolog programs are considered to be equivalent to their predicate completions. The definition of module refinement in their approach is more general than the technique presented in this paper: any implementation that satisfies the axioms is valid (cf., interpretations between theories from logic [17]). However, for modules with a larger number of procedures, presenting an axiomatic specification of how the procedures inter-relate is more problematical than with the model-based approach used in this paper. This is because axioms are required to define the possible interactions between procedures, whereas, in the approach used in this paper, each procedure is defined directly in terms of the model of the opaque type parameters. In the algebraic approach, the proof of correctness amounts to showing that all the axioms of the specification hold for the implementation [13]. For a module with a large number of procedures this can be quite complex. In comparison, the approach presented here breaks down the problem into data refinement of each procedure in isolation. Although Condition A is quite complex, in practice, many of the components of the condition are trivial (as is illustrated in the two examples), and could easily be proved automatically. Usually the only non-trivial proof is that of showing the coupling invariant is established for the opaque outputs (10).

7 Conclusion

In this paper we have outlined a technique for changing the representation of a data type defined by a module from an abstract data type that allows simple specification of the module to a concrete data type that allows a more efficient implementation of the module. Our goal is to prove that replacing the references to the abstract module with corresponding references to the concrete module results in a refinement of any program using the module, provided the program is in the appropriate form. This is done by ensuring that the concrete module faithfully preserves the observable behaviour of the abstract module (via its effects on regular parameters). Sect. 4 shows that the technique is sound for programs in the restricted form defined in Sect. 3.2. Because of the restrictions on the form of the programs that can use the module, the technique does not provide a complete method for module refinement.

We have restricted our attention to programs that use a module so that they respect the intended modes of the parameters of the procedures in the module, and so that opaque variables may not be manipulated except through the interface provided by the module. The former restriction allows us to reason about module refinement with respect to a context, which in this case is that the coupling invariant holds for the opaque inputs. The latter is required so that we know this context will not be disturbed. We also require that opaque variables not be used twice as outputs; however, this is not a fundamental restriction, as the second (and later) occurrences of a variable as an opaque output can be replaced by an explicit equality procedure defined in the module, as explained near the end of Sect. 3.2.

In our concrete implementations we are able to eliminate non-determinism that would be introduced by the coupling invariant, for instance we do not need to enumerate every list representation of a set. However, non-determinism in the abstract procedure will result in a non-deterministic concrete procedure. For instance, the *mem* procedure of the *Set* module is non-deterministic in that it may succeed with multiple instantiations of E. This cannot (and should not) be removed by the module refinement process.

In this paper we have not considered polymorphic module specifications, but we foresee no problems extending the approach to handle them. Our example made use of a set of natural numbers, but there is nothing in the approach that relied on the elements of the set being natural numbers. Hence it could easily be extended to handle modules that are polymorphic in the type of the set.

Acknowledgements

The work reported in this paper has been supported by Australian Research Council grant number A49937007 on a *Refinement Calculus for Logic Programming*. We would like to thank Ray Nickson and David Hemer for feedback on this work.

References

1. P. Bancroft and I. J. Hayes. Refining a module with opaque types. In Gopal Gupta, George Mohay, and Rodney Topor, editors, *Proceedings, 16th Australian Computer Science Conference, Bris b ane, Australian Computer Science Communications*, volume 15(1), pages 615–624, February 1993.

2. R. Colvin, I. J. Hayes, and P. Strooper. Data refining logic programs. In J. Grundy, M. Schwenke, and T. Vickers, editors, *International Refinement Workshop and Formal Methods Pacific 1998*, Discrete Mathematics and Theoretical Computer Science, pages 100–116. Springer, 1998.

3. R. Colvin, I. J. Hayes, and P. Strooper. Refining logic programs using types. In J. Edwards, editor, *Australasian Computer Science Conference (ACSC 2000)*, pages 43–50. IEEE Computer Society, 2000. For an extended version see SVRC-TR-99-25.

4. Y. Deville and K.-K. Lau. Logic program synthesis. *Journal of Logic Programming*, 19,20:321–350, 1994. Special Issue: Ten Years of Logic Programming.

5. Yves Deville. *Logic Programming: Systematic Program Development*. International series in logic programming. Addison-Wesley, 1990.

6. I. Hayes, R. Nickson, and P. Strooper. Refining specifications to logic programs. In J. Gallagher, editor, *Logic Program Synthesis and Transformation. Proc. of the 6th Int. Workshop, LOPSTR'96, Stockholm, Sweden, August 1996*, volume 1207 of *Lecture Notes in Computer Science*, pages 1–19. Springer, 1997.

7. I. Hayes, R. Nickson, P. Strooper, and R. Colvin. A declarative semantics for logic program refinement. Technical Report 00-30, Software Verification Research Centre, The University of Queensland, 2000.

8. D. Hemer. Building tool support for refinement calculus for logic programming: A comparison of interactive theorem provers. Technical Report 00-06, Software Verification Research Centre, The University of Queensland, 2000.

9. K.-K. Lau and M. Ornaghi. On specification frameworks and deductive synthesis of logic programs. In L. Fribourg and F. Turini, editors, *Proc. LOPSTR 94 and META 94, Lecture Notes in Computer Science 883*, pages 104–121. Springer-Verlag, 1994.

10. K.-K Lau and M. Ornaghi. Forms of logic specifications: A preliminary study. In J. Gallagher, editor, *Logic Program Synthesis and Transformation. Proc. of the 6th Int. Workshop, LOPSTR'96, Stockholm, Sweden, August 1996*, volume 1207 of *Lecture Notes in Computer Science*, pages 295–312. Springer, 1997.

11. B. Liskov and J. Guttag. *Abstraction and Specification in Program Development.* MIT Press, third edition, 1986.

12. C. C. Morgan. *Programming from Specifications.* Prentice Hall, second edition, 1994.

13. M. G. Read and E. Kazmierczak. Formal program development in modular Prolog. In T. P. Clement and K.-K. Lau, editors, *Logic Program Synthesis and Transformation. Proc. of LOPSTR'91, University of Manchester, July 1991*, Workshops in Computing, pages 69–93. Springer-Verlag, 1992.

14. Z. Somogyi, F. J. Henderson, and T. C. Conway. Mercury, an efficient purely declarative logic programming language. In R. Kotagiri, editor, *Proc. of the Eighteenth Australasian Computer Science Conference*, pages 499–512, Glenelg, South Australia, 1995. Australian Computer Science Communications.

15. J. M. Spivey. *The Z Notation: A Reference Manual.* Prentice Hall, second edition, 1992.

16. Y. V. Srinivas and R. Jullig. Specware: Formal support for composing software. In Bernhard Moller, editor, *Proceedings of the Conference on Mathematics of Program Construction*, volume 947 of *Lecture Notes in Computer Science*. Kloster Irsee, Germany, 1995.

17. W. M. Turski and T. S. E. Maibaum. *Specification of Computer Programs.* Addison-Wesley, 1987.

Higher-Order Transformation of Logic Programs

Silvija Seres and Michael Spivey

Oxford University Computing Laboratory,
Wolfson Building, Parks Road, Oxford OX1 3QD, UK
{Silvija.Seres,Mike.Spivey}@comlab.ox.ac.uk
http://www.comlab.ox.ac.uk/oucl/work/silvija.seres

Abstract. It has earlier been assumed that a compositional approach to algorithm design and program transformation is somehow unique to functional programming. Elegant theoretical results codify the basic laws of algorithmics within the functional paradigm and with this paper we hope to demonstrate that some of the same techniques and results are applicable to logic programming as well.

1 The Problem

The Prolog predicates *rev1* and *rev2* are both true exactly if one argument list is the reverse of the other.

$rev1([\,],[\,])$.

$rev1([X|A],C) : -$
  $rev1(A,B), append(B,[X],C)$.

$rev2(A,B) : - revapp(A,[\,],B)$.

$revapp([\,],B,B)$.

$revapp([X|A],B,C) : -$
  $revapp(A,[X|B],C)$.

These two predicates are equal according to their declarative interpretation, but they have a very different computational behaviour: the time complexity for *rev1* is quadratic while for *rev2* it is linear. The aim of this paper is to present a general technique for developing the efficient predicate from the clear but inefficient one, in this and similar examples.

Arguably the most general transformational technique in logic programming is the "rules and strategies" approach [7]. In this technique the *rules* perform operations such as an unfolding or folding of clause definitions, introduction of new clause definitions, deletion of irrelevant, failing or subsumed clauses, and certain rearrangements of goals or clauses. Subject to certain conditions, these rules can be proved correct relative to the most common declarative semantics of logic programs. The application of the transformation rules is guided by meta-rules called *strategies*, which prescribe suitable sequences of basic rule applications. The main strategies involve tupling of goals that visit the same data structure in a similar way, generalisation of goals in a clause in order to fold them with some other clause, elimination of unnecessary variables, and fusion of predicates defined by two independent recursive predicates into a single predicate. These

Kung-Kiu Lau (Ed.): LOPSTR 2000, LNCS 2042, pp. 57–68, 2001.

strategies are used as the building blocks of more complex transformation techniques, and for limited classes of predicates these complex strategies have been well understood and classified and can be seen as the backbone of a compositional method for transforming logic programs.

Our transformational example can indeed be solved by the rules and strategies approach, together with mathematical induction, needed to prove the associativity of *append* on which the transformation depends. The basic strategies involved are tupling and generalisation, and the derivation is simple and semantically correct relative to the least Herbrand model of the two programs. However, there are a few methodological problems in this approach: first, the declarative semantics does not quite capture the behaviour of logic programs when they are evaluated under the standard depth-first search strategy, and we have no clear measure of the reduction of the computation complexity. Second, the application of induction requires a separate form of reasoning. But maybe most importantly, if we did not know of this particular combination of strategies, there would be no systematic method to guide us in the derivation. As far as we know, there are no general results regarding what complex strategies can be applied for families of transformationaly similar predicates. Below we outline a general approach to logic program transformations, and argue that such an approach should be based on higher-order predicates and their properties.

2   The Proposed Solution

The problem described above has been recently explored and explained for functional programs in [2]. These results build on the ample heritage of program transformation in functional programming and are based on laws of algebra and category theory. According to this algebra of functional programming, the program transformation in the example above can be seen as an instance of a more general transformational strategy, valid for an entire family of programs based on the functions *foldl* and *foldr* and parametric in the data structure. Algebraic laws regarding such higher-order functions prove to be highly versatile for transformation of functional programs.

With this paper we begin an investigation of how these results can be translated to logic programs, and present two examples where this technique has been successfully applied to derive efficient implementations of logic programs from their specifications.

We base our transformation methods on a translation of logic programs into lazy functional programs in Haskell. Using a translation technique related to Clark completion [4], any logic program can be translated into a set of functions in a lazy functional language in such a way that the declarative semantics of the logic program is preserved. In [11] we describe an implementation of such an embedding, using a simple combinator library with only four combinators, $\doteq$, $\exists$, & and $\|$; these combinators perform respectively unification, introduction of local variables, conjunction of literals in a clause body, and disjunction of clause bodies. The combinators are implemented in such a way that they exactly mimic the SLD-resolution process.

This embedding and a set of algebraic laws valid for the basic combinators of the embedding are sketched in section 3. There are two main advantages in using this functional embedding for transformation of logic programs. The first one is that it allows us to reason about logic programs in a simple calculational style, using rewriting and the algebraic laws of combinators. The second, and the more interesting reason, is that many predicates are easily expressible using higher-order functions that accept more basic predicates as arguments. We can implement the general "prepackaged recursion operators" *foldl*, *foldr*, *map* etc. as functions from predicates to predicates, and thereby get the opportunity to use their algebraic properties for program transformation. This approach avoids the problems related to higher-order unification, while it gives us the power of generic programming and provides the appropriate language and level of abstraction to reason about logic program transformation. Even though each particular derivation can be performed in a first-order setting, the *general* strategies guiding the program transformations depend essentially on the higher-order functions. We argue that, as in functional programming, so also in logic programming it is the properties of generic recursion operators that yield generic transformation strategies.

In sections 4 and 5 we show two examples where the laws are used in logic program transformation, and in the final section we discuss related work and suggest directions for further research.

3 The Embedding

As discussed earlier, the standard approaches to logic program transformation, based purely on the declarative semantics, cannot answer questions of termination and efficiency, and consequently they can offer no guidance in deriving a more efficient program. At the other extreme, techniques that rely on operational semantics result in a tedious, low level treatment of program transformation, one that is unintuitive and difficult to generalise. We propose an intermediate approach, using a third kind of semantics for logic programs that captures the essentials of the operational behaviour of logic programs, but remains abstract enough for the techniques to be general and simple. We call this the *algebraic semantics* for logic programs.

The algebraic semantics arises from the Clark completion of the logic program. This completion translates any definite logic program to an equational, rather than implicational, form using only four basic operators: &, $\parallel$, $\exists$ and $\doteq$. The meaning that &, $\parallel$, $\exists$ are assigned by Clark is their standard interpretation in first order logic, so & is conjunction, $\parallel$ is disjunction, and $\exists$ is existential quantification. Clark defines $\doteq$ as equality, and gives an axiomatization of equality that is equivalent to unification. This is the declarative, or denotational, reading of the Clark completion of a logic program.

With a some minimal syntactic differences, the Clark completion of a predicate has essentially the same shape as the original one. For example, the standard
predicate *append* is implemented in a logic program as:

$append([\ ], XS, XS).$

$append([X|XS], YS, [X|ZS]) : - \ append(XS, YS, ZS).$

The patterns and repeated variables from the head of each clause can be replaced
by explicit equations written at the start of the body. Then each head contains
only a list of distinct variables, and renaming can ensure that these lists of
variables are same. Further steps of the completion consist of joining the clause
bodies with the $\parallel$ operator and the literals in a clause with the & operator,
existentially quantifying any variables that appear in the body but not in the
head of a clause:

$$
\begin{aligned}
append(p, q, r) = & \\
& (p \doteq nil \ \& \ q \doteq r) \\
\parallel \ & (\exists x, xs, zs. \ p \doteq cons(x, xs) \ \& \ r \doteq cons(x, zs) \ \& \\
& \qquad append(xs, q, zs)).
\end{aligned}
$$

Using Clark's form of a logic program allows us to perform equational reasoning, which simplifies program transformation. It also emphasises the similarities
between logic and functional programming. In addition, it singles out &, $\parallel$, $\exists$ and
$\doteq$ as the four basic operators which are necessary to achieve the expressiveness
of logic programs. By focusing on each of these separately, we gain a *compositional* understanding of the computational behaviour of logic programming, as
opposed to the usual monolithic view of the computation given by the standard
procedural readings of a logic program such as SLD resolution.

The declarative reading ignores evaluation issues, but these four operators
can also be given an operational reading, one that is correct with respect to SLD
resolution, for example. This operational reading can be specified in many ways:
state transition diagrams, rewrite rules, and others. We choose to specify the operational reading using an existing programming language – the lazy functional
programming language Haskell – because it allows us to give compact and clear,
yet executable, definitions to the four operators: see [11].

The Haskell evaluation of a function call in Clark's form of a logic program
mimics SLD resolution of the corresponding goal in the original logic program.
Even though it is evaluated in the functional setting of Haskell, the predicate
append behaves like a relation, i.e., one can compute the answers to goals such
as $append([1], y, [1, 2])$ or $append(x, y, [1, 2])$. The function *append* takes as input
a tuple of terms and a substitution (representing the state of knowledge about
the values of variables at the time the predicate is invoked), and produces a collection of substitutions, each corresponding to a solution of the predicate that
is consistent with the input substitution. The collection of substitutions that is
returned by *append* may be a lazy stream to model the depth-first execution
model of Prolog, or it may be a search tree in a more general execution model.

Other models of search may also be incorporated: for example, there is an implementation of a breadth-first traversal of the SLD tree that uses lazy streams of finite lists of answers (see [12] and [13]).

The relationship between the abstract logical meaning of the four basic operators and their operational meaning that arises from SLD resolution is imperfect. In other words, in order for Clark's form of the logic program to have the same *computational* meaning as SLD resolution, the operators & and $\parallel$ in the completed version of the logic program can not behave *exactly* like conjunction and disjunction in first order logic. Also, $\exists$ must introduce new variable names, rather than just existentially quantifying over a variable. The $\doteq$ needs to be understood as unification of terms. Therefore only some of the usual Boolean properties hold for these operators, and by recognising which properties of the operators hold both in first order logic and in an implementation which is correct with respect to SLD resolution, we can *distil* the algebraic semantics of a logic program.

The implementation of each of the four combinators of the embedding is strikingly simple, and can be given a clear categorical description which yields nice computational rules: it can be easily proved that (irrespectively of the search model) the operators and the primitive predicates *true* and *false* enjoy some of the standard laws of predicate calculus, e.g. & is associative and has *true* as its left and right unit and *false* as its left zero, $\parallel$ is associative and has *false* as its left and right unit and & distributes through $\parallel$ from the right. Other properties that are satisfied by the connectives of propositional logic are not shared by our operators, because the answers are produced in a definite order and with definite multiplicity. These laws are, of course, valid in the declarative reading of logic programs. Since procedural equality is too strict when reasoning about predicates with different complexity behaviour, we need to permit in our transformational proofs also the use of some of the laws that are not valid in the procedural but only in the declarative semantics, for example, the commutativity of &.

These algebraic laws can be used to prove the equivalence of two logic programs with equivalent declarative reading. The basic idea is to embed both programs in this functional setting, and then use the laws to show that the two functions satisfy the same recursive equation. Further, a result exists that guarantees that all guarded recursive predicate definitions have a unique solution. The proof for the uniqueness of fixpoints is based on metric spaces and a certain contraction property of guarded predicates. We present this result elsewhere [10].

4   Example 1: Reverse

The standard definition of the naive reverse predicate has quadratic time complexity:

$$rev1\,(l1, l2) =$$
$$(l1 \doteq nil \,\&\, l2 \doteq nil)$$
$$\parallel\ (\exists x, xs, ys.\ \ l1 \doteq cons(x, xs)\,\&$$
$$rev1\,(xs, ys)\,\&\, append(ys, cons(x, nil), l2)).$$

A better definition of reverse uses an accumulating parameter and runs in linear time:

$rev2\,(l1,l2) = revapp(l1,nil,l2)$

$revapp(l1,acc,l2) =$

$\quad (l1 \doteq nil \;\&\; l2 \doteq acc)$

$\quad \|\; (\exists x,xs.\; l1 \doteq cons(x,xs) \;\&\; revapp(xs,cons(x,acc),l2)).$

We can prove these two definitions equivalent by using the previously mentioned algebraic laws together with structural induction. This approach is similar to the rules and strategies approach for logic program transformation. However, there is a shorter and more elegant way of proving these predicates equal, by resorting to program derivation techniques based on higher-order *fold* predicates and their properties. Such fold operators have proved to be fundamental in functional programming, partly because they provide for a disciplined use of recursion, where the recursive decomposition follows the structure of the data type. They also satisfy a set of laws that are crucial in functional program transformations, and we will rely on one of those laws in our derivation. The outline of the derivation is as follows:

$rev1\,(xs,ys)$

$= foldRList\,(snoc,nil)\,(xs,ys)$ by defn. of *foldRList* and *snoc*

$= foldLList\,(flipapp,nil)\,(xs,ys)$ by duality law (1), see below

$= revapp(xs,nil,ys)$ by defn. of *foldLList*

$= rev2\,(xs,ys).$ by defn. of *rev2*

We denote this derivation by $(*)$ and justify each of the steps below.

The definitions of some families of higher-order predicates, for example the map and fold predicates over lists or other data structures, can be made without any extensions to our embedding. They can be implemented using Haskell's higher-order functions on predicates, so we do not need to resort to the higher-order unification machinery of, say, λ-Prolog. For example, the predicate *foldRList*, which holds iff the predicate p applied right-associatively to all the elements of the list l yields the term *res*, could be defined as:

$foldRList\,(p,e)\,(l,res) =$

$\quad (l \doteq nil \;\&\; e \doteq res)$

$\quad \|\; (\exists x,xs,r.\; l \doteq cons(x,xs) \;\&$

$\qquad\qquad foldRList\,(p,e)\,(xs,r) \;\&\; p(x,r,res)),$

where (p,e) are the higher-order parameters to the function *foldRList* and (l,res) are the arguments to the resulting predicate. The predicate p corresponds to a binary function to be applied to the consecutive list elements, and e denotes the initial element used to 'start things rolling'. For example, the function *foldRList* $(add,0)$ applied to $([2,7,8],res)$ produces the predicate

$(r_1 \doteq 0)$ & $add(8, r_1, r_2)$ & $add(7, r_2, r_3)$ & $add(2, r_3, res)$; when invoked with the appropriate input substitution (say the empty one), this predicate returns a substitution that maps res to 17.

In the first step of the derivation $(*)$, we use the following predicate $snoc$:

$$snoc(x, l, res) = append(l, cons(x, nil), res).$$

The pattern of recursion in the definition of $rev1$ is the same as that captured by $foldRList$. Using a result that guarantees that recursive definitions have unique fixed points, we may conclude that $rev1$ is equal to the instance of $foldRList$ shown in the second line of our derivation $(*)$.

The next step in $(*)$ involves a transition from $foldRList$ to another higher-order predicate, $foldLList$. This left-associative fold over lists could be defined as follows:

$$foldLList\ (p, e)\ (l, res) =$$
$$(l \doteq nil\ \&\ e \doteq res)$$
$$\|\ (\exists x, xs, r.\ l \doteq cons(x, xs)\ \&$$
$$p(e, x, r)\ \&\ foldLList\ (p, r)\ (xs, res)).$$

Roughly spaeaking, the function call $foldLList\ (add, 0)\ ([2, 7, 8], res)$ would return the predicate $add(0, 2, r_1)\ \&\ add(r_1, 7, r_2)\ \&\ add(r_2, 8, r_3)\ \&\ (r_3 \doteq res)$. Again, this predicate has the effect of setting res to 17, but this time the numbers are added from left to right.

The second step in $(*)$ is an instance of the duality law,

$$foldRList\ (f, e)\ (l, res) = foldLList\ (g, e)\ (l, res), \qquad (1)$$

where f is replaced by $snoc$, g by $flipapp$, and e by nil. The law above holds if f, g and e satisfy the following requirements: f and g must associate with each other, and $f(x, e, res)$ must equal $g(e, x, res)$ for all x and res. The predicates f and g associate with each other iff the predicates $\exists t.\ (f(x, t, res)\ \&\ g(y, z, t))$ and $\exists t.\ (g(t, z, res)\ \&\ f(x, y, t))$ are equal. In functional notation this corresponds to $f(x, g(y, z)) = g(f(x, y), z)$. The proof of (1) requires the following auxilliary result:

$$\exists t.\ (f(x, t, res)\ \&\ foldLList\ (g, y)\ (xs, t))$$
$$= \exists t.\ (f(x, y, t)\ \&\ foldLList\ (g, t)\ (xs, res)).$$

This is proved by induction, using the associativity assumption about f and g. Then this equality, with y instantiated to e, is used together with the assumption about the equality of $f(x, e, res)$ and $g(e, x, res)$, in the induction proof for (1).

Returning to our derivation $(*)$, we need to check that the duality law really is applicable, so we now prove that the predicates $snoc$ and $flipapp$ and term nil satisfy the requirements for f, g and e. If $flipapp$ is defined as:

$$flipapp\ (l, x, res) = append(cons(x, nil), l, res),$$

then we unfold the definition of both functions, and use the associativity of *append* in step marked with (∗∗), to get:

$$(\exists t.\ (snoc(x, t, res)\ \&\ flipapp(y, z, t)))$$
$$= (\exists t.\ (append(t, cons(x, nil), res)\ \&\ append(cons(z, nil), y, t)))$$
$$= (\exists t.\ (append(cons(z, nil), t, res)\ \&\ append(y, cons(x, nil), t)))\quad (\ast\ast)$$
$$= (\exists t.\ (flipapp(t, z, res)\ \&\ snoc(x, y, t)))$$

and similarly for $snoc(x, nil, res)$ and $flipapp(nil, x, res)$. The associativity of *append* used in (∗∗) can be shown by induction on the list argument *res*.

For the penultimate step in the our derivation (∗), we first prove that $revapp(l, acc, res)$ equals $foldLList\ (flipapp, acc)\ (l, res)$ by a simple induction proof. Then, instantiating the arbitrary term *acc* in *foldLList* to the term *nil*, we get exactly the $foldLList\ (flipapp, nil)\ (xs, ys)$ from the third line of the proof, so we can rewrite this to a call to $revapp(xs, nil, ys)$ in the fourth line. The final step follows directly from the definition of *rev2*.

5   Example 2: Sort

Our second example is inspired by [2]. We start with the standard implementation of the *naiveSort* predicate that uses the 'generate-and-test' method to sort a list:

$$naiveSort(l1, l2) = perm(l1, l2)\ \&\ isSorted(l2)$$
$$isSorted(l) =$$
$$\quad (l \doteq nil)$$
$$\parallel (\exists x.\ l \doteq cons(x, nil))$$
$$\parallel (\exists x, y, l2.\ l \doteq cons(x, cons(y, l2))\ \&$$
$$\quad\quad le(x, y)\ \&\ isSorted(cons(y, l2)))$$

where *perm* has the standard definition, using the auxiliary predicate *delete*:

$$perm(l1, l2) =$$
$$\quad (l1 \doteq nil\ \&\ l2 \doteq nil)$$
$$\parallel (\exists x, xs, zs.\ l2 \doteq cons(x, xs)\ \&$$
$$\quad\quad delete(x, l1, zs)\ \&\ perm(zs, xs))$$
$$delete(x, l1, l2) =$$
$$\quad (\exists ys.\ l1 \doteq cons(x, ys)\ \&\ l2 \doteq ys)$$
$$\parallel (\exists y, ys, zs.\ l1 \doteq cons(y, ys)\ \&\ l2 \doteq cons(y, zs)\ \&$$
$$\quad\quad delete(x, ys, zs)).$$

We now wish to show that *naiveSort* is equivalent to its more efficient variant *iSort*, which performs insertion sort. Given a predicate $insert(x, zs, l2)$ which is true if the sorted list $l2$ is the result of inserting the element x in the appropriate position in the sorted list zs, the usual implementation of the *iSort* predicate is as follows:

$$iSort(l1, l2) =$$
$$(l1 \doteq nil \ \& \ l2 \doteq nil)$$
$$\| \ (\exists x, ys. \ l1 \doteq cons(x, ys) \ \&$$
$$iSort(ys, zs) \ \& \ insert(x, zs, l2))$$
$$insert(x, l1, l2) =$$
$$(l1 \doteq nil \ \& \ l2 \doteq cons(x, nil))$$
$$\| \ (\exists y, zs. \ l1 \doteq cons(y, zs) \ \& \ l2 \doteq cons(x, cons(y, zs)) \ \&$$
$$le(x, y))$$
$$\| \ (\exists y, ys, zs. \ l1 \doteq cons(y, ys) \ \& \ l2 \doteq cons(y, zs) \ \&$$
$$gt(x, y) \ \& \ insert(x, ys, zs)).$$

The outline of this derivation is similar to the previous example, except that the essential step this time uses the fusion law for fold instead of the duality law:

$$naiveSort(l1, l2)$$

$= isSorted(l2) \ \& \ perm(l1, l2)$	by defn. of *naiveSort*
$= isSorted(l2) \ \& \ foldRList(add, nil) \ (l1, l2)$	by defn. of *foldRList*
$= foldRList(insert, nil) \ (l1, l2)$	by fusion (2), see below
$= iSort(l1, l2).$	by defn. of *iSort*

In step 1, we simply unfold the definition of $naiveSort(l1, l2)$ and use the commutativity property of &. In the next step we argue that the predicate *perm* is an instance of $foldRList(add, nil)$, where the predicate *add* is as defined below. First, we use an auxiliary result stating that the relation *perm* is symmetric, i.e. that $perm(zs, xs)$ and $perm(xs, zs)$ are equivalent. Second, we define *add* to be the converse of *delete*, i.e. $delete(x, l1, zs) = add(x, zs, l1)$, and we can now rewrite *perm* as:

$$perm(l1, l2) =$$
$$(l1 \doteq nil \ \& \ l2 \doteq nil)$$
$$\| \ (\exists x, xs, zs. \ l2 \doteq cons(x, xs) \ \&$$
$$add(x, zs, l1) \ \& \ perm(xs, zs)).$$

Then, once again using the result about the symmetricity of *perm*, we swap $l1$ and $l2$ and obtain a recursive equation equivalent to the one defining $foldRList \ (add, nil) \ (l1, l2)$.

The third step is the major step in this derivation, and it is the one where the efficiency gain is achieved, i.e. the one that captures this transformation strategy. It involves the fusion law for *foldRList*, which can be proved by induction on the length of the input list. The assumptions for this law are as follows: let predicates f, g and h, and a term e, be such that $f(e)$ holds, and that $f(res)$ & $g(x, y, res)$ rewrites to the same recursive equation as $h(x, y, res)$ & $f(y)$ for all terms x, y and res (in functional notation, $f(g \ x \ y) = h \ x \ (f \ y)$). Then, the fusion law states that:

$$f(res) \ \& \ foldRList \ (g, e) \ (l, res) = foldRList \ (h, e) \ (l, res). \tag{2}$$

If we now insert our predicate $isSorted$ for f, add for g, $insert$ for h, and nil for e, the third step in the main proof is a straight-forward application of the fusion law. We only need to prove that our choices for f, g, h, and e satisfy the two fusion law requirements. The predicate call $isSorted(nil)$ holds by definition, and the remaining condition for f, g and h is that:

$$isSorted(res) \ \& \ add(x, l, res) = insert(x, l, res) \ \& \ isSorted(l).$$

This equality can also be proved by an application of algebraic laws and induction on the lists l and res, using the lemma:

$$delete(x, zs, ys) \ \& \ isSorted(cons(y, zs))$$
$$= gt(x, y) \ \& \ delete(x, zs, ys) \ \& \ isSorted(cons(y, zs))$$

which can also be proved by induction on the argument lists zs and ys.

In the final step, we simply recognise that $isort(l1, l2)$ is equivalent to $foldRList \ (insert, nil) \ (l1, l2)$.

Following a similar approach, we can also derive the equivalence of the naive sort and, for example, $quickSort$ or $selectionSort$. Both of these derivations rely on the fusion law, but they are algebraically slightly more advanced than the above derivation of $iSort$ because they also involve properties of unfold predicates. The derivation of $quickSort$ uses fold and unfold predicates on trees. The reason for this is that even though $quickSort$ is usually represented as a flat recursive predicate, it has a compositional form which is basically a sort on trees where the intermediate tree data type has been eliminated. Essentially, the derivation of $quickSort$ involves proving the equality:

$$isSorted(l2) \ \& \ perm(l1, l2)$$
$$= mkTree(l1, t) \ \& \ flatten(t, l2)$$

where the predicate $mkTree(l1, t)$ holds if t is an ordered tree:

$$mkTree(l, t) =$$
$$\quad (l \doteq nil \ \& \ t \doteq null)$$
$$\quad \| \ (\exists x, xs, t1, t2, l1, l2, a. \ l \doteq cons(x, xs) \ \& \ t \doteq fork(t1, a, t2) \ \&$$
$$\qquad\qquad split(l, l1, a, l2) \ \& \ mkTree(l1, t1) \ \& \ mkTree(l2, t2))$$
$$split(l, l1, a, l2) =$$
$$\quad \exists y, ys. \ l \doteq cons(y, ys) \ \& \ a \doteq y \ \&$$
$$\qquad\qquad filter(\lambda x.le(x, y))(l, l2) \ \& \ filter((\lambda x.gt(x, y)(l, l1)$$

where *filter* (g) $(l, l1)$ is a higher order predicate that holds if $l1$ contains all the elements of l that satisfy g, and *flatten*(t, l) holds if the list l corresponds to the flattened tree t. The terms representing trees and fold functions on trees are defined similarly to the corresponding definitions for lists.

6   Related and Further Work

An embedding of logic programs to a functional setting has been explored by Wand [15], Baudinet [1], Ross [9] and Hinze [6], but with different motives. They all pursue an algebraic semantics for logic programming, but they do not attempt to generalise their techniques to transformation strategies. The examples presented here are mostly inspired by Bird and de Moor's work [2] on similar program synthesis and transformation techniques for functional programming. The contribution of this paper is in a translation of these techniques to logic programming. Related work in a functional setting includes, among others, Wand's work [14] on continuation based program transformation techniques. In a logic programming setting, Pettorossi and Proietti present in [8] a particular transformation strategy based on an of introduction of lists and higher-order predicates on lists.

This approach to logic program transformation opens several areas for further research. One is to apply these transformational techniques to constraint programming, which can also be translated to a functional setting by means of our embedding. Another direction is to examine what other results from [2] we can transfer to logic programming. Yet another direction is to build automatic tools for logic program transformation based on the algebraic approach described here; this has been successfully done for functional programs in [5]. All of these directions motivate a further cross-fertilisation of methods for program transformation between the two declarative paradigms.

References

1. M. Baudinet. *Logic Programming Semantics Techniques and Applications*. PhD thesis, Stanford Univeristy, 1989.
2. R. Bird and O. de Moor. *Algebra of Programming*. Prentice Hall, 1997.
3. E. Boiten. The many disguises of accumulation. Technical Report 91-26, University of Nijmegen, 1991.
4. K. L. Clark. Negation as failure. In H. Gallaire and J. Minker, editors, *Logic and Data Bases*, pages 293–322. Plenum Press, 1978.
5. O. de Moor and G. Sittampalam. Generic program transformation. In *Procs. 3rd International Summer School on Advanced Functional Programming*, pages 116–149, Springer LNCS 1608, 1998.
6. R. Hinze. Prological features in a functional setting - axioms and implementations. In *Proc. of FLOPS'98*, pages 98–122, World Scientific, Japan, 1998.
7. A. Pettorossi and M. Proietti. In *Handbook of Logic in Artificial Intelligence and Logic Programming*, volume 5, chapter Transformation of Logic Programs, pages 697–787. Oxford University Press, 1998.

8. A. Pettorossi and M. Proietti. Program derivation via list introduction. In *Proceedings of IFIP TC2 Working Conference on Algorithmic Languages and Calculi*, pages 296–323. Chapman and Hall, Le bischenberg, France, 1997.

9. B. J. Ross. Using algebraic semantics for proving Prolog termination and transformation. In *Proceedings of the ALPUK 1991*, pages 135–155. Edinburgh, Springer, 1991.

10. S. Seres. *The Algebra of Logic Programming*. PhD thesis, Oxford University, 2001 (to appear).

11. S. Seres and J. M. Spivey. Functional Reading of Logic Programs. In *Journal of Universal Computer Science*, volume 6(4), pages 433–446, 1999.

12. S. Seres, J. M. Spivey, and C. A. R. Hoare, Algrebra of Logic Programming *Proceedings of ICLP'99*, pages 184–199, Las Cruces, USA, The MIT Press, 1999.

13. J. M. Spivey. The monad of breadth-first search. *Journal of Functional Programming*, volume 10(4), pages 397–408, 2000.

14. M. Wand. Continuation-based program transformation strategies. *Journal of the ACM*, volume 27(1), pages 164–180, 1980.

15. M. Wand. A semantic algebra for logic programming. Technical Report 148, Indiana University Computer Science Department, 1983.

Non-transformational Termination Analysis of Logic Programs, Based on General Term-Orderings

Alexander Serebrenik and Danny De Schreye

Department of Computer Science, K.U. Leuven
Celestijnenlaan 200A, B-3001, Heverlee, Belgium
{Alexander.Serebrenik,Danny.DeSchreye}@cs.kuleuven.ac.be

Abstract. We present a new approach to termination analysis of logic programs. The essence of the approach is that we make use of general term-orderings (instead of level mappings), like it is done in transformational approaches to logic program termination analysis, but that we apply these orderings directly to the logic program and not to the term-rewrite system obtained through some transformation. We define some variants of acceptability, based on general term-orderings, and show how they are equivalent to LD-termination. We develop a demand driven, constraint-based approach to verify these acceptability-variants.
The advantage of the approach over standard acceptability is that in some cases, where complex level mappings are needed, fairly simple term-orderings may be easily generated. The advantage over transformational approaches is that it avoids the transformation step all together.

Keywords: termination analysis, acceptability, term-orderings.

1 Introduction

There are many different approaches to termination analysis of logic programs. One particular distinction is between *transformational* approaches and *"direct"* ones. A transformational approach first transforms the logic program into an "equivalent" term-rewrite system (or, in some cases, into an equivalent functional program). Here, equivalence means that, at the very least, the termination of the term-rewrite system should imply the termination of the logic program, for some predefined collection of queries[1]. Direct approaches do not include such a transformation, but prove the termination directly on the basis of the logic program.

Besides the transformation step itself, there is one other technical difference between these approaches. Direct approaches usually prove termination on the basis of a well-founded ordering over the natural numbers. More specifically,

---

[1] The approach of Arts [4] is exceptional in the sense that the termination of the logic program is concluded from a weaker property of *single-redex normalisation* of the term-rewrite system.

Kung-Kiu Lau (Ed.): LOPSTR 2000, LNCS 2042, pp. 69–85, 2001.

they use a *level mapping*, which maps atoms to natural numbers, and, they verify appropriate decreases of this level mapping on the atoms occuring in the clauses. On the other hand, transformational approaches make use of more general well-founded orderings over terms, such as reduction orders, or more specifically a simplification order, or others (see [11]).

At least for the direct approaches the systematic choice for level mappings and norms, instead of general term orders, seems arbitrary and ad hoc. This has been the main motivation for this paper. We present an initial study on the use of general well-founded term-orderings as a means of directly proving the termination of logic programs—without intermediate transformation. In particular,

- we study whether the theoretical results on acceptability can be reformulated on the basis of general term orders,
- we evaluate to what extent the use of the general term orderings (instead of level mappings) either improves or deteriorates the direct approaches.

To illustrate the latter point, consider the following program, that formulates some of the rules for computing the repeated derivative of a linear function in one variable u (see also [13]) :

Example 1.

$$d(der(u), 1).$$
$$d(der(A), 0) \leftarrow number(A).$$
$$d(der(X + Y), DX + DY) \leftarrow d(der(X), DX), d(der(Y), DY).$$
$$d(der(X * Y), X * DY + Y * DX) \leftarrow d(der(X), DX), d(der(Y), DY).$$
$$d(der(der(X)), DDX) \leftarrow d(der(X), DX), d(der(DX), DDX).$$

Proving termination of this program on the basis of a level-mapping is hard. For this example, the required level-mapping is a non-linear function. In particular, a level mapping, such that: $|d(X, Y)| = \|X\|$, $|number(X)| = 0$, $\|der(X)\| = 2^{\|X\|}$, $\|X + Y\| = max(\|X\|, \|Y\|) + 1$, $\|X * Y\| = max(\|X\|, \|Y\|) + 1$, $\|u\| = 2$, $\|n\| = 2$, if n is a number,would be needed. No automatic system for proving termination on the basis of level mappings is able to generate such mappings. Moreover, we believe, that it would be very difficult to extend existing systems to support generation of appropriate non-linear mappings.   □

Although we have not yet presented our general-well-founded term ordering approach, it should be intuitively clear, that we can capture the decrease in order between the $der(X)$ and DX by using an ordering on terms that gives the highest "priority" to the functor *der*.

As an example of the fact that moving to general ordering can also introduce deterioration, consider the following program from [7,10].

Example 2. This program defines a predicate *conf* that decreases a list provided as an argument, by two elements, and then adds a new element to it.

$$conf(X) \leftarrow delete_2(X, Z), delete(U, Y, Z), conf(Y).$$

$delete_2(X, Y) \leftarrow delete(U, X, Z), delete(V, Z, Y).$

$delete(X, [X|T], T).$

$delete(X, [H|T], [H|T1]) \leftarrow delete(X, T, T1).$

Note that by reasoning in terms of sizes of terms, we can infer that the size decreases by 2 after the call to $delete_2$ predicate in the first clause and then increases by 1 in the subsequent call to the $delete$ predicate. In total, sizes allow to conclude a decrease. Reasoning in terms of order relations only, however, does not allow to conclude the overall decrease from the inequalities $arg3 < arg2$ for the $delete$ predicate and $arg1 > arg2$ for the $delete_2$ predicate.   □

As can be expected, theoretically both approaches are essentially equivalent, that is existence of a level-mapping or an order is equivalent to termination. We will introduce a variant of the notion of acceptability, based on general term orders, which is again equivalent to termination in a similar way as in the level mapping based approach. On the more practical level, as illustrated in the two examples above, neither of the approaches is strictly better: the general term orders provide a larger set of orders to select from (in particular, note that orders based on level mappings and norms are a term order), the level mapping approach provides arithmetic, on top of mere ordering.

In the remainder of this paper, we will start off from a variant of the notion of *acceptability with respect to a set*, as introduced in [8], obtained by replacing level mappings by term orderings. We show how this variant of acceptability remains equivalent to termination under the left-to-right selection rule, for certain goals. Then, we illustrate how this result can be used to prove termination with some examples. We also provide a variant of the *acceptability* condition, as introduced in [3], and discuss advantages and disadvantages of each approach. Next, we discuss automation of the approach. We elaborate on a demand-driven method to set-up and verify sufficient preconditions for termination. In this method, the aim is to derive—in, as much as possible, a constructive way—a well-founded ordering over the set of all atoms and terms of the language underlying the program, that satisfies the termination condition.

2   Preliminaries

2.1   Term Ordering

An *quasi-order* over a set S is a reflexive, asymmetric and transitive relation $\geq$ defined on elements of S. We define the associated equivalence relation $=_>$ as $s =_> t$, if and only if $s \geq t$ and $t \geq s$, and the associated strict *partial ordering* $>$ if and only if $s \geq t$ but not $t \geq s$. If neither $s \geq t$, nor $t \geq s$ we write $s\|_> t$. Sometimes, in order to distinguish between different orders we also use $\succeq$, $\succ$, $=_\succ$ and $\|_\succ$

An ordered set S is said to be *well-founded* if there are no infinite descending sequences $s_1 > s_2 > \dots$ of elements of S. If the set S is clear from the context we will say that the order, defined on it, is well-founded. We'll also say that a quasi-order is well-founded if the strict partial order associated with it, is well-founded.

Definition 1. *Let $\geq$ be a quasi-order on a set T. A quasi-order $\succeq$ defined on a set $S \supseteq T$ is called a* proper extension *of $\geq$ if*

- *$t_1 \geq t_2$ implies $t_1 \succeq t_2$ for all $t_1, t_2 \in T$.*
- *$t_1 > t_2$ implies $t_1 \succ t_2$ for all $t_1, t_2 \in T$.*

The study of termination of term-rewriting systems caused intensive study of term orderings. A number of useful properties of term orderings were established.

Definition 2. *Let $>$ be an ordering on terms.*

- *$>$ is called* monotonic *if $s_1 > s_2$ implies $f(\bar{t}_1, s_1, \bar{t}_2) > f(\bar{t}_1, s_2, \bar{t}_2)$ and $p(\bar{t}_1, s_1, \bar{t}_2) > p(\bar{t}_1, s_2, \bar{t}_2)$ for any terms s_1 and s_2, sequences of terms $\bar{t}_1$ and $\bar{t}_2$, function symbol f and predicate p.*
- *$>$ is said to have the* subterm *property if $f(\bar{t}_1, s, \bar{t}_2) > s$ holds for any term $f(\bar{t}_1, s, \bar{t}_2)$.*

These properties can be analogously defined for quasi-orders. The following are examples of strict orderings: $>$ on the set of numbers, the lexicographic order on the set of strings (this is the way entries are ordered in dictionaries), the multiset ordering and the recursive path ordering [11]. The following are examples of quasi-orders: $\geq$ on the set of numbers, $\supseteq$ on the power set of some set.

For our purposes monotonicity and subterm properties are too restrictive. Thus, we assign to each predicate or functor a subset of the argument positions, such that for the argument positions in this subset the specified properties hold. We will say that a predicate p (a functor f) is monotone (has a subterm property) on a specified subset of argument positions. The formal study of these weaker notions may be found in [20].

Example 3. Let f be a functor of arity two, and a, b two terms, such that $a > b$. Let f be monotone in the first argument position. Then, $f(a, c) > f(b, c)$ holds for any term c, but there might be some term c, such that $f(c, a) \not> f(c, b)$.

One of the strict orderings that is useful for proving termination is the recursive path ordering. We define this ordering formally, following [11].

We start with defining *multisets* that are similar to sets, but allow multiple occurrences of identical elements. An ordering $>$, defined on S, can be extended to an ordering on finite multisets of S, $M(S)$. This ordering is denoted $\gg$ and formally is defined as following.

Definition 3. *For a partially-ordered set $(S, >)$, the* multiset ordering $\gg$ *on $M(S)$ is defined as follows: $M \gg M'$ if, and only if, for some multisets $X, Y \in M(S)$, where X is a nonempty subset of M,*

$$M' = (M - X) \cup Y$$

and for all $y \in Y$ there is an $x \in X$, such that $x > y$.

Example 4. If S is a set of integers, then $\{\!\{1, 1, 2, 2, -3, \}\!\}$ and $\{\!\{1, 2, 2, -3, -3\}\!\}$ are two different multisets on S. If $>$ is a usual order on integers and $\gg$ is its extension to $M(S)$, then $\{\!\{1, 1, 2, 2, -3, \}\!\} \gg \{\!\{1, 2, 2, -3, -3\}\!\}$.

Now we are going to use this notion to define a recursive path ordering. Recursive path ordering starts with a partial ordering on a set of operators and based on it, defines an order on terms.

Definition 4. *Let $\succ$ be a partial order on a set of operators F. The recursive path ordering $>$ on the set of terms over F is defined recursively as follows:*

$$s = f(s_1, \ldots, s_m) > g(t_1, \ldots, t_n) = t$$

if

- $s_i \geq t$ *for some* $i = 1, \ldots, m$
- $f \succ g$ *and* $s > t_j$ *for all* $j = 1, \ldots, n$
- f *is identical to* g *and* $\{s_1, \ldots, s_m\} \gg \{t_1, \ldots, t_n\}$*, where* $\gg$ *is the extension of* $>$ *to multisets, and* $\geq$ *means* $>$ *or equivalent up to permutation of subterms.*

2.2 Logic Programs

We follow the standard notation for terms and atoms. A *query* is a finite sequence of atoms. Given an atom A, $rel(A)$ denotes the predicate occuring in A. $Term_P$ and $Atom_P$ denote, respectively, sets of all terms and atoms that can be constructed from the language underlying P. The extended Herbrand Universe U_P^E (the extended Herbrand base B_P^E) is a quotient set of $Term_P$ ($Atom_P$) modulo the variant relation.

We refer to an SLD-tree constructed using the left-to-right selection rule of Prolog, as an LD-tree. We will say that a goal G *LD-terminates* for a program P, if the LD-tree for (P, G) is finite.

The following definition is borrowed from [1].

Definition 5. *Let P be a program and p, q be predicates occurring in it.*

- *We say that p refers to q in P if there is a clause in P that uses p in its head and q in its body.*
- *We say that p depends on q in P and write $p \sqsupseteq q$, if (p, q) is in the transitive, reflexive closure of the relation refers to.*
- *We say that p and q are mutually recursive and write $p \simeq q$, if $p \sqsupseteq q$ and $q \sqsupseteq p$. We also write $p \sqsupset q$ when $p \sqsupseteq q$ and $q \not\sqsupseteq p$.*

3 Term-Acceptability with Respect to a Set

In this section we present and discuss some of the theory we developed to extend acceptability to general term orders. In the literature, there are different variants of acceptability. The most well-known of these is the acceptability as introduced by Apt and Pedreschi [3]. This version is defined and verified on the level of ground instances of clauses, but draws its practical power mostly from the fact that termination is proved for *any bounded* goal. Here, boundedness is a notion related to the selected level mapping and requires that the set $\{|G\theta| \mid \theta$ is a grounding substitution for goal $G\}$ is bounded in the natural numbers, where $|\cdot| : B_P \to \mathcal{N}$ denotes the level mapping.

Another notion of acceptability is the "acceptability with respect to a set of goals", introduced by De Schreye et. al. in [8]. This notion allows to prove termination with respect to any set of goals. However, it relies on procedural concepts, such as calls and computed answer substitution. It was designed to be verified through global analysis, for instance through abstract interpretation.

A variant of acceptability w.r.t. a set that avoids the drawbacks of using procedural notions and that can be verified on a local level was designed in [10]. This variant required that the goals of interest are *rigid* under the given level mapping. Here, rigidity means that $|G\theta| = |G|$, for any substitution θ, where $|\cdot| : B_P^E \to \mathcal{N}$ now denotes a generalised level mapping, defined on the extended Herbrand base.

Comparing the notions of boundedness and rigidity in the context of a level mapping based approach, it is clear that boundedness is more general than rigidity. If the level mapping of a goal is invariant under substitution, then the level mapping is bounded on the set of instances of the goal, but not conversely.

Given the latter observation and given that acceptability of [3] is a more generally known and accepted notion, we started our work by generalising this variant.

However, generalising the concept of boundedness to general term orders proved to be very difficult. We postpone the discussion on this issue until after we formulated the results, but because of these complications, we only arrived at generalised acceptability conditions that are useful in the context of well-moded, simply moded programs and goals.

Because of this, we then turned our attention to acceptability with respect to a set. Here, the generalisation of rigidity was less complicated, so that in the end we obtained the strongest results for this variant of acceptability. Therefore, we first present term-acceptability with respect to a set of goals. We need the following notion.

Definition 6. *[9] Let P be a definite program and S be a set of atomic queries. The call set, Call(P, S), is the set of all atoms A, such that a variant of A is a selected atom in some derivation for $P \cup \{\leftarrow Q\}$, for some $Q \in S$ and under the left-to-right selection rule.*

To illustrate this definition recall the following example [1,10].

Example 5.

$$perm([], []).$$
$$perm(L, [El|T]) \leftarrow del(El, L, L1), perm(L1, T).$$

$$del(X, [X|T], T).$$
$$del(X, [H|T], [H|T1]) \leftarrow del(X, T, T1).$$

Let S be $\{perm(t_1, t_2) \mid t_1$ is a nil-terminated list and t_2 is a free variable$\}$. Then, $Call(P, S) = S \cup \{ del(t_1, t_2, t_3) \mid t_1$ and t_3 are free variables and t_2 is a nil-terminated list$\}$. Such information about S could for instance be expressed in terms of the rigid types of [16] and $Call(P, S)$ could be computed using the type inference of [16]. □

The following definition generalises the notion of acceptability w.r.t. a set [9] in two ways: 1) it generalises it to general term orders, 2) it generalises it to mutual recursion, using the standard notation of mutual recursion [1]—the original definition of acceptability required decrease only for calls to the predicate that appears in the head of the clause. This restriction limited the approach to programs with direct recursion only.

Definition 7. *Let S be a set of atomic queries and P a definite program. P is term-acceptable w.r.t. S if there exists a well-founded order $>$, such that*

- *for any $A \in Call(P, S)$*
- *for any clause $A' \leftarrow B_1, \ldots, B_n$ in P, such that $\mathrm{mgu}(A, A') = \theta$ exists,*
- *for any atom B_i, such that $rel(B_i) \simeq rel(A)$*
- *for any computed answer substitution σ for $\leftarrow (B_1, \ldots, B_{i-1})\theta$:*

$$A > B_i\theta\sigma$$

The following establishes the connection between term-acceptability w.r.t. a set S and LD-termination for queries in S.

Theorem 1. *Let P be a program. P is term-acceptable w.r.t. a set of atomic queries S if and only if P is LD-terminating for all queries in S.*

Proof. For all proofs we refer to [20].

This theorem is similar to Proposition 2.8 [10]. However, since the definition of term-acceptability deals correctly with mutual recursion, termination is established not only for directly recursive programs.

We postpone applying the Theorem 1 to Example 5 until a more syntactic way of verifying term-acceptability w.r.t. a set is developed.

To do this, we extend the sufficient condition of [8], that impose the additional requirement of rigidity of the level mapping on the call set, to the case of general term orders.

First we adapt the notion of rigidity to general term orders.

Definition 8. *(see also [6]) The term or atom $A \in U_P^E \cup B_P^E$ is called rigid w.r.t. a quasi-order $\geq$ if for any substitution θ, $A =_> A\theta$. In this case $\geq$ is said to be rigid on A.*

The notion of the rigidity on a term (an atom) is naturally extended to the notion of rigidity on a set of atoms (terms). In particular, we will be interested in orders that are rigid on $Call(P, S)$ for some P and S.

We also need interargument relations based on general term orders.

Definition 9. *Let P be a definite program, p/n a predicate in P. An interargument relation is a relation $R_p \subseteq \{p(t_1, \ldots, t_n) \mid t_i \in Term_P\}$. R_p is a valid interargument relation for p/n if and only if for every $p(t_1, \ldots, t_n) \in Atom_P$: if $P \models p(t_1, \ldots, t_n)$ then $p(t_1, \ldots, t_n) \in R_p$.*

Usually, the interargument relation will be defined based on a quasi-order used for proving termination. However, in general, this needs not be the case.

Example 6. Consider the following program.

$$p(0, []). \quad p(f(X), [X|T]) \leftarrow p(X, T)$$

The following interargument relations can be considered for p: $\{p(t_1, t_2) \mid t_2 > t_1 \vee t_1 =_> t_2\}$, valid if $>$ is a part of a quasi-order imposed by a list-length norm, $\| \cdot \|_l$. Recall, that for lists $\|[t_1|t_2]\|_l = 1 + \|t_2\|_l$, while the list-length of other terms is considered to be 0. On the other hand, $\{p(t_1, t_2) \mid t_1 > t_2 \vee t_1 =_> t_2\}$ is valid, if $>$ and $=_>$ are parts of a quasi-order imposed by a term-size norm.

Using general (non-norm based) quasi-orders, $\{p(t_1, t_2) \mid t_1 > t_2\}$ is valid, for example, for the recursive path ordering [11] with the following order on functors: $f/1 \succ ./2$ and $0 \succ []$. Alternatively, $\{p(t_1, t_2) \mid t_2 > t_1\}$ is valid, for example, for the recursive path ordering with the following order on functors: $./2 \succ f/1$ and $[] \succ 0$. $\square$

Using the notion of rigidity a sufficient condition for term-acceptability w.r.t. a set is presented. We call this condition *rigid term-acceptability w.r.t. a set of queries*.

Theorem 2. *Let S be a set of atomic queries and P be a definite program. Let $\geq$ be a quasi-order on U_P^E and for each predicate p in P, let R_p be a valid interargument relation for p. If there exists a well-founded proper extension $\succeq$ of $\geq$ to $U_P^E \cup B_P^E$, which is rigid on $Call(P, S)$ such that*

- *for any clause $H \leftarrow B_1, \ldots, B_n \in P$, and*
- *for any atom B_i in its body, such that $rel(B_i) \simeq rel(H)$,*
- *for substitution θ, such that the arguments of the atoms in $(B_1, \ldots, B_{i-1})\theta$ all satisfy their associated relations $R_{rel(B_1)}, \ldots, R_{rel(B_{i-1})}$*

$$H\theta \succ B_i\theta$$

then P is term-acceptable w.r.t. S

We continue the analysis of Example 5.

Example 7. Let $\succeq$ be a well-founded quasi-order on $U_P^E \cup B_P^E$, such that:

- for all terms t_1, t_{21} and t_{22}: $perm(t_1, t_{21}) =_{\succ} perm(t_1, t_{22})$.
- for all terms $t_{11}, t_{12}, t_2, t_{31}, t_{32}$: $del(t_{11}, t_2, t_{31}) =_{\succ} del(t_{12}, t_2, t_{32})$.
- for all terms t_{11}, t_{12} and t_2: $[t_{11}|t_2] =_{\succ} [t_{12}|t_2]$.

That is, we impose that the ordering is invariant on predicate argument positions and functor argument positions that may occur with a free variable in $Call(P, S)$. Furthermore, we impose that $\succeq$ has the subterm and monotonicity properties at all remaining predicate or functor argument positions.

First we investigate the rigidity of $\succeq$ on $Call(P, S)$, namely: $G\theta =_{\succ} G$ for any $G \in Call(P, S)$ and any θ. Now any effect that the application of θ to G may have on G needs to be through the occurrence of some variable in G. However, because we imposed that $\succeq$ is invariant on all predicate and functor argument positions that may possibly contain a variable in some call, $G\theta =_{\succ} G$.

Associate with del the interargument relation $R_{del} = \{del(t_1, t_2, t_3) \mid t_2 \succ t_3\}$. First, we verify that this interargument relationship is valid. Note, that an interargument relationship is valid whenever it is a model for its predicate. Thus, to check whether R_{del} is valid, $T_P(R_{del}) \subseteq R_{del}$ is checked. For the non-recursive clause of del the inclusion follows from the subset property of $\succeq$, while for the recursive one, from the monotonicity of it.

Then, consider the recursive clauses of the program.

- $perm$. If $del(El, L, L1)\theta$ satisfies R_{del}, then $L\theta \succ L1\theta$. By the monotonicity, $perm(L, T)\theta \succ perm(L1, T)\theta$ and, by the first condition on the quasi-order $\succeq$, $perm(L, [El|T])\theta =_{\succ} perm(L, T)\theta$. Thus, the decrease $perm(L, [El|T])\theta \succ perm(L1, T)\theta$ holds.
- del. By the properties of $\succ$: $del(X, [H|T], [H|T1]) \succ del(X, T, [H|T1])$ and $del(X, T, [H|T1]) =_{\succ} del(X, T, T1)$, i.e., $del(X, [H|T], [H|T1]) \succ del(X, T, T1)$.

We have shown that all the conditions of Theorem 2 are satisfied, and thus, P is term-acceptable w.r.t. S. By Theorem 1, P terminates for all queries in S.

We do not need to construct the actual order, but only to prove that there is one, that meets all the requirements. In our case, the requirement (subterm and monotonicity on the remaining argument positions) is satisfiable.   □

4   The Results for Standard Acceptability

In this section we briefly discuss some of the results we obtained in generalising the acceptability notions of [3,14]. Since these results are weaker than those presented in the previous section, we do not elaborate on them in full detail. In particular, we do not recall the definitions of well-moded programs and goals, nor those of simply moded programs and goals, that we use below, but instead refer to [1], respectively [2]. Below, we assume that in-output modes for the program and goal are given. For any atom A and a mode m_A for A, we denote by A^{inp} the atom obtained from A by removing all output arguments. E.g., let $A = p(f(2), 3, X)$ and $m_A = p(in, in, out)$, then $A^{inp} = p(f(2), 3)$.

Definition 10. *Let $\geq$ be a quasi-order on B_P^E. We call $\geq$ output-independent if for any two moded atoms A and B: $A^{\mathrm{inp}} = B^{\mathrm{inp}}$ implies $A =_> B$.*

For well-moded programs, term-acceptability in the style of [3] can now be defined as follows.

Definition 11. *Let P be a well-moded program, $\geq$ an output-independent well-founded order and I a model for P. The program P is called term-acceptable w.r.t. $\geq$ and I if for all $A \leftarrow B_1, \ldots, B_n$ in P, all i, $1 \leq i \leq n$, and all substitutions θ, such that $(A\theta)^{\mathrm{inp}}$ and $B_1\theta, \ldots, B_{i-1}\theta$ are ground and $I \models B_1\theta \wedge \ldots \wedge B_{i-1}\theta$ holds: $A\theta > B_i\theta$.*

P is called *term-acceptable* if it is term-acceptable with respect to some output-independent well-founded quasi-order and some model. Note the similarity and the difference with the notion of *well-acceptability* introduced by Etalle, Bossi and Cocco [14]—both notions relay on "ignoring" the output positions. However, the approach suggested in [14] measures atoms by level-mappings, while our approach is based on general term orders. In addition [14] requires a decrease only between atoms of mutually recursive predicates. Similarly, one might use the notion of term-acceptability that requires a decrease only between atoms of mutually recursive predicates. This definition will be equivalent to the one we used, since for atoms of non-mutually recursive predicates the dependency relation, $\sqsupset$, can always be used to define an order. Since every level mapping naturally gives rise to the order on atoms, that is $A_1 \succ A_2$ if $\mid A_1 \mid > \mid A_2 \mid$, we conclude that *every well-acceptable program is term-acceptable.*

The following theorem states that term-acceptability of a well-moded program is sufficient for LD-termination of all well-moded goals w.r.t. this program. Etalle, Bossi and Cocco [14] call such a program *well-terminating.*

Theorem 3. *Let P be a well-moded program, that is term-acceptable w.r.t. an output-independent well-founded quasi-order $\geq$ and a model I. Let G be a well-moded goal, then G LD-terminates.*

If the requirement of well-modedness is relaxed the theorem ceases to hold.

Example 8.

$$p(a) \leftarrow q(X) \qquad q(f(X)) \leftarrow q(X)$$

with the modes $p(in), q(in)$. This program is not well-moded w.r.t. the given modes, but satisfies the remaining conditions of term-acceptability with respect to the following quasi-order: $p(a) > q(t)$ and $q(f(t)) > q(t)$ for any term t and $t =_> s$ only if t and s are syntactically identical, and the following model $\{p(a), q(a), q(f(a)), \ldots\}$. However, well-moded goal $p(a)$ is non-terminating. $\Box$

Unfortunately, well-modedness is not sufficient to make the converse to hold. That is, there is a well-moded program P and a well-moded goal G, such that G is LD-terminating w.r.t. P, but P is not term-acceptable.

Example 9. Consider the following program:

$$p(f(X)) \leftarrow p(g(X))$$

with the mode $p(out)$. This program is well-moded, the well-moded goal $p(X)$ terminates w.r.t. this program, but it is not term-acceptable, since the required decrease $p(f(X)) > p(g(X))$ violates output-independence of $>$.   □

Intuitively, the problem in the example occured, since some information has been passed via the output positions, i.e, P is not simply moded. Indeed, if P is simply-moded,[2], the second direction of the theorem holds as well. This was already observed in [14] in the context of well-acceptability and well-termination. The following is an immediate corollary to Theorem 5.1 in [14]. As that theorem states for well-moded simply moded programs well-termination implies well-acceptability. Therefore, well-terminating programs are term-acceptable.

Corollary 1. *Let P be a well-moded and simply moded program, LD-terminating for any well-moded goal. Then there exists a model I and an output-independent well-founded quasi-order $\geq$, such that P is term-acceptable w.r.t. I and $>$.*

To conclude, we briefly discuss why it is difficult to extend the notions of term-acceptability to the non well-moded case, using a notion of boundedness, as it was done for standard acceptability [3]. In acceptability based on level mappings, boundedness ensures that the level mapping of a (non-ground) goal can only increase up to some finite bound when the goal becomes more instantiated. Observe that every ground goal is trivially bounded.

One particular possible generalisation of boundedness to term-orderings, which is useful for maintaining most of our results, is:

An atom A is *bounded* with respect to an ordering $>$, if there exists an atom C such that for all ground instances $A\theta$ of A: $C > A\theta$, and $\{B \in B_P^E \mid C > B\}$ is finite.

Such a definition imposes constraints which are very similar to the ones imposed by standard boundedness in the context of level mappings. However, one thing we lose is that it is no longer generalisation of groundness. Consider an atom $p(a)$ and assume that our language contains a functor $f/1$ and a constant b. Then one particular well-founded ordering is

$$p(a) > \ldots > p(f(f(b))) > p(f(b)) > p(b).$$

So, $p(a)$ is not bounded with respect to this ordering.

Because of such complications, we felt that the rigidity-based results of the previous section are the preferred generalisations to general term orders.

5   Towards Automation of the Approach

In this section we present an approach leading towards automatic verification of the term-acceptability condition. The basic idea for the approach is inspired on the "constraint based" termination analysis proposed in [10]. We start off from the conditions imposed by term-acceptability, and systematically reduce these conditions to more explicit constraints on the objects of our search: the quasi-order $\geq$ and the interargument relations, R_p, or model I.

The approach presented below has been applied successfully to a number of examples that appear in the literature on termination, such as different versions of *permute* [5,17,10], *dis-con* [7], *transitive closure* [17], *add-mult* [19], *combine, reverse, odd-even, at_least_double* and *normalisation* [10], *quicksort* program [21,1], *derivative* [13], *distributive law* [12], *boolean ring* [15], *flatten* [4].

In the remainder of the paper, we explain the approach using some of these examples. We start by showing how the analysis of Example 5, presented before, can be performed systematically. We stress the main points of the methodology.

Example 10. $\geq$ should be rigid on $Call(P, S)$. To enforce the rigidity, $\geq$ should ignore all argument positions in atoms in $Call(P, S)$ that might be occupied by free variables, i.e., the second argument position of *perm* and the first and the third argument positions of *del*. Moreover, since for the elements of $Call(P, S)$ the first argument of *perm* and the second argument of *del* are general nil-terminated lists, the first argument of ./2 should be ignored as well.

The $>$-decreases imposed in the term-acceptability w.r.t. a set S are:

$del(X, [H|T], [H|T1])\theta > del(X, T, T1)\theta$

$del(El, L, L_1)\theta$ satisfies R_{del} implies $perm(L, [El|T])\theta > perm(L_1, T)\theta$

Each of these conditions we simplify by replacing the predicate argument positions that should be ignored by some arbitrary term—one of $v_1, v_2, \ldots$. The following conditions are obtained:

$$del(v_1, [H|T]\theta, v_2) > del(v_3, T\theta, v_4) \tag{1}$$

$$del(El, L, L_1)\theta \text{ satisfies } R_{del} \text{ implies } perm(L\theta, v_1) > perm(L_1\theta, v_2) \tag{2}$$

Observe that this only partially deals with the requirements that the rigidity conditions expressed above impose: rigidity on functor arguments (the first argument of ./2 should be invariant w.r.t. the order) is not expressed. We keep track of such constraints implicitly, and only verify them at a later stage when additional constraints on the order are derived.

For each of the conditions we have two options on how to enforce it:

Option 1): The decrease required in the condition can be achieved by imposing some property on $\geq$, which is consistent with the constraints that were already imposed on $\geq$ before.

In our example, condition (1) is satisfied by imposing the subterm property for the second argument of ./2 and monotonicity on the second argument of *del*. The second argument of ./2 does not belong to a set of functor argument positions that should be ignored. Then, $[t_1|t_2] > t_2$ holds for any terms t_1 and t_2, and by the monotonicity of $>$ in the second argument of *del* (1) holds.

In general we can select from a bunch of term-order properties, or even specific term-orders, that were proposed in the literature.

Option 2): The required decrease is imposed as a constraint on the interargument relation(s) R of the preceding atoms.

In the *perm* example, the decrease $perm(L\theta, v_1) > perm(L_1\theta, v_2)$ cannot directly be achieved by imposing some constraint on $\geq$. Thus, we impose that the underlying decrease $L\theta > L_1\theta$ should hold for the intermediate body atoms $(del(El, L, L_1)\theta)$ that satisfy the interargument relation R_{del}.

Thus, in the example, the constraint is that R_{del} should be such that for all $del(t_1, t_2, t_3)$ that satisfy R_{del}: $t_2 > t_3$. Recall that the interargument relation is valid if it forms a model for its predicate. Thus, one way to verify that a valid interargument relation R_{del} as required exists, is to impose that $M = \{del(t_1, t_2, t_3) \mid t_2 > t_3\}$ itself is a model for the *del* clauses in the program, i.e., $T_P(M) \subseteq M$. As shown in [20], this reduces to "$[t_1|t_2] > t_2$" and "$t_2 > t_3$ implies $[t|t_2] > [t|t_3]$". These are fed into our Option 1) step, imposing a monotonicity property on the second argument of ./2 for $>$, completing the proof.   □

The previous example does not illustrate the approach in full generality. It might happen that more than one intermediate goal preceded the recursive atom in the body of the clause. In this case we refer to the whole conjunction as to "one" subgoal. Formally, given a sequence of intermediate body atoms $B_1, \ldots, B_n$ a (generalised) clause $B_1, \ldots, B_n \leftarrow B_1, \ldots, B_n$ is constructed and one step of unfolding is performed on each atom in its body, producing a generalised program P'.

Example 11. The following version of the *perm* program appeared in [17].

$$perm([], []). \qquad ap_1([], L, L).$$
$$perm(L, [H|T]) \leftarrow \quad ap_1([H|L1], L2, [H|L3]) \leftarrow$$
$$ap_2(V, [H|U], L), \qquad ap_1(L1, L2, L3).$$
$$ap_1(V, U, W), \qquad ap_2([], L, L).$$
$$perm(W, T). \qquad ap_2([H|L1], L2, [H|L3]) \leftarrow$$
$$ap_2(L1, L2, L3).$$

This example is analysed, based on Theorem 3 for the well-moded case. We would like to prove termination of the goals $perm(t_1, t_2)$, where t_1 is a ground list and t_2 a free variable. Assume the modes $perm(in, out)$, $ap_1(in, in, out)$, $ap_2(out, out, in)$.

The term-acceptability imposes, among the others, the following $>$-decrease: $I \models ap_2(V, [H|U], L)\theta \wedge ap_1(V, U, W)\theta$ implies $perm(L)\theta > perm(W)\theta$. The underlying decrease $L\theta > W\theta$ cannot be achieved by reasoning on $ap_1/3$ or $ap_2/3$ alone. Therefore, we construct a following generalised program P':

$$ap_2([], [t_1|t_2], [t_1|t_2]), ap_1([], t_2, t_2).$$
$$ap_2([t_6|t_1], [t_5|t_2], [t_6|t_3]), ap_1([t_6|t_1], t_2, [t_6|t_4]) \leftarrow$$
$$ap_2(t_1, [t_5|t_2], t_3), ap_1(t_1, t_2, t_4).$$

Now, we need to very that $M = \{ap_2(a_1, a_2, a_3), ap_1(b_1, b_2, b_3) \mid a_3 > b_3\}$ satisfies $T_{P'}(M) \subseteq M$. Using the 2 clauses, this is reduced to "$[t_1|t_2] > t_2$" and

"$t_3 > t_4$ implies $[t_6|t_3] > [t_6|t_4]$", imposing monotonicity and subterm properties on $>$. The proof is completed analogously to the previous example. $\square$

As a last example, we return to the motivating Example 1, on computing higher derivatives of polynomial functions in one variable.

Example 12. We are interested in proving termination of the queries that belong to $S = \{d(t_1, t_2) \mid t_1$ is a repeated derivative of a function in a variable u and t_2 is a free variable$\}$. So S consists of atoms of the form $d(der(u), X)$ or $d(der(u*u+u), Y)$ or $d(der(der(u+u)), Z)$, etc. Observe, that $Call(P, S) = S$.

We start by analysing the requirements that imposes the rigidity of $\geq$ on $Call(P, S)$. First, the second argument position of d should be ignored, since it might be occupied by a free variable. Second, the first argument position of d is occupied by a ground term. Thus, rigidity does not pose any restrictions on functors argument positions.

Then, we construct the $>$-decreases implied by the rigid term-acceptability. The arguments that should be ignored are replaced by anonymous terms $v_1, v_2, \ldots$ For the sake of brevity we omit most of these $>$-decreases, since the only requirement they pose is monotonicity and subterm properties on the first argument of d. However, in order to satisfy the following $>$-decrease:

$$d(der(X), DX)\theta \text{ satisfies } R_d \text{ implies } d(der(der(X))\theta, v_1) > d(der(DX)\theta, v_2)$$

more complicated analysis should be performed. It is sufficient to prove that for any $(t_1, t_2) \in R_d$ holds that $t_1 > t_2$. That is if $M = \{d(t_1, t_2) \mid t_1 > t_2\}$ then $T_P(M) \subseteq M$. This may be reduced to the following conditions:

$$der(u) > 1 \tag{3}$$
$$t_1 \in R_{number} \text{ implies } der(t_1) > 0 \tag{4}$$
$$der(t_1) > t_2 \ \& \ der(t_3) > t_4 \text{ implies } der(t_1 + t_3) > t_2 + t_4 \tag{5}$$
$$der(t_1) > t_2 \ \& \ der(t_3) > t_4 \text{ implies } der(t_1 * t_3) > t_1 * t_4 + t_2 * t_3 \tag{6}$$
$$der(t_1) > t_2 \ \& \ der(t_2) > t_3 \text{ implies } der(der(t_1)) > t_3 \tag{7}$$

Condition (7) follows from monotonicity and transitivity of $>$. However, (4)-(6) are not satisfied by general properties of $>$ and we choose, to specify the order. The order that meets these conditions is the recursive path ordering [11] with der having the highest priority, i.e. $der \succ +$ and $der \succ *$. $\square$

This example demonstrates the main points of our methodology. First, given a program P and a set S of goals, *compute the set of calls* $Call(P, S)$ (for instance through the abstract interpretation of [16]). Second, *enforce the rigidity of* $\geq$ *on* $Call(P, S)$, i.e., ignore all predicate or functor argument positions that might be occupied by free variables in $Call(P, S)$. Third, repeatedly *construct* $>$-*decreases*, such that rigid term-acceptability condition will hold and check if those can be verified by some of the predefined orders.

6   Conclusion

We have presented a non-transformational approach to termination analysis of logic programs, based on general term-orderings. The problem of termination was studied by a number of authors (see [7] for the survey). More recent work on this topic can be found in [18,9,14,10].

Our approach gets it power from integrating the traditional notion of acceptability [3] with the wide class of term-orderings that have been studied in the context of the term-rewriting systems. In theory, such an integration is unnecessary: acceptability (based on level mappings only) is already equivalent to LD-termination. In practice, the required level mappings may sometimes be very complex (such as for Example 1 or *distributive law* [12], *boolean ring* [15] or *flattening of a binary tree* [4]), and automatic systems for proving termination are unable to generate them. In such cases, generating an appropriate term-ordering, replacing the level mapping, may often be much easier, especially since we can reuse the impressive machinery on term-orders developed for term-rewrite systems. In some other cases, such as *turn* [6], simple level mappings do exist (in the case of *turn*: a norm counting the number of 0s before the first occurrence of 1 in the list is sufficient), but most systems based on level mappings will not even find this level mapping, because they only consider mappings based on term-size or list-length norms. Again, our approach is able to deal with such cases.

Additional extensions of acceptability [3], such as semi-acceptability [1], well-acceptability [14] appeared in the literature. For the well-moded programs term-acceptability implies acceptability (or, equivalently, semi-acceptability). As illustrated by Example 9, not every acceptable program is term-acceptable. Similarly, well-acceptability implies term-acceptability. Moreover, for well-moded simply moded programs well-acceptability is equivalent to term-acceptability. In [20] we have proved that, under certain conditions, term-acceptability w.r.t. a set implies term-acceptability (w.r.t. the least Herbrand model).

Unlike transformational approaches, that establish the termination results for logic programs by the reasoning on termination of term-rewriting systems, we apply the term-orderings directly to the logic programs, thus, avoiding transformations. This could both be regarded as an advantage and as a drawback of our approach. It may be considered as a drawback, because reasoning on successful instances of intermediate body-atoms introduces an additional complication in our approach, for which there is no counterpart in transformational methods (except for in the transformation step itself). On the other hand, we consider it as an advantage, because it is precisely this reasoning on intermediate body atoms that gives more insight in the property of *logic program termination* (as opposed to *term-rewrite system termination*).

So, in a sense our approach provides the best of both worlds: a means to incorporate into 'direct' approaches the generality of general term-orderings.

We consider as a future work a full implementation of the approach. Although we already tested very many examples manually, an implementation will allow us to conduct a much more extensive experimentation, comparing the technique also in terms of efficiency with other systems. Since we apply a demand-driven approach, systematically reducing required conditions to more simple constraints on the ordering and the model, we expect that the method can lead to very efficient verification.

Acknowledgement

Alexander Serebrenik is supported by GOA: "LP^+: a second generation logic programming language". We thank anonymous referees for very useful comments.

References

1. K. R. Apt. *From Logic Programming to Prolog.* Prentice-Hall Int. Series in Computer Science. Prentice Hall, 1997.
2. K. R. Apt and S. Etalle. On the unification free Prolog programs. In A. M. Borzyszkowski and S. Sokolowski, editors, *18th Int. Symp. on Mathematical Foundations of Computer Science,* pages 1–19. Springer Verlag, 1993. LNCS 711.
3. K. R. Apt and D. Pedreschi. Studies in Pure Prolog: Termination. In J. W. Lloyd, editor, *Proc. Esprit Symp. on Comp. Logic,* pages 150–176. Springer Verlag, 1990.
4. T. Arts. *Automatically proving termination and innermost normalisation of term rewriting systems.* PhD thesis, Universiteit Utrecht, 1997.
5. T. Arts and H. Zantema. Termination of logic programs using semantic unification. In M. Proietti, editor, *5th Int. Workshop on Logic Programming Synthesis and Transformation,* pages 219–233. Springer Verlag, 1995. LNCS 1048.
6. A. Bossi, N. Cocco, and M. Fabris. Norms on terms and their use in proving universal termination of a logic program. *Theoretical Computer Science,* 124(2):297–328, February 1994.
7. D. De Schreye and S. Decorte. Termination of logic programs: The never-ending story. *J. Logic Programming,* 19/20:199–260, May/July 1994.
8. D. De Schreye, K. Verschaetse, and M. Bruynooghe. A framework for analyzing the termination of definite logic programs with respect to call patterns. In I. Staff, editor, *Proc. of the Int. Conf. on Fifth Generation Computer Systems.,* pages 481–488. IOS Press, 1992.
9. S. Decorte and D. De Schreye. Termination analysis: some practical properties of the norm and level mapping space. In J. Jaffar, editor, *Proc. of the 1998 Joint Int. Conf. and Symp. on Logic Programming,* pages 235–249. MIT Press, June 1998.
10. S. Decorte, D. De Schreye, and H. Vandecasteele. Constraint-based termination analysis of logic programs. *ACM Transactions on Programming Languages and Systems (TOPLAS),* 21(6):1137–1195, November 1999.
11. N. Dershowitz. Termination. In C. Kirchner, editor, *First Int. Conf. on Rewriting Techniques and Applications,* pages 180–224. Springer Verlag, 1985. LNCS 202.
12. N. Dershowitz and C. Hoot. Topics in termination. In C. Kirchner, editor, *Rewriting Techniques and Applications, 5th Int. Conf.,* pages 198–212. Springer Verlag, 1993. LNCS 690.
13. N. Dershowitz and Z. Manna. Proving termination with multiset orderings. *Communications of the ACM (CACM),* 22(8):465–476, August 1979.
14. S. Etalle, A. Bossi, and N. Cocco. Termination of well-moded programs. *J. Logic Programming,* 38(2):243–257, February 1999.

15. J. Hsiang. Rewrite method for theorem proving in first order theory with equality. *Journal of Symbolic Computation*, 8:133–151, 1987.
16. G. Janssens and M. Bruynooghe.   Deriving descriptions of possible values of program variables by means of abstract interpretation. *J. Logic Programming*, 13(2&3):205–258, July 1992.
17. M. Krishna Rao, D. Kapur, and R. Shyamasundar. Transformational methodology for proving termination of logic programs. *J. Logic Programming*, 34:1–41, 1998.
18. N. Lindenstrauss and Y. Sagiv. Automatic termination analysis of logic programs. In L. Naish, editor, *Proc. of the Fourteenth Int. Conf. on Logic Programming*, pages 63–77. MIT Press, July 1997.
19. L. Plümer. *Termination Proofs for Logic Programs*. LNAI 446. Springer Verlag, 1990.
20. A. Serebrenik and D. De Schreye.   Termination analysis of logic programs using acceptability with general term orders. Technical Report CW 291, Departement Computerwetenschappen, K. U.Leuven, Leuven, Belgium, 2000. Available at http://www.cs.kuleuven.ac.be/publicaties/rapporten/CW2000.html.
21. L. Sterling and E. Shapiro. *The Art of Prolog*. The MIT Press, 1994.

A Model for Inter-module Analysis and Optimizing Compilation

Francisco Bueno[1], María García de la Banda[2], Manuel Hermenegildo[1], Kim Marriott[2], Germán Puebla[1], and Peter J. Stuckey[3]

[1] Technical University of Madrid (UPM), Spain
{bueno,herme,german}@fi.upm.es
[2] Monash University, Australia
{mbanda,marriott}@csse.monash.edu.au
[3] University of Melbourne, Australia
pjs@cs.mu.oz.au

Abstract. Recent research into the implementation of logic programming languages has demonstrated that global program analysis can be used to speed up execution by an order of magnitude. However, currently such global program analysis requires the program to be analysed as a whole: separate compilation of modules is not supported. We describe and empirically evaluate a simple model for extending global program analysis to support separate compilation of modules. Importantly, our model supports context-sensitive program analysis and multi-variant specialization of procedures in the modules.

1 Introduction

Decades of software development have demonstrated that the use of modules to structure programs is crucial to the development of large software systems. It has also shown that separate compilation of these modules is vital since it is too inefficient to have to compile the entire program including library files each time something is changed. Thus, virtually all commercially used compilers for almost all programming languages allow compilation of modules in isolation. Typically this is achieved by import and export declarations in the module providing information about each module's interface to other modules.

Recent research into the implementation of logic programming languages has demonstrated that information from global program analysis can be used, for example, to guide compile-time optimizations which can speed up execution by an order of magnitude [8] or to guide automatic parallelization [3]. In order to perform such optimizations, program analyses must determine useful information at compile-time about the run-time behavior of the program. However, a severe limitation of most existing analyses is that they require the program to be analysed as a whole: thus separate compilation of modules is not supported.

One of the main reasons to need the whole program is that, at least for logic programs, accurate program analysis seems to require *context-sensitive* analysis in which procedures are analysed with respect to a number of calling patterns,

Kung-Kiu Lau (Ed.): LOPSTR 2000, LNCS 2042, pp. 86–102, 2001.

rather than a *context-free* analysis in which analysis is only performed once for each procedure. Context-sensitive analysis is also important because it naturally supports specialization of the program procedures for particular cases. Such *multi-variant specialization* [19] allows different optimizations to be performed on the same procedure, a technique which has been shown to be quite important in practice [8,10].

Here we describe and empirically evaluate a rather simple model for extending abstract interpretation based global program analysers for logic programming languages to support separate module compilation. Our model supports a program development scenario in which the program is divided into modules and each module is developed separately, possibly by different programmers. Each module may be compiled separately, taking into account the available analysis information of the modules it imports for optimization. Each compilation updates available analysis information as well as marking other modules where recompilation could improve performance. The whole process migrates towards a point equivalent to that obtained by analysing and optimizing the whole program at once. Importantly, the model supports context-sensitive program analysis and multi-variant specialization of procedures in the modules.

The issue of how to combine global program analysis with separate compilation of modules is not new: however, most work has been limited to context-free program analysis. In this context, make style dependencies [6] can be used to order compilation of modules. If a module is modified, other modules depending upon it must be recompiled if the changes may have affected them. Thus, one area of research has been to determine precisely which changes to a module force recompilation of another module [13,14,16]. These approaches do not extend naturally to context-sensitive analyses.

Another proposal consists in a two stage approach to program analysis, in which a fast imprecise global analysis is applied to the whole program, then more precise analysis (possibly context sensitive) is applied to each module in turn [12]. Similarly, the work described in [4] proposes an approach to analysis of Prolog modules in which the system first pre-analyses modules, and then analyses the program as a whole by combining the result of these pre-analyses. This method is basically restricted to context-free analyses. These approaches contrast to our approach in which no analysis of the whole program is ever required.

In the specific context of logic programming languages, Mercury [15] is a modular logic programming language which makes use of sophisticated modular analyses to improve execution speed, but context sensitive analysis information is required to be specified by the user for exported predicates.

The present paper extends our previous work on the incremental analysis of logic programs [7] (although this work did not consider modules as such) and also [11] which contains a general discussion of different scenarios and the overall issues which appear in the analysis and specialization of programs decomposed into modules. The paper is organized as follows. In the next section we introduce our notation. Then, Section 3 gives our model for modular compilation where modules are not changing. Section 4 extends this to the edit-compile-test cycle. Some brief experimental results are provided in Section 5, while Section 6 concludes.

2 Preliminaries and Notation

We assume the reader is familiar with the concepts of abstract interpretation [5] which underlie most analyses of logic programs.

The context-sensitive analysis of a module starts from descriptions of the initial calls to the module. The analysis computes descriptions of all the possible calls to the procedures in the module and, for each possible call, a description of its possible answers (returns of the calls). Descriptions of procedure calls and answers are "abstract" values in a domain $\mathcal{D}$ of descriptions, which is a poset with ordering relation $\preceq$. The infimum and supremum of the poset are denoted $\perp$ and $\top$, respectively, while the operations of least upper bound and greatest lower bound are denoted $\sqcup$ and $\sqcap$, respectively.

A *call pattern* is a pair $P : CP$ of a procedure P and a description CP of the values of the arguments of P (in logic programming terms, the head variables) when it is called. We assume for simplicity that all procedures P appear with a unique set of arguments (head variables), so we can refer to the argument positions in the description. An *answer pattern* is a triple $P : CP \mapsto AP$ where AP is a description of the values of the argument positions of P on return of calls described by call pattern $P : CP$. Analysis of a module M proceeds from a call pattern $P : CP$ for a procedure P exported by M and computes a set of answer patterns for all procedures that are visible in M and are reachable from $P : CP$. The description $\perp$ indicates an unreachable situation (e.g. an unreachable program point) while the description $\top$ conveys no information. The answer patterns computed by analysis are kept in the *answer table* of module M. There will be only one answer pattern per call pattern.

A *call dependency* is an arc $P : CP \rightarrow P' : CP'$ between call patterns which indicates that calls of the form $P' : CP'$ (might) occur during execution of calls of the form $P : CP$. The analysis also computes all possible call dependencies in the module, which are kept in the *call dependency graph*.

Example 1 A widely used analysis domain in the context of (constraint) logic programs is groundness analysis using the *Pos* abstract domain [1]. Descriptions in *Pos* are positive Boolean functions denoting groundness dependencies, for example the description $X \wedge (Y \leftrightarrow Z)$ denotes that X is ground and Y is ground iff Z is ground. In this domain the least description $\perp_{Pos}$ is *false*, and the greatest description $\top_{Pos}$ is *true*, least upper bound $\sqcup_{Pos}$ is $\vee$ and greatest lower bound $\sqcap_{Pos}$ is $\wedge$.

Consider the top-down analysis of the following module, from the initial call pattern $app(X, Y, Z) : X$, that is, where app is called with the first argument ground.

```
:- module app.
app(X,Y,Z) :- X = [], Y = Z.
app(X,Y,Z) :- X = [A|X1], Z = [A|Z1], app(X1,Y,Z1).
```

Analysis proceeds by iterative fixpoint evaluation. The first iteration through the program produces answer pattern $app(X, Y, Z) : X \mapsto X \wedge (Y \leftrightarrow Z)$ (the answer from the first rule), as well as a call dependency $app(X, Y, Z) : X \to app(X, Y, Z) : X$. In the second iteration the same answer pattern is produced and so we have reached a fixpoint.   □

3   A Model for Separate Module Compilation

The principal idea of our compilation model is that at each stage the analysis information and associated executable code is correct, but recompilation may use more accurate analysis information to better optimize the generated code. Each compilation of a module asks the modules it calls for new (more accurate) analyses of the procedures it calls, and tells its calling modules whether more accurate information is available for their use. In this section we present a framework where the individual modules are not being modified and, thus, the information inferred during each compilation is never invalidated. In the next section we examine the use of the separate compilation model in the edit-compile-test cycle, where modules are being modified.

During modular analysis, information about each exported procedure is kept in the *analysis registry*. The analysis registry, or registry for short, is an extended answer table with the most up to date analysis information about procedures together with book keeping information for the compilation process. It is used when compiling a module to access information about procedures in other modules. Information about procedures is updated when their module is (re-)compiled. For simplicity, we assume that the analysis registry is global, but in practice we will store each answer pattern $P : CP \mapsto AP$ attached to the module M in which procedure P resides (see Section 5 for more details).

Entries in the analysis registry may be marked, written $P : CP \mapsto^{\bullet} AP$. A marked entry indicates that recompilation of the module containing P may infer better information. Entries may also be followed by another call pattern $P : CP'$ for the same procedure P, written $P : CP \mapsto AP \ (P : CP')$, where $P : CP'$ is called the *version call pattern*. At any time there is only one entry of the form $P : CP \mapsto \_$ (with or without version call pattern) for each $P : CP$.

A version call pattern indicates that a specialized procedure for $P : CP$ does not exist and instead the specialized procedure for $P : CP'$ should be used for linking. It also indicates that the compiler has not (yet) performed context sensitive analysis for $P : CP$, but rather has used information in the analysis registry to infer the answer pattern for $P : CP$. In an entry $P : CP \mapsto AP \ (P : CP')$ it is always the case that $CP \preceq CP'$ since it must be legitimate to use the existing procedure $P : CP'$ for calls of the form $P : CP$.

The analysis registry is initialized with (marked) entries of the form $P : \top \mapsto^{\bullet} \top$ for each exported procedure P in the program. This gives no information, but ensures a correct answer is available for each procedure.

The *inter-module dependency graph* is a call dependency graph with entries of the form $P_1 : CP_1 \to P_2 : CP_2$ where P_1 and P_2 are procedures exported by different modules. It is used to assess which modules may benefit from recompilation after the module exporting P_2 is (re-)compiled.

The key to the method is that the analysis registry always contains correct information, hence (optimizing) compilation of a module can safely make use of this information.

3.1 Compiling a Single Module

The first step in compiling a module M is determining its initial call patterns. This is simply the list of $P : CP$ appearing in a marked entry in the analysis registry where P is a procedure exported by M. Analysis proceeds from these initial call patterns as usual. During analysis of M, information for procedures in other modules is accessed by looking in the analysis registry. Suppose imported procedure P is being called with call pattern CP. Two cases are considered:

1. If $P : CP \mapsto AP$ (or $P : CP \mapsto AP$ ($P : CP'$)) exists in the analysis registry then the analysis can use AP as the answer description.
2. Otherwise, the analysis selects an entry in the registry of the form $P : CP' \mapsto AP'$ (or $P : CP' \mapsto AP'$ ($P : CP''$)) such that $CP \preceq CP'$ and uses AP' as a correct (but possibly inaccurate) answer description. Note that such an entry must exist since there is always an entry $P : \top \mapsto AP'$ for every exported procedure.

   If there are several entries of the appropriate form, analysis will choose one whose answer is no less accurate than the rest, i.e., an AP' will be chosen such that for all other entries of the form $P : CP'_i \mapsto AP'_i$ or $P : CP'_i \mapsto AP'_i$ ($P : CP''_i$) in the registry for which $CP \preceq CP'_i$ we have that $AP'_i \not\prec AP'$.[1]

   A new entry $P : CP \mapsto^\bullet AP'$ ($P : CP_{imp}$) is then added to the analysis registry, where $P : CP_{imp}$ is either $P : CP'$ if the selected entry does not have a version call pattern or $P : CP''$ otherwise. The mark indicates that the new call pattern could be refined by recompilation, and the version call pattern indicates its best current implementation.

The algorithm get_answer($P : CP$) below defines the answer pattern returned for a calling pattern $P : CP$. For the purposes of matching in the algorithm we assume that an entry without version call pattern $P : CP \mapsto AP'$ is equivalent to an entry with the version call pattern $P : CP \mapsto AP'$ ($P : CP$).

get_answer($P : CP$)
    if exists $P : CP \mapsto AP'$ ($P : CP'$) in registry
        return AP'

---

[1] If the behaviour of code resulting from multivariant specialisation is the same as the original program code with respect to the analysis domain, then a better choice for AP' is $\sqcap_i AP'_i$. Even better, if the analysis domain is downwards closed, the answer description $CP \sqcap AP'$ is also correct for $P : CP$ and, in general, more accurate since $CP \sqcap AP' \preceq AP'$. Thus, in this case, we can choose AP' to be $CP \sqcap (\sqcap_i AP'_i)$.

else
  $AP := \top;\ CP_{imp} := \top$
  foreach $P : CP' \mapsto AP'\ (P : CP'')$ in registry
    if $CP \preceq CP'$ and $AP' \preceq AP$
      $AP := AP'$
      $CP_{imp} := CP''$
  add $P : CP \mapsto^\bullet AP\ (P : CP_{imp})$ to the registry
  return AP

Once analysis is complete, the analysis registry is updated as follows. For each initial call pattern $P : CP$ the entry in the analysis registry is modified to $P : CP \mapsto AP$ as indicated by the answer table for module M. Note that any previous mark or additional version call pattern is removed. If the answer pattern has changed then, for each $P_1 : CP_1 \to P : CP$ appearing in the inter-module dependency graph, the entry in the analysis registry for $P_1 : CP_1$ is marked. Note that after analysis of a module, none of its procedures will be marked or have version call patterns in the analysis registry.

The inter-module dependency graph is updated as follows. For each initial call pattern $P : CP$ any entries of the form $P : CP \to P_2 : CP_2$ are removed. For each $P_3 : CP_3$, where P_3 is an imported procedure reachable from $P : CP$, the entry $P : CP \to P_3 : CP_3$ is added to the inter-module dependency graph.

Example 2 Consider the analysis of a simple program consisting of the modules

```
:- module main.
:- import rev.
main(X) :- A = [1,2,3], rev(A,X).

:- module rev.
:- import app.
rev(X,Y) :- X = [], Y = [].
rev(X,Y) :- X = [A|X1], rev(X1,Y1), B = [A], app(Y1,B,Y).

:- module app.
app(X,Y,Z) :- X = [], Y = Z.
app(X,Y,Z) :- X = [A|X1], Z = [A|Z1], app(X1,Y,Z1).
```

using groundness analysis domain *Pos*. Assume we want to compile module `rev` after we have compiled modules `main` and `app`, with current analysis registry

$$main(X) : true \mapsto true,$$
$$rev(X,Y) : true \mapsto^\bullet true,$$
$$rev(X,Y) : X \mapsto^\bullet true\ (rev : true),$$
$$app(X,Y,Z) : true \mapsto (X \wedge Y) \leftrightarrow Z,$$

and inter-module dependencies $main(X) : true \to rev(X,Y) : X$. See Example 5 to determine how the compilation process might reach this state.

Given the above analysis registry, the initial call patterns are $rev(X, Y) : true$ and $rev(X, Y) : X$. Analyzing both of them we obtain answer table

$$rev(X, Y) : true \mapsto true,$$
$$rev(X, Y) : X \mapsto X \wedge Y$$

and call dependency arcs

$$rev(X, Y) : true \rightarrow rev(X, Y) : true,$$
$$rev(X, Y) : X \rightarrow rev(X, Y) : X,$$
$$rev(X, Y) : true \rightarrow app(X, Y, Z) : true,$$
$$rev(X, Y) : X \rightarrow app(X, Y, Z) : X \wedge Y.$$

During the analysis the new calling pattern $app(X, Y, Z) : X \wedge Y$ is generated and it uses the answer for $app(X, Y, Z) : true$ adding the entry $app(X, Y, Z) : X \wedge Y \mapsto^{\bullet} (X \wedge Y) \leftrightarrow Z$ $(app(X, Y, Z) : true)$ to the registry.

The updating stage moves the answer patterns to the registry, marks the entry $main(X) : true \mapsto true$, and adds the inter-module dependency arcs (the last two call dependency arcs) to the inter-module dependency graph. □

3.2 Obtaining an Executable without Recompilation

The single module compilation algorithm must generate correct answers since it uses the information from the analysis registry, and that information is known to be correct (of course we assume the underlying local analysis algorithm is correct). Hence, the analysis information generated can be safely used to guide the optimization of the compiled code of the module. In particular, information about different call patterns facilitates multivariant specialisation of the procedure. Different variants of a procedure are generated if different optimizations can be performed depending on the different call patterns of the procedure.

Example 3 Several variants may be generated for the same procedure. We distinguish them by replacing the name of the procedure by the corresponding call pattern. Continuing with Example 2, compilation produces two variants for procedure rev, identified by 'rev:$true$' and 'rev:X', respectively. The second one can be optimized to:

```
'rev:X'(X, Y) :-
  ( X == []
  -> Y = []
  ;  X =: [A|X1],
     'rev:X'(X1,Y1),
     B := [A],
     'app:X∧Y'(Y1,B,Y)
  ).
```

where == is a test, := is an assignment and =: is a deconstruction. □

Once an object file exists for each module, an executable for the entire program can be produced by simply linking all the object files as usual (modulo the small change to the linker described below). The resulting executable is correct and any optimizations performed for specialized procedures are guaranteed to be valid.

Linking is made between specialized procedures as usual. From the linkers point of view the pair $P : CP$ is just a unique identifier for a specialized variant of procedure P. There is one additional complexity. The linker must use the analysis registry information to handle non-existent specialized variants. If the specialized procedure $P : CP$ does not exist then the link is made instead to the procedure $P : CP'$ where the entry in the analysis registry is $P : CP \mapsto AP (P : CP')$.

Example 4 After the compilation in Example 3, the call to 'app:$X \wedge Y$' in the body of 'rev:X' is linked to the procedure 'app:*true*'.   □

3.3   Obtaining an Executable by Performing Recompilation

Although linking can be performed at any time in the program development process without requiring any additional work, recompilation of module M might improve the analysis information if there is a procedure P in M with a marked entry $P : CP \mapsto^{\bullet} AP$ in the analysis registry. In turn, recompiling a module may mark procedures in modules that it calls (if new call patterns are created) and in modules that call it (if more accurate answer information is obtained).

We may continue choosing a module M which can benefit from recompilation and recompile it as above until either there are no marked entries in the analysis registry anymore (a "completely optimized" version of the program has been reached) or we decide not to perform any further recompilation. The latter is possible because the algorithm guarantees that after any number of recompilation steps the compiled program and the corresponding linked object is correct, even if marked entries still remain in the registry. This is important since the aim of the separate compilation model we propose is not to use a long full optimization process often. Instead, during the lifetime of the program various modules move towards fully optimized status as the program is modified and recompiled.

The process of repeated compilation is guaranteed to terminate if the abstract domain has no infinite descending chains. This is because every new answer description is guaranteed to be more specific than the previous answer description, and any new call pattern must be more specific than previous call patterns. More importantly, as long as there are no cyclic inter-module dependencies the process of repeated compilation is guaranteed to be as accurate as the analysis of the entire program at once. Essentially, this is because since there are no cycles there is only one fixpoint and the greatest fixpoint discovered by repeated compilation is equivalent to the least fixpoint discovered by a usual analysis of the entire program at once (see [2] for the formal proof).

Example 5 Consider compiling the program of Example 2 from scratch. Initially the analysis registry contains

$$main(X) : true \mapsto^{\bullet} true,$$
$$rev(X, Y) : true \mapsto^{\bullet} true,$$
$$app(X, Y, Z) : true \mapsto^{\bullet} true.$$

Compiling module `rev` first we obtain answer table $rev(X, Y) : true \mapsto true$ and call dependency arcs $rev(X, Y) : true \rightarrow app(X, Y, Z) : true$ and $rev(X, Y) : true \rightarrow rev(X, Y) : true$. The analysis registry has the mark removed from the $rev(X, Y) : true \mapsto true$ entry and the arc $rev(X, Y) : true \rightarrow app(X, Y, Z) : true$ is added to the inter-module dependency graph.

Compiling module `app` we obtain answer pattern $app(X, Y, Z) : true \mapsto (X \wedge Y) \leftrightarrow Z$. This replaces the entry in the registry and the entry for $rev(X, Y) : true \mapsto true$ is marked.

During analysis of `main` the new call pattern $rev(X, Y) : X$ is generated, which causes an entry $rev(X, Y) : X \mapsto^{\bullet} true$ ($rev(X, Y) : true$) to be added to the registry. The answer $main(X) : true \mapsto true$ overwrites the previously marked version while the inter-module dependency $main(X) : true \rightarrow rev(X, Y) : X$ is added to the inter-module dependency graph. At this point we could link together an executable.

Recompiling `rev` is described in Example 2. An executable could be produced also at this point, where calls to $app(X, Y, Z) : X \wedge Y$ will be linked to the code for $app(X, Y, Z) : true$.

Recompiling `main` only changes its registry entry to $main(X) : true \mapsto X$. Recompiling `app` replaces entry

$$app(X, Y, Z) : X \wedge Y \mapsto^{\bullet} (X \wedge Y) \leftrightarrow Z \ (app(X, Y, Z) : true)$$

by

$$app(X, Y, Z) : X \wedge Y \mapsto X \wedge Y \wedge Z$$

and marks entry $rev(X, Y) : X \mapsto X \wedge Y$. An optimized version for $app(X, Y, Z) : X \wedge Y$ is produced. Recompiling `rev` produces no changes. The program is now completely optimized.   □

4   The Compilation Model in the Edit-Compile-Test Cycle

Editing a module might invalidate the analysis information appearing in the registry. Hence, we need to be able to recover a correct state for the program. In this section we provide an algorithm which guarantees that the analysis information for all modules in the program is correctly updated after editing a module.

Given a sensible interface between modules we believe that, for many analyses, even substantial changes to a module are unlikely to invalidate the answer patterns in the analysis registry. Hence many edits will not cause the invalidation of information previously used in other modules and thus often it will require recompilation of few or no modules to regain a correct state.

4.1   Recompiling an Edited Module

Recompilation of an edited module is almost identical to the simple compilation described in Section 3.1 above. The only changes are that the initial call patterns used are all those $P : CP$ appearing in the analysis registry[2] rather than just marked ones, and that the analysis registry is updated differently.

The updating of the analysis registry is as follows. As before, for each initial call pattern $P : CP$ the entry $P : CP \mapsto AP$ in the registry is replaced by the answer pattern $P : CP \mapsto AP'$ appearing in the answer table for module M. As before, any mark or additional version call pattern of the entry is removed. If $AP' \prec AP$, then, as before, for each $P_1 : CP_1 \to P : CP$ appearing in the inter-module dependency graph the entry for $P_1 : CP_1$ is marked. If $AP' \npreceq AP$ the answer pattern has changed in a way that invalidates old information. Then, for each $P_2 : CP_2$ such that there is an arc $P_2 : CP_2 \to P : CP$ in the inter-module dependency graph, the entry $P_2 : CP_2 \mapsto AP_2$ is changed to $P_2 : CP_2 \mapsto^{\perp} AP_2$ to indicate that the current specialized procedure is invalid.

The algorithm update_registry below describes how the registry is updated from answer table $Answers$, obtained by having analysed module M.

> update_registry($Answers$)
>   **foreach** $P : CP \mapsto AP'$ in $Answers$
>   **let** $e \equiv P : CP \mapsto AP$ $(P : CP')$ be the matching entry in registry
>   replace e in registry by $P : CP \mapsto AP$
>   **if** $AP' \prec AP$
>   **foreach** $P_1 : CP_1 \to P : CP$ in inter-module dependency graph
>   mark the entry $P_1 : CP_1 \mapsto AP_1$ with a $\bullet$
>   **else if** $AP \prec AP'$
>   **foreach** $P_2 : CP_2 \to P : CP$ in inter-module dependency graph
>   mark the entry $P_2 : CP_2 \mapsto AP_2$ with a $\perp$

Example 6 Consider what happens if module app is changed to

```
:- module app.
app(X,Y,Z) :- X = [], Y = Z.
app(X,Y,Z) :- X = [A], Z = [A].
```

Recompilation finds information $app(X, Y, Z) : true \mapsto (X \wedge (Y \leftrightarrow Z)) \vee X \leftrightarrow Z$ and $app(X, Y, Z) : X \wedge Y \mapsto X \wedge Y \wedge Z$. Because of the change in the answer pattern for $app(X, Y, Z) : true$ the entry $rev(X, Y) : true \mapsto true$ is updated to $rev(X, Y) : true \mapsto^{\perp} true$. The entry for $rev(X, Y) : X$ remains unchanged. $\square$

---

[2] By comparing the original and edited versions of the module we could determine the procedures P that might have been affected by the edits and only reanalyse them. Of course, this would require us to have saved the previous version of the module code, as well as the answer table of the last analysis. If we also had saved the (intra-module) dependency graph, then incremental analysis can be used to reanalyse the module (see [7]).

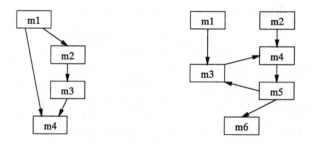

Fig. 1. Two example inter-module dependency graphs, one with a cycle

Note that any specialized procedure $P' : CP'$ from where there is a path to $P : CP$ in the inter-module dependency graph is potentially invalidated. We do not mark them all since we may be able to determine that they are not invalidated and prevent additional work.

Example 7 Consider the module import graph on the left of Figure 1. An arc from module m to m' indicates that module m imports module m'. If module $m4$ is edited then modules $m1$ and $m3$ may have entries marked as invalid. It may also mean that some procedures in module $m2$ are invalid, but we will defer marking them until we have recompiled $m3$ to determine if the invalidation of $m4$ has actually invalidated answer patterns in $m3$. □

4.2   Recompiling an Invalidated Module

Recompilation of an invalidated module is similar to normal compilation. The important difference is that care must be taken in order to avoid using invalid analysis information. An invalidated module can be recompiled if there are no paths in the inter-module dependency graph from its invalidated call patterns to other invalidated call patterns. Clearly for such modules we will not use (even indirectly) any invalidated information in the analysis registry, and hence the result of the recompilation will be guaranteed to be correct.

The recompilation procedure is as for an edited module but only marked entries (marked with either • or ⊥) are used as initial call patterns.

Example 8 Continuing Example 7, the first module to be recompiled must be $m3$, assuming $m1$ has a path to an invalid procedure in $m3$. For the cyclic import graph on the right there may be no module that can be recompiled first after $m6$ is edited. □

Example 9 Continuing after the edit made in Example 6 module **rev** must be recompiled. The only invalidated call pattern is $rev : true$ and the same answer pattern $rev : true \mapsto true$ is found. Since it matches the old answer no further invalidation is required and the program is again in a correct state. □

The process of recompilation must continue until there are no entries marked $\perp$ in the registry before we can rebuild a valid executable.

4.3   Cyclic Inter-module Dependencies

If there are no cycles in the inter-module dependency graph (true if, for example, there are no cycles in the module import graph) then there is always an invalidated call pattern which does not depend on another invalidated call pattern. But if cycles exists we cannot simply recompile a single module; instead a different approach must be taken.

The simplest solution is to throw away all the possibly invalid information. For each $P : CP$ in the strongly connected component that contains an invalidated entry, we can reset the analysis registry entry to $P : CP \mapsto^{\bullet} \top$ (we could do better than this with some care). For each $P' : CP'$ not in the strongly connected component with an arc $P' : CP' \rightarrow P : CP$, we mark the entry as invalid. Each module involved in the strongly connected component can now be recompiled, since they now do not depend on invalid information. Note that for simplicity we may treat cycles in the import graph as an overestimation of cycles in the inter-module dependency graph (as we do in the examples below).

Example 10 Consider the module import graph on the right of Figure 1. If $m6$ is edited then $m5$ is invalidated and (assuming the cycle exists at the procedure level) all procedures in $m3$, $m4$ and $m5$ must be reset to $\top$ and the calling procedures in $m1$ and $m2$ invalidated to achieve a correct state.   □

The above approach is simple, but may lead to considerably more recompilation than is really required. A better approach is to break a cycle by choosing a module to start (re)analyse from. We then "zero" the information for those modules which it depends on and which have invalid information. We repeat this, choosing modules that depend on modules that have just been reanalysed.

Example 11 Consider again the import graph illustrated on the right of Figure 1. If $m6$ is edited causing an invalidation of old information, then all the other modules are now potentially invalidated. By resetting all the answer information in $m3$ (instead of $m3$, $m4$ and $m5$) to $\top$ we could now safely recompile $m5$, since it does not depend on any invalid information. Since there is no longer a cycle of invalidated information we can continue as in Section 4.2.   □

5   Implementation

We now show the first results of very preliminary experimentation with the implementation of our modular analysis system. The aim of this section is not to report on a complete evaluation, but rather to show the feasibility of the approach and the possible advantages in terms of (memory) performance.

The modular analysis has been integrated in the Plai analysis system, written in Ciao Prolog. The current implementation uses a global analysis registry, which is kept in memory throughout the analysis of a program until a fixpoint is reached (memory consumption could be optimised by keeping the analysis registry entries for each module in a separate file). The registry entries are asserted in the Prolog database. They include answer patterns (without version call patterns) but no call dependencies; instead, dependencies are stored at the module level, that is, when a new answer pattern is found in module M, all exported procedures of each module M' importing M are marked for re-analysis. This results in more processing than required, since only a few (or none) of the procedures of module M' may depend on the procedures in M which actually changed.

The registry is initially empty, but the analyser assumes a topmost answer when no applicable entry can be found in the registry, which is equivalent to initializing the registry with topmost answer patterns for all exported procedures in the program.

The current implementation's use of a single global registry is for simplicity. It would be better if the analysis registry and inter-module dependency graph was stored as a separate *info file* associated with each module. The info file for module M stores, for procedures P defined in M, answer patterns of the form $P : CP \mapsto AP$, as well as the call dependencies of the form $P' : CP' \to P : CP$ where P' is a procedure from another module M'. When compiling module M we then update the answer patterns in its info file and add the new call patterns that may have appeared to the info files of the imported modules. To determine when a module needs be recompiled, we simply examine its info file for marked entries. Note that using this arrangement, all the information required to compile a module M is found in its info files and those of the modules it imports. Our implementation works with this storage methodology. However, info files are cached in memory, so that the overall effect is that of a global analysis registry, as mentioned before.

In our experiment we analyse a set of benchmarks[3] using our modular approach: during the first iteration each module is analysed; in following iterations only those modules which have marked entries in their info files will be analysed, until no marked entry remains. This approach is compared to that of analysing the whole program at once. The comparison has been carried out on three analysis domains, namely *shf* (set-sharing and freeness information, see [9]), *son* (pair-sharing and linearity information, see [18]), and *def* (a simplified version of the *Pos* domain, see [1]).

The following table shows size statistics for each benchmark program: the number of predicates, clauses and literals in the program as well as the average and maximum number of variables per literal. The analysis results given are the the analysis time of the whole non-modular program (Whole) and of the modular program (Module) in seconds, the number of iterations of the modular analysis (#IT) and the number of modules analysed in each iteration (#Mods); the first of these numbers is the number of modules forming the complete program. The analysis times shown in the table are an average of the analysis (wall-)times for 10 executions of the analyser, performed in a PC with two Intel PII processors at

---

[3] The benchmarks used are available at http://www.clip.dia.fi.upm.es/bueno.

400MHz, SuperMicro motherboard at 100MHz, 512Mb ram, and running Red Hat Linux 6.2. Note that we do not take into account any Ciao libraries the benchmarks might use, i.e., the libraries are assumed to be previously analysed and thus do not contribute to the analysis time.

Program	Preds	Clauses	Lits	Vars/Cls Ave	Vars/Cls Max	Dom	Whole	Module	#IT	#Mods
boyer	29	144	64	3	6	shf	1	1.8	2	3-2
						son	0.5	0.8	2	3-2
						def	0.6	0.8	2	3-2
wms2	63	1339	269	6	22	shf	–	–		
						son	–	12.6	3	7-5-1
						def	5.1	32.5	2	7-2
chat80	459	2822	1416	6	27	shf	–	–		
						son	–	–		
						def	–	34.4	2	21-8
icost	1159	2681	6203	6	100	shf	–	–		
						son	–	–		
						def	–	219.6	4	12-12-12-2

The size of the programs vary considerably, and the complexity of each program is also different. The core of boyer is a pair of recursive predicates, one of which is also mutually recursive with a third one. In wms2, the central part is a multiply recursive predicate based on another two multiply recursive predicates; there is no mutual recursion. Programs chat80 and icost have a large number of multiply and mutually recursive predicates.

Regarding the modular versions, only chat80 and icost have cycles in the module import graph (which the implementation takes as an overestimation of the inter-module dependency graph). There is only one cycle in chat80, which includes two modules. In contrast, in icost there are many cycles, which basically amounts to ten of the twelve modules being included in a single strongly connected component.

The program boyer is a simplified version of the Boyer-Moore theorem prover (written by Evan Tick). The core part of the program has been divided in two separate modules (plus a third one providing data to both these). These two modules need a second iteration of modular analysis to complete. Obviously there is overhead in the modular analysis of a program that can be analysed all at once. The boyer benchmark shows that this is not overwhelming.

The program wms2 solves a job allocation problem (written by Kish Shen). Analysis of the whole program with domains shf and son runs out of memory. However, a simple modularization (i.e., taking the tables of data to different modules) allows analysis with the son domain. The difficulty in analysing the whole program seems simply to be the large amount of code to analyse.

On the other hand, having the data in different modules increases the overhead in modular analysis in the case of domain def, compared to that of boyer. In this domain, the lack of information on the data slows down the analysis of the core part of the algorithm in the first iteration. In the second iteration, once the data modules are analyzed, this does not happen.

The program chat80 is the famous natural language query answering system of F. Pereira and D. H. D. Warren. Again in this case, the analysis of the whole program runs out of memory. Converting each of the original files in the program in a different module, the program can now be analysed in two iterations. The difficulty in this program seems to be the amount of analysis information that needs be handled: It can be handled separately for each module, but not when it is put together.

A similar thing happens with program icost. This one is a version of Caslog, originally developed by Nai-Wei Lin, which has been further developed by Pedro López. In this case, every subpart of the original program has been converted into a module (which includes the time complexity, size, number of solutions, dependency and determinacy analyses which are part of the functionality of the program). This allows modular analysis with domain *def*, while the analysis of the whole program was not possible.

6   Conclusion

We have presented a simple algorithm for context sensitive analysis and optimization of modular programs. It is efficient in the sense that it keeps track of which information can be improved through reanalysis, and only performs this reanalysis. It has the advantage that correct executables can be produced after compiling each module just once and, if there are no cycles in the import graph, the final result from repeated recompilation is as accurate as analyzing the entire program globally. Our experimental results illustrate that modular analysis allows global optimization to be applied to much larger programs than if we are forced to analyse the whole program at once. To our knowledge, this is the first generic proposal for a context sensitive analysis that truly allows separate compilation of modules.

The technique may produce multiple versions of predicates to allow different optimizations. It may appear that the proliferation of different specialized versions will result in an excessive program size. However, in our experience with the CLP(R) optimizing compiler [8] and the Ciao Prolog parallelizing compiler [10] the resulting sizes are reasonable. Also, it is easy to modify the approach to only allow two versions of a procedure P, the most general $P : \top$ and a single specialized version $P : CP$. Whenever a new call pattern $P : CP'$ is generated it is compared with the (unique) specialized version in the registry $P : CP \mapsto AP$. If $CP' \preceq CP$ then there is no change. Otherwise, the entry is replaced with $P : (CP \sqcup CP') \mapsto^{\bullet} AP_\top$ ($P : \top$) where $AP_\top$ is the answer pattern for $P : \top$.

Although throughout the paper we have used logic programs as our examples, the approach is relatively independent of the underlying language. The same approach is applicable to context sensitive analysis of other programming languages with a clean separation of exported and private parts of a module. Of course other issues which complicate the context sensitive analysis, such as tracking global state, dynamic scheduling and higher-order function calls, may require considerable additional machinery to handle.

Acknowledgements

The work of the authors from Technical University of Madrid (UPM) has been partially supported by Spanish research project EDIPIA, TIC99-1151.

References

1. T. Armstrong, K. Marriott, P. J. Schachte, and H. Søndergaard. Boolean functions for dependency analysis: Algebraic properties and efficient representation. In *Proceedings of the 1st International Static Analysis Symposium*, B. Le Charlier, Ed. Lecture Notes in Computer Science, vol. 864. Springer-Verlag, Berlin, 266–280, 1994.
2. F. Bueno, M. García de la Banda, M. Hermenegildo, K. Marriott, G. Puebla, and P. J. Stuckey. Inter-module Analysis and Optimizing Compilation. Department of Computer Science and Software Engineering, University of Melbourne, Forthcoming Technical Report, 2001.
3. F. Bueno, M. García de la Banda, M. Hermenegildo, and K. Muthukumar. Automatic compile-time parallelization of logic programs for restricted, goal-level, independent and-parallelism. *Journal of Logic Programming 38*, 2, 165–218.
4. M. Codish, S. K. Debray, and R. Giacobazzi. Compositional analysis of modular logic programs. In *ACM SIGPLAN-SIGACT Symposium on Principles of Programming Languages POPL'93*, pages 451–464, Charleston, South Carolina, 1993. ACM.
5. P. Cousot and R. Cousot. Abstract Interpretation: a unified lattice model for static analysis of programs by construction or approximation of fixpoints. In *Fourth ACM Symposium on Principles of Programming Languages*, 238–252, 1977.
6. S. I. Feldman. Make–a program for maintaining computer programs. *Software – Practice and Experience*, 1979.
7. M. Hermenegildo, G. Puebla, K. Marriott, and P. J. Stuckey. Incremental analysis of constraint logic programs. *ACM Transactions on Programming Languages and Systems*, 22(2):187–223, 2000.
8. A. Kelly, A. Macdonald, K. Marriott, H. Søndergaard, and P. J. Stuckey. Optimizing compilation for CLP($\mathcal{R}$). *ACM Transactions on Programming Languages and Systems*, 20(6):1223–1250, 1998.
9. K. Muthukumar and M. Hermenegildo. Compile-time Derivation of Variable Dependency Using Abstract Interpretation. *Journal of Logic Programming*, 13(2/3):315–347, July 1992.
10. G. Puebla and M. Hermenegildo. Abstract multiple specialization and its application to program parallelization. *J. of Logic Programming. Special Issue on Synthesis, Transformation and Analysis of Logic Programs*, 41(2&3):279–316, 1999.
11. G. Puebla and M. Hermenegildo. Some issues in analysis and specialization of modular Ciao-Prolog programs. In [20].
12. A. Rountev, B. G. Ryder, and W. Landi. Data-flow analysis of program fragments. In *Proceedings of ESEC/FSE '99*, volume 1687 of *LNCS*, pages 235–252. Springer-Verlag, 1999.

13. Z. Shao and A. Appel. Smartest recompilation. In *ACM SIGPLAN-SIGACT Symposium on Principles of Programming Languages POPL'93*, pages 439–450, Charleston, South Carolina, 1993. ACM.
14. R. W. Schwanke and G. E. Kaiser. Smarter recompilation. *ACM Transactions on Programming Languages and Systems*, 10(4):627–632, 1988.
15. Z. Somogyi, F. Henderson and T. Conway. The execution algorithm of Mercury: an efficient purely declarative logic programming language. *Journal of Logic Programming*, 29(1-3):17-64, 1996.
16. W. Tichy. Smart recompilation. *ACM Transactions on Programming Languages and Systems*, 8(3):273–291, 1986.
17. W. Vanhoof and M. Bruynooghe. Towards modular binding-time analysis for first-order Mercury. In [20].
18. H. Sondergaard. An application of abstract interpretation of logic programs: occur check reduction. In *European Symposium on Programming, LNCS 123*, pages 327–338. Springer-Verlag, 1986.
19. W. Winsborough. Multiple specialization using minimal-function graph semantics. *Journal of Logic Programming*, 13(2 and 3):259–290, July 1992.
20. *Special Issue on Optimization and Implementation of Declarative Programming Languages*, volume 30 of *Electronic Notes in Theoretical Computer Science*. Elsevier - North Holland, March 2000.

Measuring the Effectiveness of Partial Evaluation in Functional Logic Languages

Elvira Albert[1], Sergio Antoy[2], and Germán Vidal[1]

[1] DSIC, Technical University of Valencia
{ealbert,gvidal}@dsic.upv.es
[2] Department of Computer Science, Portland State University
antoy@cs.pdx.edu

Abstract. We introduce a framework for assessing the effectiveness of partial evaluators in functional logic languages. Our framework is based on properties of the rewrite system that models a functional logic program. Consequently, our assessment is independent of any specific language implementation or computing environment. We define several criteria for measuring the cost of a computation: number of steps, number of function applications, and pattern matching effort. Most importantly, we express the cost of each criterion by means of recurrence equations over algebraic data types, which can be automatically inferred from the partial evaluation process itself. In some cases, the equations can be solved by transforming their arguments from arbitrary data types to natural numbers. In other cases, it is possible to estimate the improvement of a partial evaluation by analyzing the associated cost recurrence equations.

1 Introduction

Partial evaluation is a source-to-source program transformation technique for specializing programs w.r.t. parts of their input (hence also called *program specialization*). This technique has been studied, among others, in the context of functional [12,21], logic [14,25], and functional logic [6,22] programming languages. A common motivation of all partial evaluation techniques is to improve the efficiency of a program while preserving its meaning. Rather surprisingly, relatively little attention has been paid to the development of formal methods for reasoning about the effectiveness of this program transformation; usually, only experimental tests on particular languages and compilers are undertaken. Clearly, a machine-independent way of measuring the effectiveness of partial evaluation would be useful to both users and developers of partial evaluators.

Predicting the speedup achieved by partial evaluators is generally undecidable. We mention below some approaches to this problem. Andersen and Gomard's *speedup analysis* [8] predicts a relative interval of the speedup achieved by a program specialization. Nielson's type system [29] formally expresses when a partial evaluator is better than another. Other interesting efforts investigate *cost analyses* for logic and functional programs which may be useful for determining the effectiveness of program transformations. For instance, Debray and

Kung-Kiu Lau (Ed.): LOPSTR 2000, LNCS 2042, pp. 103–124, 2001.

Lin's method [13] for the semiautomatic analysis of the worst-case cost of a large class of logic programs and Sands's theory of cost equivalence [31] for reasoning about the computational cost of *lazy* functional programs. Laziness introduces a considerable difficulty since the cost of lazy (call-by-name) computations is not *compositional* [31]. Although both the above cost analyses can be used to study the effectiveness of partial evaluation, their authors did not address this issue.

All these efforts mainly base the cost of executing a program on the number of steps performed in a computation. However, simple experiments show that the number of steps and the computation time are not easily correlated. Consider, for instance, the positive supercompiler described in [35]. As noted by Sørensen in [34, Chapter 11], the residual program obtained by positive supercompilation —without the *postunfolding* phase—performs *exactly* the same number of steps as the original one. This does not mean that the process is useless. Rather, all intermediate data structures are gone, and such structures take up space and garbage collection time in actual implementations. Furthermore, the reduction in number of steps of a computation does not imply a proportional reduction in its execution time. The following example illustrates this point. In this work we consider a first-order language. However, we use a curried notation in the examples as usual in functional languages.

Example 1. Consider the well-known operation app to concatenate lists:

$$\text{app } [] \ y \quad \rightarrow y$$
$$\text{app } (x_1 : x_s) \ y \rightarrow x_1 : \text{app } x_s \ y$$

and the following partial evaluation w.r.t. app x y obtained by the partial evaluator INDY [2]:

$$\text{app2s } [] \ y \quad \rightarrow y$$
$$\text{app2s } (x : []) \ y \quad \rightarrow x : y$$
$$\text{app2s } (x_1 : x_2 : x_s) \ y \rightarrow x_1 : x_2 : (\text{app2s } x_s \ y)$$

Note that no input data have been provided for the specialization. In spite of this, INDY can still improve programs by shortening computations and removing intermediate data structures. In particular, this residual program computes the same function as the original one but in approximately half the number of steps. This might suggest that the execution time of app2s (for sufficiently large inputs) should be about one half the execution time of app. However, executions of function app2s in several environments (e.g., in the lazy functional language Hugs [19] and the functional logic language Curry [17]) show that speedup is only around 10%.

In order to reason about these counterintuitive results, we introduce several formal criteria to measure the efficiency of a functional logic computation. We consider *inductively sequential* rewrite systems as programs. Inductive sequentiality ensures strong desirable properties of evaluations. In particular, if a term has a value, there is a sound, complete and efficient algorithm to find this value. Inductive sequentiality is not a limiting condition for programming. In fact, the first order components of many functional programs, e.g., Haskell and ML, are inductively sequential. Essentially, a rewrite system is *inductively sequential* when all its operations are defined by rewrite rules that, recursively, make on their arguments a case distinction analogous to a data type (or structural) induction.

The strategy that determines what to evaluate in a term is based on this case distinction and is called *needed narrowing* [10]. Needed narrowing, which extends the usual call-by-name semantics of functional computations, has been proved *optimal* for functional logic computations as well. We formally define the cost of evaluating an expression in terms of the number of steps, the number of function applications, and the complexity of pattern-matching or unification involved in the computation. Similar criteria are taken into account (though experimentally) in traditional profiling approaches (e.g., [33]). Let us remark that our aim is not to define a complex cost analysis for functional logic programs, but to introduce some representative cost criteria and then investigate their variations by the application of a particular partial evaluation method. The above criteria seem specially well-suited to estimate the speedup achieved by the narrowing-driven partial evaluation scheme of [6]. Nevertheless, our technique can be easily adapted to other related partial evaluation methods, like partial deduction [25] and positive supercompilation [35]. In particular, we use *recurrence equations* to compare the cost of executing the original and residual programs. These equations can be automatically derived from the partial evaluation process itself and are parametric w.r.t. the considered cost criteria. Unlike traditional recurrence equations used to reason about the complexity of programs, our equations are defined on data structures rather than on natural numbers. This complicates the computation of their solutions, although in some cases useful statements about the improvements achieved by partial evaluation can be made by a simple inspection of the sets of equations. In other cases, these equations can be transformed into traditional recurrence equations and then solved by well-known mathematical methods.

The remainder of the paper is organized as follows. Section 2 introduces some preliminary definitions. Section 3 defines several formal criteria to measure the cost of a computation. Section 4 addresses the problem of determining the improvement achieved by the partial evaluation process in the context of a functional logic language and Sect. 5 illustrates its usefulness by showing some possible applications. Section 6 discusses some related work and Sect. 7 concludes. An extended version of this paper can be found in [3].

2   Preliminaries

For the sake of completeness, we recall in this section some basic notions of term rewriting [11] and functional logic programming [16]. We consider a (*many-sorted*) *signature* Σ partitioned into a set $\mathcal{C}$ of *constructors* and a set $\mathcal{F}$ of (defined) *functions* or *operations*. We write $c/n \in \mathcal{C}$ and $f/n \in \mathcal{F}$ for n-ary constructor and operation symbols, respectively. There is at least one sort *Bool* containing the constructors `True` and `False`. The set of *terms* and *constructor terms* with *variables* (e.g., x, y, z) from $\mathcal{V}$ are denoted by $\mathcal{T}(\mathcal{C}\cup\mathcal{F}, \mathcal{V})$ and $\mathcal{T}(\mathcal{C}, \mathcal{V})$, respectively. The set of variables occurring in a term t is denoted by $Var(t)$. A term is *linear* if it does not contain multiple occurrences of one variable.

A *pattern* is a term of the form $f(d_1, \ldots, d_n)$ where $f/n \in \mathcal{F}$ and $d_1, \ldots, d_n \in \mathcal{T}(\mathcal{C}, \mathcal{V})$. A term is *operation-rooted* if it has an operation symbol at the root. A *position* p in a term t is represented by a sequence of natural numbers (Λ denotes the empty sequence, i.e., the root position). $t|_p$ denotes the *subterm* of t at position p, and $t[s]_p$ denotes the result of *replacing the subterm* $t|_p$ by the term s. We denote a *substitution* σ by $\{x_1 \mapsto t_1, \ldots, x_n \mapsto t_n\}$ with $\sigma(x_i) = t_i$ for $i = 1, \ldots, n$ (with $x_i \neq x_j$ if $i \neq j$), and $\sigma(x) = x$ for all other variables x. The set $\mathcal{D}om(\sigma) = \{x \in \mathcal{V} \mid \sigma(x) \neq x\}$ is called the *domain* of σ. A substitution σ is *constructor*, if $\sigma(x)$ is a constructor term for all x. The identity substitution is denoted by $\{\,\}$. A substitution θ is more general than σ, in symbols $\theta \leq \sigma$, iff there exists a substitution γ such that $\gamma \circ \theta = \sigma$. A term t' is a (constructor) *instance* of t if there is a (constructor) substitution σ with $t' = \sigma(t)$.

A set of rewrite rules $l \to r$ such that $l \notin \mathcal{V}$, and $Var(r) \subseteq Var(l)$ is called a *term rewriting system* (TRS). Terms l and r are called the *left-hand side* and the *right-hand side* of the rule, respectively. A TRS $\mathcal{R}$ is *left-linear* if l is linear for all $l \to r \in \mathcal{R}$. A TRS is *constructor-based* if each left-hand side l is a pattern. In the following, a functional logic *program* is a left-linear constructor-based TRS. A *rewrite step* is an application of a rewrite rule to a term, i.e., $t \to_{p,R} s$ if there exists a position p in t, a rewrite rule $R = l \to r$ and a substitution σ with $t|_p = \sigma(l)$ and $s = t[\sigma(r)]_p$. The instantiated left-hand side $\sigma(l)$ of a reduction rule $l \to r$ is called a *redex* (*red*ucible *ex*pression). Given a relation $\to$, we denote by $\to^+$ its transitive closure, and by $\to^*$ its transitive and reflexive closure.

To evaluate terms containing variables, *narrowing* non-deterministically instantiates these variables so that a rewrite step is possible. Formally, $t \rightsquigarrow_{(p,R,\sigma)} t'$ is a *narrowing step* if p is a non-variable position in t and $\sigma(t) \to_{p,R} t'$. We often write $t \rightsquigarrow_\sigma t'$ when the position and the rule are clear from the context. We denote by $t_0 \rightsquigarrow_\sigma^n t_n$ a sequence of n narrowing steps $t_0 \rightsquigarrow_{\sigma_1} \ldots \rightsquigarrow_{\sigma_n} t_n$ with $\sigma = \sigma_n \circ \cdots \circ \sigma_1$. (If $n = 0$ then $\sigma = \{\,\}$.) Due to the presence of free variables, an expression may be reduced to different values after instantiating free variables to different terms. Given a narrowing derivation $t_0 \rightsquigarrow_\sigma^* t_n$, we say that t_n is a *computed value* and σ is a *computed answer* for t_0. To avoid unnecessary narrowing computations and to provide computations with infinite data structures, as well as a demand-driven generation of the search space, the most recent work has advocated *lazy* narrowing strategies (e.g., [15,26,28]). In this paper we consider *needed* narrowing [10], an evaluation strategy which is based on the idea of evaluating only subterms that are needed, in a precise technical sense, to obtain a result.

Needed Narrowing. Needed narrowing is an optimal evaluation strategy w.r.t. both the length of derivations and the independence of computed solutions [10]. It extends the Huet and Lévy notion of a needed rewrite step [18] to functional logic programming. Following [10], a narrowing step $t \rightsquigarrow_{(p,R,\sigma)} t'$ is called *needed* iff, for every substitution θ such that $\sigma \leq \theta$, p is the position of a needed redex of $\theta(t)$ in the sense of [18]. A narrowing derivation is called *needed* iff every step of the derivation is needed.

An efficient implementation of needed narrowing exists for *inductively sequential* programs. The formal definition of inductive sequentiality is rather technical. In this paper, for the sake of completeness, we give a more intuitive account of this concept. The complete technical details are in [9].

A rewrite system is *inductively sequential* when all its operations are defined by rewrite rules that, recursively, make on their arguments a case distinction analogous to a data type (or structural) induction. Both definitions of Example 1 show this point. In fact, operation app makes a case distinction on its first argument. The type of this argument is *list*. A structural induction on *list* needs to consider two cases, namely [] and a list consisting of a head and a tail. The advantage of this disciplined approach is that in any term app x y, it is necessary and sufficient to evaluate argument x to a head normal form in order to fire a rule of app. Operations defined according to this principle are called *inductively sequential* as well and their rules can be organized in a hierarchical structure called a *definitional tree*. We show below these trees for the operations of Example 1.

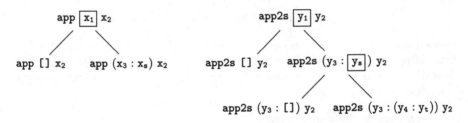

The leaves of these trees are (modulo a renaming of variables) the left-hand sides of the operations' rewrite rules. It is easy to see that operation app2s makes an initial case distinction on its first argument. Then, it makes a second case distinction that leads to its three rewrite rules. The arguments' target of a case distinction are shown in a box and are usually called the *inductive positions* of the tree. Thus, to evaluate an expression app2s y_1 y_2, we first evaluate y_1 to a head normal form. If the result of this evaluation is [], we apply the first rule. If the result of this evaluation is of the form $y_3 : y_s$, we evaluate y_s to a head normal form which will eventually determine which rule, if any, to fire.

There exists a needed narrowing strategy, denoted by λ in [10, Def. 13], which determines what to evaluate in a term based on this case distinction. Following [10], to compute needed narrowing steps for an operation-rooted term t, we take a definitional tree $\mathcal{P}$ for the root of t and compute $\lambda(t, \mathcal{P})$. Then, for all $(p, l \rightarrow r, \sigma) \in \lambda(t, \mathcal{P})$, we say that $t \leadsto_{(p,l \rightarrow r,\sigma)} t'$ is a *needed narrowing step*, where $t' = \sigma(t[r]_p)$. Informally speaking, given an operation-rooted term and an associated definitional tree for the root of this term, needed narrowing applies a rule to the entire term, if possible, or checks the subterm corresponding to an inductive position of the tree: if it is a variable, it is instantiated to the constructor of a child; if it is already a constructor, we proceed with the corresponding child; finally, if it is a function, we evaluate it by recursively applying needed narrowing. The extension of function λ to constructor-rooted terms is straightforward. Essentially, to compute a needed narrowing step of a constructor-rooted term, it suffices to compute a needed narrowing step of any of its maximal operation-rooted subterms. We call λ-*derivation* a narrowing derivation computed by λ.

Example 2. Consider the following rules which define the less-or-equal relation "$\leqslant$" and the addition on natural numbers which are represented by terms built from 0 and Succ:

$$
\begin{array}{rcl rcl}
0 \leqslant n & \rightarrow & \text{True} & 0 + n & \rightarrow & n \\
(\text{Succ } m) \leqslant 0 & \rightarrow & \text{False} & (\text{Succ } m) + n & \rightarrow & \text{Succ } (m+n) \\
(\text{Succ } m) \leqslant (\text{Succ } n) & \rightarrow & m \leqslant n & & &
\end{array}
$$

Then the function λ computes the following set for the initial term $x \leqslant (x + x)$:

$$\{(\Lambda, 0 \leqslant n \rightarrow \text{True}, \{x \mapsto 0\}), \ (2, (\text{Succ } m) + n \rightarrow \text{Succ } (m+n), \{x \mapsto \text{Succ } m\})\}$$

These steps yield the λ-derivations:

$$x \leqslant (x+x) \rightsquigarrow_{\{x \mapsto 0\}} \quad \text{True}$$

$$x \leqslant (x+x) \rightsquigarrow_{\{x \mapsto \text{Succ } m\}} (\text{Succ } m) \leqslant (\text{Succ } (m + (\text{Succ } m)))$$

Needed narrowing derivations can be represented by a (possibly infinite) finitely branching *tree*. Formally, given an inductively sequential program $\mathcal{R}$ and an operation-rooted term t, a *needed narrowing tree* for t in $\mathcal{R}$ is a tree satisfying the following conditions:

- Each node of the tree is a term.
- The root node is t.
- Let s be a node in the tree and assume that $\mathcal{P}$ is a definitional tree for the root of s. Then, for each tuple $(p, l \rightarrow r, \sigma) \in \lambda(s, \mathcal{P})$, the node has a child $\sigma(s[r]_p)$.
- Nodes which are constructor terms have no children.

Each branch of the needed narrowing tree is a λ-derivation for t in $\mathcal{R}$.

3   Formal Criteria for Measuring Computational Cost

The cost criteria that we introduce below are independent of the particular implementation of the language. Rather, they are formulated for a rewrite system, which we intend as a program, and are based on operations that are, in one form or another, performed by likely implementations of rewriting and narrowing.

The first cost criterion that we consider has been widely used in the literature. This is the *number of steps*, or *length*, of the evaluation of a term. The following trivial definition is presented only for uniformity with the remaining costs.

Definition 1 (number of steps). *We denote by $\mathcal{S}$ a function on rewrite rules, called the number of steps, as follows. If R is a rewrite rule, then $\mathcal{S}(R) = 1$.*

The second cost criterion is the number of symbol *applications* that occur within a computation. Counting applications is interesting because, in most implementations of a functional logic language, an evaluation will execute some machine instructions that directly correspond to each symbol application. The following definition bundles together all applications. It can be easily specialized to constructor or defined symbol applications only, denoted by $\mathcal{A}_c$ and $\mathcal{A}_d$ respectively.

Definition 2 (number of applications). *We denote by $\mathcal{A}$ a function on rewrite rules, called the number of applications, as follows. If $R = l \rightarrow r$ is a rewrite rule, then $\mathcal{A}(R)$ is the number of occurrences of non-variable symbols in r.*

The above definition is appropriate for a first-order language in which function applications are not curried. In a fully curried language, $\mathcal{A}(l \rightarrow r)$ would be one less the number of symbols in r (including variables).

The third cost criterion that we consider abstracts the effort performed by *pattern matching*. We assume that the number of rewrite rules in a program does not affect the efficiency of a computation. The reason is that in a first-order language a reference to the symbol being applied can be resolved at compile-time. However, when a defined operation f is applied to arguments, in non-trivial cases, one needs to inspect (at run-time) certain occurrences of certain arguments of the application of f to determine which rewrite rule of f to fire. This cost is determined by the pattern matching effort.

Definition 3 (pattern matching effort). *We denote by $\mathcal{P}$ a function on rewrite rules, called pattern matching effort, as follows. If $R = l \rightarrow r$ is a rewrite rule, then $\mathcal{P}(R)$ is the number of constructor symbols in l.*

We note that $\mathcal{P}$ gives a worst-case measure of the pattern matching effort. In particular, if a ground expression e is evaluated using rule R, then $\mathcal{P}(R)$ returns exactly the number of constructor symbols of e whose inspection is required. However, whenever e contains free variables, the value returned by $\mathcal{P}(R)$ represents an upper bound.

For simplicity, we do not consider non-deterministic computations, although our cost measures could be extended along the lines of [13]. On the other hand, many partial evaluation methods do not change the non-determinism of computations, i.e., although some paths become shorter, the *search spaces* of a given goal in the original and residual programs have essentially the same structure. In particular, this is the case of the narrowing-driven partial evaluation method (see discussion in Sect. 5.2). Therefore, a cost measure which quantifies the amount of non-determinism would not be affected by our partial evaluation method.

In the remainder of this paper, we denote by C any cost criterion, i.e., C stands for $\mathcal{S}$, $\mathcal{A}$ or $\mathcal{P}$. Furthermore, most of the developments in the following sections are independent of the considered criteria; thus, C could also denote more elaborated criteria, like the number of variable bindings, the "size" of the reduced expression, etc.

The previous definitions allow us to define the cost of a derivation as the total cost of its steps.

Definition 4 (cost of a derivation). *Let $\mathcal{R}$ be a program and t_0 a term. Let C denote a cost criterion. We overload function C by partially defining it on derivations as follows. If $D : t_0 \rightsquigarrow_{(p_1,R_1,\sigma_1)} t_1 \rightsquigarrow_{(p_2,R_2,\sigma_2)} \cdots \rightsquigarrow_{(p_n,R_n,\sigma_n)} t_n$ is a derivation for t_0 in $\mathcal{R}$, then $C(D) = \sum_{i=1}^{n} C(R_i)$.*

For the developments in the next section, it is more convenient to reason about the efficiency of programs when a cost measure is defined over terms rather than entire *computations*. We use "computation" as a generic word for the *evaluation* of a term, i.e., a narrowing derivation ending in a constructor term. In general, different strategies applied to a same term may produce evaluations of different lengths and/or fail to terminate. For instance, if term t contains uninstantiated variables, there may exist distinct evaluations of t obtained by distinct instantiations of t's variables. Luckily, needed narrowing gives us some leeway. We allow uninstantiated variables in a term t as long as these variables are not instantiated during its evaluation, i.e., we have a derivation of the form $t \rightsquigarrow^*_{\{\}} d$. In this case, there is a concrete implementation of needed narrowing, i.e., that denoted by λ in Sect. 2, in which $t \rightsquigarrow^*_{\{\}} d$ is the only possible derivation computed from t (see Lemma 1 in [3]). Therefore, to be formal, we consider only λ-derivations in the technical results of this paper. Note that this is not a practical restriction in our context, since λ-derivations are efficient, easy to compute, and used in the implementations of modern functional logic languages such as Curry [17] and Toy [27]. The above property allows us to define the cost of a term as the cost of its λ-derivation when the computed substitution is empty (since it is unique).

Definition 5 (cost of a term). *Let $\mathcal{R}$ be a program and t a term. Let C denote a cost criterion. We overload function C by partially defining it on terms and programs as follows. If $t \rightsquigarrow_{(p_1,R_1,\sigma_1)} \cdots \rightsquigarrow_{(p_k,R_k,\sigma_k)} d$ is a λ-derivation, where d is a constructor term and $\sigma_1 = \cdots = \sigma_k = \{\}$ (i.e., $\sigma_i = \{\}$, for $i = 1, 2, \ldots, k$), we define $C(t, \mathcal{R}) = \sum_{i=1}^{k} C(R_i)$.*

In the following, we often write $C(t)$ to denote the cost of a term when the program $\mathcal{R}$ is clear from the context.

We apply the previous definitions to Example 1. The next table summarizes (with minor approximations to ease understanding) the cost of computations with both functions when the arguments are constructor terms:

	$\mathcal{S}$	$\mathcal{A}_c$	$\mathcal{A}_d$	$\mathcal{P}$
app	n	n	n	n
app2s	$0.5\,n$	n	$0.5\,n$	n

Here n represents the *size* of the inputs to the functions, i.e., the number of elements in the first argument of app and app2s (the second argument does not affect the cost of computations). The first observation is that not all cost criteria have been improved. In fact, the number of constructor applications and the pattern matching effort remain unchanged. To obtain a "global" value of the improvement achieved by a partial evaluation, one might assume an equal unit cost for all criteria. In this way, the total cost of a computation using app is $4\,n$. Likewise, the cost of a computation using app2s is $3\,n$. The speedup is only 25%. In general, one should determine the appropriate weight of each cost criterion for a specific language environment. For instance, if we increase the unit cost of $\mathcal{A}_c$ and decrease that of $\mathcal{S}$—a more realistic choice in our environment—the improvement of app2s over app estimated by our criteria closely explains the lower speedup measured experimentally (10%).

4   Measuring the Effectiveness of a Partial Evaluation

In this section, we are concerned with the problem of determining the improvement achieved by a partial evaluation in the context of a functional logic language.

4.1   Narrowing-Driven Partial Evaluation

We briefly recall the partial evaluation scheme of [6] which is based on needed narrowing. An intrinsic feature of this approach is the use of the same operational mechanism—needed narrowing—for both execution and partial evaluation. Informally speaking, a *partial evaluation* for a term s in a program $\mathcal{R}$ is computed by constructing a finite (possibly incomplete) needed narrowing tree for this term, and then extracting the *resultants* associated to the root-to-leaf derivations of this tree. Resultants are defined as follows:

Definition 6 (resultant). *Let $\mathcal{R}$ be a program and s be a term. Given a needed narrowing derivation $s \leadsto^{+}_{\sigma} t$, its associated resultant is the rewrite rule $\sigma(s) \to t$.*

The potential value of resultants is that they compute in a single step a non-null derivation of the original program.

Example 3. Consider the function app of Example 1 and the following needed narrowing derivations:

$$\text{app } (\text{app } x_s \ y_s) \ z_s \leadsto_{\{x_s \mapsto []\}} \quad \text{app } y_s \ z_s$$
$$\text{app } (\text{app } x_s \ y_s) \ z_s \leadsto_{\{x_s \mapsto x' : x'_s\}} \text{app } (x' : \text{app } x'_s \ y_s) \ z_s$$
$$\leadsto_{\{\}} \qquad x' : \text{app } (\text{app } x'_s \ y_s) \ z_s$$

Then, the associated resultants are:

$$\text{app } (\text{app } [] \ y_s) \ z_s \qquad \to \text{app } y_s \ z_s$$
$$\text{app } (\text{app } (x' : x'_s) \ y_s) \ z_s \to x' : \text{app } (\text{app } x'_s \ y_s) \ z_s$$

We note that, whenever the specialized call s is not a linear pattern, the left-hand sides of resultants may not be linear patterns either and hence resultants may not be legal program rules (as the above example shows). To overcome this problem, we introduce a post-processing of renaming which also eliminates redundant structures from residual rules. Informally, the renaming transformation proceeds as follows. First, an *independent renaming* ρ for a set of terms S is constructed, which consists of a mapping from terms to terms such that for all $s \in S$, we have $\rho(s) = f(x_1, \ldots, x_n)$, where $x_1, \ldots, x_n$ are the distinct variables in s in the order of their first occurrence and f is a *fresh* function symbol. We also let $\rho(S)$ denote the set $S' = \{\rho(s) \mid s \in S\}$. While the independent renaming suffices to rename the left-hand sides of resultants (since they are constructor instances of the specialized calls), right-hand sides are renamed by means of the auxiliary function ren_ρ, which *recursively* replaces each call in the expression by a call to the corresponding renamed function (according to ρ).

Given an independent renaming ρ for a set of terms, the auxiliary function ren_ρ is formally defined as follows.

Definition 7. *Let S be a set of terms, t a term, and ρ an independent renaming of S. The partial function $ren_\rho(S, t)$ is defined inductively as follows:*

$$
ren_\rho(S, t) = \begin{cases}
t & \text{if } t \in \mathcal{V} \\
c(t'_1, \ldots, t'_n) & \text{if } t = c(t_1, \ldots, t_n), \ c \in \mathcal{C}, \ n \geq 0, \text{ and} \\
& \quad t'_i = ren_\rho(S, t_i), \ i = 1, \ldots, n \\
\theta'(\rho(s)) & \text{if } \exists \theta, \exists s \in S \text{ such that } t = \theta(s) \text{ and} \\
& \quad \theta' = \{x \mapsto ren_\rho(S, \theta(x)) \mid x \in \mathcal{D}om(\theta)\}
\end{cases}
$$

The above mapping is non-deterministic. An operation-rooted term can be possibly renamed by different symbols obtained using different sequences of terms in S (according to the third case). The mapping can be made deterministic by some simple heuristics (as it is done in the INDY system [2]).

Example 4. Consider the set of terms:

$$S = \{\text{app (app } x_s \ y_s) \ z_s, \ \text{app } x_s \ y_s\}$$

A possible independent renaming ρ for S is the mapping:

$$\{\text{app (app } x_s \ y_s) \ z_s \mapsto \text{dapp } x_s \ y_s \ z_s, \ \text{app } x_s \ y_s \mapsto \text{app1s } x_s \ y_s\}$$

By using this independent renaming, we can rename arbitrary expressions by means of function ren_ρ. Consider, for instance:

$$
\begin{aligned}
ren_\rho(\text{app [] } (x : x_s)) &= \text{app1s [] } (x : x_s) \\
ren_\rho(\text{app (app [] } y_s) \ (z : z_s)) &= \text{dapp [] } y_s \ (z : z_s) \\
ren_\rho(\text{app (app [] } y_s) \ (\text{app } z_s \ [])) &= \text{dapp [] } y_s \ (\text{app1s } z_s \ [])
\end{aligned}
$$

Observe that the renaming of the term app (app [] y_s) (z : z_s) could be app1s (app1s [] y_s) (z : z_s) as well.

Following [25], in this work we adopt the convention that any derivation is potentially *incomplete* in the sense that at any point we are allowed to simply not select any redex and terminate the derivation; a branch thus can be failed, incomplete, successful, or infinite. A *failing derivation* is a needed narrowing

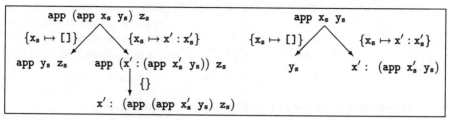

Fig. 1. Needed narrowing trees for "app (app x_s y_s) z_s" and "app x_s y_s"

derivation ending in an expression that is neither a constructor term nor can be further narrowed. Given a needed narrowing tree $\mathcal{N}$ for a term t in program $\mathcal{R}$, a *partial* (or *incomplete*) needed narrowing tree $\mathcal{N}'$ for t in $\mathcal{R}$ is obtained by considering only the narrowing derivations from t down to some terms $t_1, \ldots, t_n$ such that $t_1, \ldots, t_n$ appear in $\mathcal{N}$ and each non-failing branch of $\mathcal{N}$ contains exactly one of them. Partial evaluation can be formally defined as follows.

Definition 8 (partial evaluation). *Let $\mathcal{R}$ be a program, $S = \{s_1, \ldots, s_n\}$ a finite set of operation-rooted terms, and ρ an independent renaming of S. Let $\mathcal{N}_1, \ldots, \mathcal{N}_n$ be finite (possibly incomplete) needed narrowing trees for s_i in $\mathcal{R}$, $i = 1, \ldots, n$. A partial evaluation of S in $\mathcal{R}$ (under ρ) is obtained by constructing a renamed resultant, $\sigma(\rho(s)) \to ren_\rho(t)$, for each non-failing needed narrowing derivation $s \rightsquigarrow_\sigma^+ t$ in $\mathcal{N}_1, \ldots, \mathcal{N}_n$.*

We note that [6] requires, additionally, that no constructor-rooted term is evaluated at partial evaluation time. This restriction is necessary in order to preserve the correctness of the partial evaluation transformation in the context of lazy functional logic languages (see [6] for details). We now illustrate this definition with an example.

Example 5. Consider again the function app together with the set of calls:

$$S = \{\text{app (app } x_s \text{ } y_s) \text{ } z_s, \text{ app } x_s \text{ } y_s\}$$

Given the (incomplete) needed narrowing trees of Figure 1, we produce the following resultants:

$$
\begin{aligned}
\text{app (app [] } y_s) \text{ } z_s &\quad \to \text{ app } y_s \text{ } z_s \\
\text{app (app (x : } x_s) \text{ } y_s) \text{ } z_s &\to \text{ x : app (app } x_s \text{ } y_s) \text{ } z_s \\
\text{app [] } y_s &\quad \to y_s \\
\text{app (x : } x_s) \text{ } y_s &\quad \to \text{ x : app } x_s \text{ } y_s
\end{aligned}
$$

Now, if we consider the independent renaming ρ for S of Example 4:

$$\{\text{app (app } x_s \text{ } y_s) \text{ } z_s \mapsto \text{dapp } x_s \text{ } y_s \text{ } z_s, \text{ app } x_s \text{ } y_s \mapsto \text{app1s } x_s \text{ } y_s\}$$

we compute the following partial evaluation of $\mathcal{R}$ w.r.t. S (under ρ):

$$
\begin{aligned}
\text{dapp [] } y_s \text{ } z_s &\quad \to \text{ app1s } y_s \text{ } z_s \\
\text{dapp (x : } x_s) \text{ } y_s \text{ } z_s &\to \text{ x : dapp } x_s \text{ } y_s \text{ } z_s \\
\text{app1s [] } y_s &\quad \to y_s \\
\text{app1s (x : } x_s) \text{ } y_s &\quad \to \text{ x : app1s } x_s \text{ } y_s
\end{aligned}
$$

We will not discuss in details this transformation since it is not essential for the forthcoming sections, where we mainly deal with the notion of resultant. Nevertheless, a full description of the narrowing-driven approach to partial evaluation, as well as a comparison to related partial evaluation techniques, can be found in [5,6].

4.2   Automatic Generation of Recurrence Equations

In this section we propose the use of recurrence equations to analyze how a cost criterion is affected by the partial evaluation process. Although we will illustrate our proposal over the cost criteria introduced in the previous section, our developments are parametric w.r.t. the considered cost criteria. Our approach is inspired by the standard use of recurrence equations to analyze the complexity of algorithms in terms of their inputs (see, e.g., [1] for imperative, [31] for functional, and [13] for logic programs).

Definition 9 (recurrence equation). *Let $\mathcal{R}$ be a program and s be a term. Given a needed narrowing derivation $s \leadsto_\sigma^+ t$, its associated recurrence equation is: $C(\sigma(s)) = C(t) + k$, where $k = C(s \leadsto_\sigma^+ t)$.*

However, we are not interested in arbitrary recurrence equations, or sets of equations, since in general they would not be useful. Rather, we present a technique for deriving sets of recurrence equations tightly associated with the partial evaluation process. These equations, specifically the form in which we present them, are informative about the effectiveness of partial evaluation even in the absence of an explicit solution of the equations.

Definition 10. *Let $\mathcal{R}$ be a program, S a finite set of operation-rooted terms, and ρ an independent renaming for S. Let $\mathcal{R}'$ be a partial evaluation of $\mathcal{R}$ w.r.t. S (under ρ) computed from the finite (possibly incomplete) needed narrowing trees $\mathcal{N}_1, \ldots, \mathcal{N}_n$. We produce a pair of equations:*

$$C(\sigma(s)) \;=\; C(t) + k \quad / \quad C(\sigma(\rho(s))) \;=\; C(ren_\rho(t)) + k'$$

for each non-failing needed narrowing derivation $s \leadsto_\sigma^+ t$ in $\mathcal{N}_1, \ldots, \mathcal{N}_n$. Constants k and k' denote the observable cost of the considered derivation in the original and residual programs, respectively, i.e., $k = C(s \leadsto_\sigma^+ t)$ and $k' = C(\rho(s) \leadsto_\sigma ren_\rho(t))$.

Informally, for each needed narrowing derivation used to construct the partial evaluation, we generate a pair of recurrence equations representing the computational cost of executing goals in the original and residual programs, respectively. We use the notation $equation_1$ / $equation_2$ to emphasize that they represent a kind of *ratio* between the cost of the original and residual programs, as we will discuss later in Sect. 5.2. We note that there is no risk of ambiguity in using the same symbol, C, for the (cost) equations associated to both the original and residual programs, since the signatures of $\mathcal{R}$ and $\mathcal{R}'$ are disjoint by definition of partial evaluation. Observe also that if $C = \mathcal{S}$, then $k \geq 1$ and $k' = 1$, i.e., the application of each resultant corresponds to a sequence of one or more rules in the original program.

Example 6. Consider the operation app of Example 1 and the needed narrowing derivation:

$$\overbrace{\text{app (app x y) z}}^{s} \leadsto_{\{x\mapsto x':x_s\}} \text{app (x' : app } x_s \text{ y) z} \leadsto_{\{\}} \overbrace{x' : \text{app (app } x_s \text{ y) z}}^{t}$$

Then, we produce the associated resultant:

$$\underbrace{\text{dapp (x' : } x_s\text{) y z}}_{\sigma(\rho(s))} \rightarrow \underbrace{\text{x' : dapp } x_s \text{ y z}}_{ren_\rho(t)}$$

with $\sigma = \{x \mapsto x' : x_s\}$ and $\rho = \{\text{app (app x y) z} \mapsto \text{dapp x y z}\}$. According to Def. 10, we produce the following equations for the cost criteria of Sect. 3:

$$
\begin{array}{lll}
\mathcal{S}(\sigma(s)) = \mathcal{S}(t) + 2 & / & \mathcal{S}(\sigma(\rho(s))) = \mathcal{S}(ren_\rho(t)) + 1 \\
\mathcal{A}(\sigma(s)) = \mathcal{A}(t) + 4 & / & \mathcal{A}(\sigma(\rho(s))) = \mathcal{A}(ren_\rho(t)) + 2 \\
\mathcal{P}(\sigma(s)) = \mathcal{P}(t) + 2 & / & \mathcal{P}(\sigma(\rho(s))) = \mathcal{P}(ren_\rho(t)) + 1
\end{array}
$$

which represent the cost of performing the above narrowing derivation in the original / residual program. Note that some useful conclusions about the improvement achieved by this residual rule can be easily inferred from the equations. For instance, we can see that all the cost criteria have been halved.

The following result establishes the *local* correctness of the equations generated according to Def. 9, i.e., each single equation is correct w.r.t. the definition of the different cost measures.

Theorem 1 (local correctness). *Let $\mathcal{R}$ be an inductively sequential program and u a term such that $C(u) = n$ in $\mathcal{R}$. If there exists an equation $C(s) = C(t)+k$ (associated to a λ-derivation in $\mathcal{R}$) with $u = \theta(s)$, then $C(\theta(t)) = n - k$.*

In particular, the above result applies to the sets of equations constructed according to Def. 10. However, reasoning about recurrence equations of the above kind is not easy. The problem comes from the laziness of the computation model, since interesting cost criteria are not compositional for non-strict semantics [31]. In particular, the cost of evaluating an expression of the form $f(e)$ will depend on how much function f needs argument e. In eager (call-by-value) languages, the cost of $f(e)$ can be obtained by first computing the cost of evaluating e to some normal form d and, then, adding the cost of evaluating $f(d)$. Trivially, this procedure can be used to compute an *upper-bound* for $f(e)$ under a lazy semantics. Nevertheless, we have identified a class of recurrence equations for which we can state a stronger result.

Definition 11 (closed set of recurrence equations). *Let $\mathcal{R}$ be a program and $S = \{s_1, \ldots, s_n\}$ a finite set of operation-rooted terms. Let $\mathcal{N}_1, \ldots, \mathcal{N}_n$ be finite (possibly incomplete) needed narrowing trees for s_i in $\mathcal{R}$, $i = 1, \ldots, n$. Let E be the set of recurrence equations associated to the narrowing derivations in $\mathcal{N}_1, \ldots, \mathcal{N}_n$. We say that E is S-closed iff for each equation in E of the form:*

$$C(s) = C(t) + k$$

t is either a constructor term or a constructor instance of some term in S.

The relevance of closed recurrence equations stems from their use to *compute* the cost of a term:

Theorem 2 (cost computation). *Let $\mathcal{R}$ be an inductively sequential program and $S = \{s_1, \ldots, s_k\}$ a finite set of operation-rooted terms. Let $\mathcal{N}_1, \ldots, \mathcal{N}_k$ be finite (possibly incomplete) needed narrowing trees (using λ-derivations) for s_i in $\mathcal{R}$, $i = 1, \ldots, k$. Let E be a set of S-closed recurrence equations associated to the λ-derivations in $\mathcal{N}_1, \ldots, \mathcal{N}_k$. If t is a constructor instance of some term in S and $C(t) = n$, then there is a rewrite sequence $C(t) \rightarrow^* n$ using the (oriented) equations in E and the definition of "$+$".*

Roughly speaking, this result states that, by considering the set of recurrence equations as a rewrite system (implicitly oriented from left to right) and performing additions as usual, we have all the necessary information for computing the associated cost of a term (whenever the cost of this term is defined, i.e., it is narrowable to a constructor term with the empty substitution). Therefore, if the cost of term t is $C(t) = n$ in program $\mathcal{R}$, then there exists a rewrite sequence which *computes* this cost: $C(t) \rightarrow^* n$ in E.

This result shows that, under appropriate conditions, a finite set E of recurrence equations captures the cost of an infinite set of derivations or terms. For example, E could be used to mechanically compute the cost of a term according to the considered cost criteria. Observe that the rewrite strategy for E is irrelevant, since in E the only defined functions are C and $+$ (any function defined in the original and residual programs plays now the role of a constructor), and $+$ is strict in its both arguments.

Theorem 2 becomes useful when the sets of recurrence equations associated to a concrete partial evaluation are closed. Indeed, the characterization of closed recurrence equations is related to the "closedness" condition employed in some partial evaluation methods. In particular, given a partial evaluation $\mathcal{R}'$ of $\mathcal{R}$ w.r.t. S (under ρ), we compute a set of recurrence equations $E = E_{\mathcal{R}} \cup E_{\mathcal{R}'}$ (according to Def. 10), where $E_{\mathcal{R}}$ (resp. $E_{\mathcal{R}'}$) is the subset of recurrence equations associated to program $\mathcal{R}$ (resp. $\mathcal{R}'$). Then, Theorem 2 can be applied whenever $E_{\mathcal{R}}$ is S-closed (and, thus, $E_{\mathcal{R}'}$ is $\rho(S)$-closed). Note that this is always ensured if one considers the *perfect* ("α-identical") closedness test of [35] or the *basic* notion of closedness of [5] during partial evaluation. However, this property is not guaranteed when stronger notions of closedness are considered during partial evaluation (e.g., the recursive closedness of [5]) or when some partitioning techniques are used (as in conjunctive partial deduction [23]).

According to Def. 11, the equations of Example 6 are not closed due to calls like $S(\mathsf{x} : \mathsf{app} \ (\mathsf{app} \ \mathsf{x_s} \ \mathsf{y}) \ \mathsf{z})$. However, this is not a problem. We can simplify constructor-rooted calls using the following (straightforward) properties:

$$C(x) = 0, \text{ for all } x \in \mathcal{V} \tag{1}$$
$$C(t) = C(t_1) + \ldots + C(t_n), \text{ if } t = c(t_1, \ldots, t_n), c \in \mathcal{C}, n \geq 0 \tag{2}$$

This amounts to say that the cost of reducing constructor constants and variables is zero. Furthermore, the cost to evaluate a constructor-rooted term is the total cost to evaluate all its arguments. In the following, we assume that recurrence equations are possibly simplified using the above properties.

5   Usefulness of Recurrence Equations

The previous section presents a formal approach for assessing the effectiveness of partial evaluation. Here, we illustrate its usefulness by showing several possible applications of our recurrence equations.

5.1   Recurrence Equations over Natural Numbers

Our recurrence equations provide a formal characterization of the computational cost of executing a program w.r.t. a class of goals (those which are constructor instances of the left-hand sides). Therefore, as a first approach to analyze the improvement achieved by a concrete partial evaluation, one can *solve* the recurrence equations associated to both the original and partially evaluated programs and determine the speedup. In general, it is hard to find explicit solutions of these equations. Nevertheless, we can use a *size* function that maps the arguments of an expression to natural numbers. In some cases, using this function one can transform a cost C over terms into a cost T over natural numbers. Intuitively, for each recurrence equation

$$C(\sigma(s)) = C(t) + k$$

we define an associated equation

$$T_s(n_1, \ldots, n_i) = T_t(m_1, \ldots, m_j) + k$$

where $n_1, \ldots, n_i$ is a sequence of natural numbers representing the sizes of arguments $\sigma(x_1), \ldots, \sigma(x_i)$, with $x_1, \ldots, x_i$ the distinct variables of s. Similarly, $m_1, \ldots, m_j$ denote the sizes of the different variables in t. Note that the subscript s of T_s is only a device to uniquely identify the recurrence equations associated to term s.

Example 7. Consider the following recurrence equations defining $\mathcal{S}$:

$$
\begin{array}{lll}
\mathcal{S}(\sigma(\text{app (app x y) z})) & = \mathcal{S}(\text{app y z}) + 1 & \text{with } \sigma = \{x \mapsto [\,]\} \\
\mathcal{S}(\sigma(\text{app (app x y) z})) & = \mathcal{S}(\text{app (app x}_s \text{ y) z}) + 2 & \text{with } \sigma = \{x \mapsto x' : x_s\} \\
\mathcal{S}(\sigma(\text{app x y})) & = 1 & \text{with } \sigma = \{x \mapsto [\,]\} \\
\mathcal{S}(\sigma(\text{app x y})) & = \mathcal{S}(\text{app x}_s \text{ y}) + 1 & \text{with } \sigma = \{x \mapsto x' : x_s\}
\end{array}
$$

We can transform them into the following standard recurrence equations over natural numbers:

$$
\begin{array}{lll}
T_1(0, n_2, n_3) & = T_2(n_2, n_3) + 1 & \\
T_1(n_1, n_2, n_3) & = T_1(n_1 - 1, n_2, n_3) + 2 & n_1 > 0 \\
T_2(0, n_3) & = 1 & \\
T_2(n_2, n_3) & = T_2(n_2 - 1, n_3) + 1 & n_2 > 0
\end{array}
$$

where n_1, n_2 and n_3 denote the length of the corresponding lists $\sigma(x)$, $\sigma(y)$ and $\sigma(z)$, respectively. Here, T_1 stands for $T_{\text{app (app (x y) z)}}$ and T_2 for $T_{\text{app x y}}$. The *explicit solutions* of these equations are the functions:

$$T_1(n_1, n_2, n_3) = 2\,n_1 + n_2 + 2$$
$$T_2(n_2, n_3) \quad = n_2 + 1$$

Generalizing and formalizing a useful notion of size does not seem to ease the understanding or manipulation of recurrence equations because one must carefully distinguish different occurrences of a same constructor. In practice, the occurrences to be counted in sizing a constructor term depend on specific computations. For example, if x is a list of lists, only the "top-level" occurrences of the constructors of list x affect to the length of the evaluation of app x y. The number of occurrences of constructors in an element of x is irrelevant. However, these additional occurrences should be counted in sizing an argument of operation `flatten` defined below:

```
flatten []              → []
flatten ([] : y)        → flatten y
flatten ((x₁ : xₛ) : y) → x₁ : flatten (xₛ : y)
```

Furthermore, a solution of arbitrary recurrence equations does not always exist. In particular, *non-linear* recurrence equations, which might arise in some cases, do not always have a mathematical explicit solution (i.e., a solution in terms of some size-measure of the arguments).

Nevertheless, in the following we present some alternative approaches. Basically, we are interested in computing the improvement achieved by partial evaluation. Therefore, it may suffice to compute a speedup interval from the corresponding sets of equations, rather than their exact solutions.

5.2   Bounds for the Effectiveness of Partial Evaluation

In this section, we are concerned with the estimation of the speedup (or slowdown) produced by partial evaluation from the associated recurrence equations.

Let us denote by $|s, \mathcal{P}|$ the execution time of evaluating a term s in the program $\mathcal{P}$. Consider a program $\mathcal{R}$, a set of terms S, and an independent renaming ρ for S. Let $\mathcal{R}_S$ be a partial evaluation of $\mathcal{R}$ w.r.t. S (under ρ). Then, for a given term t, the speedup achieved by partial evaluation is:

$$\frac{|t, \mathcal{R}|}{|ren_\rho(t), \mathcal{R}_S|}$$

Following [8], we say that partial evaluation accomplishes *linear speedup* on $\mathcal{R}$ if for all S there exists a constant k such that for all term t

$$k \leq \frac{|t, \mathcal{R}|}{|ren_\rho(t), \mathcal{R}_S|}$$

Let, for each S, k_S be the least upper bound of the possible values for k. We call k_S the *speedup on $\mathcal{R}$ for S*. Jones [20] posed as an open question the possibility of accomplishing superlinear speedups; equivalently: "does there exist a set S for which k_S is not defined?".

It is well-known that, in general, partial evaluation cannot accomplish superlinear speedups; intuitively, the assumption that partial evaluation terminates can be used to place a bound on k_S (see, e.g., [8]). Only a *constant* speedup is usually achieved, i.e., the complexity of the original and partially evaluated programs differs by a constant factor (or, equivalently, the worst-case complexity —"big O" notation— is the same); see, for instance, [7,8,21] for traditional partial evaluation and [34] for positive supercompilation. This is also true in partial deduction if the same execution model is also used for performing computations during partial evaluation. Of course, if one uses a different computational mechanism at partial evaluation time, superlinear speedup becomes possible. For instance, one can use call-by-name evaluation at partial evaluation time when specializing call-by-value functional languages, or a refined selection rule when specializing Prolog programs (see, e.g., the discussion in [7]).

In our case, where we use the same mechanism both for execution and for partial evaluation, it is obvious from Def. 10 that the recurrence equations associated to the original and residual programs have exactly the same structure, i.e., they are identical except for the renaming of terms and the associated costs. Hence, it is straightforward to conclude that narrowing-driven partial evaluation cannot achieve superlinear speedups, as well.

An important observation is that the overall speedup of a program is determined by the speedups of loops, since sufficiently long runs will consume most of the execution time inside loops. In our method, loops are represented by recurrence equations. Since the recurrence equations associated to the original and residual programs have the same structure, as justified in the above paragraph, they constitute by themselves a useful aid to the user for determining the speedup (or slowdown) associated to each loop. Moreover, this information is inexpensive to obtain since the recurrence equations can be generated from the same partial derivations used to produce residual rules.

In principle, we can easily modify existing partial evaluators for functional logic programs [2,4] to provide rules decorated with the associated cost improvement. Each resultant rule can be augmented with a pair of integers, (k, k'), for each cost criterion. This pair describes a cost variation (according to Def. 10) of the resultant rule in the original and in the residual program.

For instance, given the partial derivation of Example 6, we produce the (decorated) residual rule:

$$\mathsf{dapp}\ (\mathsf{x}' : \mathsf{x_s})\ \mathsf{y}\ \mathsf{z}\ \rightarrow\ \mathsf{x}' : \mathsf{dapp}\ \mathsf{x_s}\ \mathsf{y}\ \mathsf{z}\quad /*\ \{(2,1), (4,2), (2,1)\}\ */$$

From this information, we immediately see that all cost criteria have been improved and, moreover, we can quantify this improvement.

However, as residual programs grow larger, it becomes more difficult to estimate the effectiveness of a particular partial evaluation from the decorated rules.

In this case, it would be valuable to design an automatic speedup analysis tool to determine (at least in some cases) the improvement achieved by the whole program w.r.t. each cost criterion. For instance, we could define a simple speedup analysis along the lines of [8]. For this purpose, it suffices to consider a speedup interval $\langle l, u \rangle$ where l and u are, respectively, the smallest and largest ratios k'/k among all the computed recurrence equations.

6 Related Work

A considerable effort has been devoted to reason about the complexity of imperative programs (see, e.g., [1]). However, relatively little attention has been paid to the development of methods for reasoning about the computational cost of declarative programs. For logic programs, [13] introduces a method for the (semi-)automatic analysis of the worst-case cost of a large class of logic programs, including nondeterminism and the generation of multiple solutions via backtracking. Regarding eager (call-by-value) functional programs, [24] describes a general approach for time-bound analysis of programs. Essentially, it is based on the construction of time-bound functions which mimic the original functions but compute the associated cost of evaluations. The techniques of [24] cannot be easily adapted to lazy (call-by-name) functional languages since cost criteria are not usually compositional. A similar approach can be found in [30], where a *step-counting* version of a functional program is produced automatically. This version, when called with the same arguments as the original program, returns the computation time for the original program. In a second phase, a *time bound* function (or worst-case complexity) is expressed as an abstract interpretation of the step-counting version. Rosendahl's work [30] is defined for (first-order) call-by-value functional languages, although it contains some hints about how to adapt the method to different languages. We note that, in contrast to [24] and [30], our (cost) recurrence equations are tightly associated to the partial evaluation process and, thus, they allow us to assess more easily the effectiveness achieved by the partial evaluation transformation. On the other hand, [31] develops a theory of cost equivalence to reason about the cost of lazy functional programs. Essentially, [31] introduces a set of *time rules* extracted from a suitable operational semantics, together with some equivalence laws. The aim of this calculus is to reveal enough of the "algorithmic structure" of operationally opaque lazy functional programs to permit the use of more traditional techniques developed in the context of imperative programs.

None of the above references apply the introduced analyses to predict the improvement achieved by partial evaluation techniques. Indeed, we found very little work directed to the formal study of the cost variation due to partial evaluation techniques. For instance, [29] introduces a type system to formally express when a partial evaluator is better than another, i.e., when a residual program is more *efficient* than another. The aim of [7] is on the definition of a general framework to study the effects of several unfolding-based transformations over logic programs. The framework is applied to partial evaluation, but the considered measures are very simple (e.g., unification is not taken into account). A well-known technique appears in [8] and [21, Chapter 6]. They introduce a simple *speedup analysis* which predicts a relative interval of the speedup achieved by a partial evaluation. Finally, [34, Chapter 11] presents a theoretical study of the efficiency of residual programs by positive supercompilation, a partial evaluation technique closely related to narrowing-driven partial evaluation. It proves that the number of steps is not improved by positive supercompilation alone (a post-unfolding phase is necessary). This would be also true in our context if resultants were constructed only from one-step derivations. However, as discussed in [34], this does not mean that the process is useless, since intermediate data structures are frequently eliminated.

All the cited references study the effectiveness of partial evaluation by taking into account only the number of steps in evaluations. Although this is an important measure, we think that other criteria should also be considered (as in traditional experimental profiling approaches [33]). The discussion in [34] (see above) as well as situations like that in Example 1 justify this position.

7   Conclusions and Future Work

To the best of our knowledge, this is the first attempt to formally measure the effectiveness of partial evaluation with cost criteria different from the number of evaluation steps. Our characterization of cost enables us to estimate the effectiveness of a partial evaluation in a precise framework. We also provide an automatic method to infer some recurrence equations which help us to reason about the improvement achieved. The combination of these contributions helps us to reconcile theoretical results and experimental measures. Although the introduced notions and techniques are specialized to narrowing-driven partial evaluation, they could be adapted to other related partial evaluation methods (e.g., positive supercompilation [35] or partial deduction [25]).

There are several possible directions for further research. On the theoretical side, we plan to study several properties of partial evaluation within the formal framework presented so far. Two well-known facts motivate our interest: (1) partial evaluation techniques cannot, in general, increase the number of steps required to perform a particular computation (under a call-by-name evaluation model, see [32]); and (2) partial evaluation sometimes degrades program efficiency. By experimenting with a preliminary implementation of the analysis outlined in the present paper, we discovered that some cost criteria can be actually degraded (producing a slowdown in the residual program). The formal study of the conditions under which an improvement is guaranteed for each cost criteria is the subject of ongoing research. On the practical side, we plan to develop an analytical tool for estimating the improvements achieved by residual programs.

Acknowledgements

We gratefully acknowledge the anonymous referees and the participants of LOP-STR'2000 for their comments on this paper. We are also grateful to Mark Jones for helping us to benchmark Hugs programs. Part of this research was done while Elvira Albert and Germán Vidal were visiting the Department of Computer Science at Portland State University. They gratefully acknowledge this department's hospitality.

This work has been partially supported by CICYT TIC 98-0445-C03-01 and the National Science Foundation under grant INT-9981317.

References

1. A. V. Aho, J. E. Hopcroft, and J. D. Ullman. *The Design and Analysis of Computer Algorithms.* Addison-Wesley, Reading, MA, 1974.
2. E. Albert, M. Alpuente, M. Falaschi, and G. Vidal. INDY User's Manual. Technical Report DSIC-II/12/98, UPV, 1998.
3. E. Albert, S. Antoy, and G. Vidal. A Formal Approach to Reasoning about the Effectiveness of Partial Evaluation. Technical Report DSIC, UPV, 2000. Available from URL: http://www.dsic.upv.es/users/elp/papers.html.
4. E. Albert, M. Hanus, and G. Vidal. Using an Abstract Representation to Specialize Functional Logic Programs. In *Proc. of the 7th Int'l Conf. on Logic for Programming and Automated Reasoning (LPAR'2000)*, pages 381–398. Springer LNAI 1955, 2000.
5. M. Alpuente, M. Falaschi, and G. Vidal. Partial Evaluation of Functional Logic Programs. *ACM Transactions on Programming Languages and Systems*, 20(4):768–844, 1998.
6. M. Alpuente, M. Hanus, S. Lucas, and G. Vidal. Specialization of Functional Logic Programs Based on Needed Narrowing. *ACM Sigplan Notices*, 34(9):273–283, 1999.
7. T. Amtoft. Properties of Unfolding-based Meta-level Systems. In *Proc. of PEPM'91*, pages 243–254. ACM Press, 1991.
8. L. O. Andersen and C. K. Gomard. Speedup Analysis in Partial Evaluation: Preliminary Results. In *Proc. of PEPM'92*, pages 1–7. Yale University, 1992.
9. S. Antoy. Definitional trees. In *Proc. of the 3rd Int'l Conference on Algebraic and Logic Programming (ALP'92)*, pages 143–157. Springer LNCS 632, 1992.
10. S. Antoy, R. Echahed, and M. Hanus. A Needed Narrowing Strategy. *Journal of the ACM*, 47(4):776–822, 2000.
11. F. Baader and T. Nipkow. *Term Rewriting and All That.* Cambridge University Press, 1998.
12. C. Consel and O. Danvy. Tutorial notes on Partial Evaluation. In *Proc. of the Annual Symp. on Principles of Programming Languages (POPL'93)*, pages 493–501. ACM, New York, 1993.
13. S. K. Debray and N. W. Lin. Cost Analysis of Logic Programs. *ACM Transactions on Programming Languages and Systems*, 15(5):826–975, 1993.
14. J. Gallagher. Tutorial on Specialisation of Logic Programs. In *Proc. of PEPM'93*, pages 88–98. ACM, New York, 1993.
15. E. Giovannetti, G. Levi, C. Moiso, and C. Palamidessi. Kernel Leaf: A Logic plus Functional Language. *Journal of Computer and System Sciences*, 42:363–377, 1991.

16. M. Hanus. The Integration of Functions into Logic Programming: From Theory to Practice. *Journal of Logic Programming*, 19&20:583–628, 1994.

17. M. Hanus (ed.). Curry: An Integrated Functional Logic Language. Available at http://www-i2.informatik.rwth-aachen.de/~hanus/curry, 2000.

18. G. Huet and J. J. Lévy. Computations in orthogonal rewriting systems, Part I + II. In J. L. Lassez and G. D. Plotkin, editors, *Computational Logic – Essays in Honor of Alan Robinson*, pages 395–443, 1992.

19. M. P. Jones and A. Reid. The Hugs 98 User Manual. Available at http://haskell.cs.yale.edu/hugs/, 1998.

20. N. D. Jones. Partial Evaluation, Self-Application and Types. In M. S. Paterson, editor, *Proc. of 17th Int'l Colloquium on Automata, Languages and Programming (ICALP'90)*, pages 639–659. Springer LNCS 443, 1990.

21. N. D. Jones, C. K. Gomard, and P. Sestoft. *Partial Evaluation and Automatic Program Generation*. Prentice-Hall, Englewood Cliffs, NJ, 1993.

22. Laura Lafave. *A Constraint-based Partial Evaluator for Functional Logic Programs and its Application*. PhD thesis, University of Bristol, 1999.

23. M. Leuschel, D. De Schreye, and A. de Waal. A Conceptual Embedding of Folding into Partial Deduction: Towards a Maximal Integration. In M. Maher, editor, *Proc. of the Joint Int'l Conf. and Symp. on Logic Programming (JICSLP'96)*, pages 319–332. The MIT Press, Cambridge, MA, 1996.

24. Y. A. Liu and G. Gomez. Automatic Accurate Time-Bound Analysis for High-Level Languages. In *Proc. of ACM SIGPLAN Workshop on Languages, Compilers, and Tools for Embedded Systems*, pages 31–40. Springer LNCS 1474, 1998.

25. J. W. Lloyd and J. C. Shepherdson. Partial Evaluation in Logic Programming. *Journal of Logic Programming*, 11:217–242, 1991.

26. R. Loogen, F. López-Fraguas, and M. Rodríguez-Artalejo. A Demand Driven Computation Strategy for Lazy Narrowing. In *Proc. of 5th Int'l Symp. on Programming Language Implementation and Logic Programming (PLILP'93)*, pages 184–200. Springer LNCS 714, 1993.

27. F. J. López-Fraguas and J. Sánchez-Hernández. TOY: A Multiparadigm Declarative System. In *Proc. of the 10th Int'l Conf. on Rewriting Techniques and Applications (RTA'99)*, pages 244–247. Springer LNCS 1631, 1999.

28. J. J. Moreno-Navarro and M. Rodríguez-Artalejo. Logic Programming with Functions and Predicates: The language Babel. *Journal of Logic Programming*, 12(3):191–224, 1992.

29. F. Nielson. A Formal Type System for Comparing Partial Evaluators. In *Proc. of the Int'l Workshop on Partial Evaluation and Mixed Computation*, pages 349–384. N-H, 1988.

30. M. Rosendahl. Automatic Complexity Analysis. In *Proc. of the Int'l Conf. on Functional Programming Languages and Computer Architecture*, pages 144–156, New York, NY, 1989. ACM.

31. D. Sands. A Naive Time Analysis and its Theory of Cost Equivalence. *Journal of Logic and Computation*, 5(4):495–541, 1995.

32. D. Sands. Total Correctness by Local Improvement in the Transformation of Functional Programs. *ACM Transactions on Programming Languages and Systems*, 18(2):175–234, March 1996.

33. P. M. Sansom and S. L. Peyton-Jones. Formally Based Profiling for Higher-Order Functional Languages. *ACM Transactions on Programming Languages and Systems*, 19(2):334–385, 1997.

34. M. H. Sørensen. Turchin's Supercompiler Revisited: An Operational Theory of Positive Information Propagation. Technical Report 94/7, Master's Thesis, DIKU, University of Copenhagen, Denmark, 1994.
35. M. H. Sørensen, R. Glück, and N. D. Jones. A Positive Supercompiler. *Journal of Functional Programming*, 6(6):811–838, 1996.

Automated Strategies for Specializing Constraint Logic Programs

Fabio Fioravanti[1], Alberto Pettorossi[2], and Maurizio Proietti[1]

[1] IASI-CNR
Viale Manzoni 30, I-00185 Roma, Italy
{fioravanti,proietti}@iasi.rm.cnr.it
[2] DISP, University of Roma Tor Vergata
I-00133 Roma, Italy
adp@iasi.rm.cnr.it

Abstract. We consider the problem of specializing constraint logic programs w.r.t. constrained queries. We follow a transformational approach based on rules and strategies. The use of the rules ensures that the specialized program is equivalent to the initial program w.r.t. a given constrained query. The strategies guide the application of the rules so to derive an efficient specialized program. In this paper we address various issues concerning the development of an automated transformation strategy. In particular, we consider the problems of when and how we should unfold, replace constraints, introduce generalized clauses, and apply the contextual constraint replacement rule. We propose a solution to these problems by adapting to our framework various techniques developed in the field of constraint programming, partial evaluation, and abstract interpretation. In particular, we use: (i) suitable solvers for simplifying constraints, (ii) well-quasi-orders for ensuring the termination of the unfoldings and for activating clause generalizations, and (iii) widening operators for ensuring the termination of the generalization process.

1 Introduction

Program specialization is a powerful methodology for automated software engineering and, in particular, for program reuse. Program specialization, in fact, may adapt a generic program to the specific context where it has to be used and this adaptation process may be done via automatic or semiautomatic techniques. One such technique is *partial evaluation*. Partial evaluation has been proposed and studied for various programming languages [14] and it has been shown to be very powerful. In particular, via partial evaluation one can perform many sophisticated program optimizations by taking advantage of the context of use of the programs. In this paper we address the problem of automating some techniques for the *contextual specialization* [8] of *constraint logic programs* over a domain $\mathcal{D}$ (CLP, for short, or CLP($\mathcal{D}$) when we want to make the domain explicit) [12]. Contextual specialization is defined as follows. We are given a CLP($\mathcal{D}$) program P and a constrained atom c, A and we want to derive a program P_s and an atom

Kung-Kiu Lau (Ed.): LOPSTR 2000, LNCS 2042, pp. 125–146, 2001.

A_s such that, for every variable assignment σ that assigns an element of $\mathcal{D}$ to each free variable in the constrained atom c, A, we have that:

$$lm(P, \mathcal{D}) \models_\sigma c, A \quad \text{iff} \quad lm(P_s, \mathcal{D}) \models_\sigma c, A_s \quad \text{(1: Contextual Specialization)}$$

where $lm(P, \mathcal{D})$ denotes the *least $\mathcal{D}$-model* of P [13].

Contextual specialization is more general than the partial evaluation of $CLP(\mathcal{D})$ programs based on Lloyd and Shepherdson's approach [17,18,26]. Indeed, partial evaluation is defined as follows. We are given a $CLP(\mathcal{D})$ program P and a constrained atom c, A and we want to derive a program P_{pe} and an atom A_{pe} such that, for every variable assignment σ, we have that:

$$lm(P, \mathcal{D}) \models_\sigma c, A \quad \text{iff} \quad lm(P_{pe}, \mathcal{D}) \models_\sigma A_{pe} \quad \text{(2: Partial Evaluation)}$$

Now we present a very simple example which illustrates the difference between contextual specialization of CLP programs and partial evaluation. More significant examples and experimental results will be discussed in Sections 5 and 6. Let us consider the following $CLP(\mathcal{R})$ program P over the domain $\mathcal{R}$ of real numbers:

$$p(X) \leftarrow X \geq 0, q(X) \qquad\qquad \text{(Program } P\text{)}$$

where q is a predicate which does not depend on p. By contextual specialization of P w.r.t. the constrained atom $X \geq 3, p(X)$ we derive the program P_s:

$$p_s(X) \leftarrow q(X) \qquad\qquad \text{(Program } P_s\text{)}$$

together with the atom $p_s(X)$.

Instead, by partial evaluation of program P w.r.t. the same constrained atom $X \geq 3, p(X)$ we derive the program P_{pe}:

$$p_{pe}(X) \leftarrow X \geq 3, q(X) \qquad\qquad \text{(Program } P_{pe}\text{)}$$

together with the atom $p_{pe}(X)$.

Thus, the partially evaluated program P_{pe} is less efficient than the program P_s derived by contextual specialization, because P_{pe} redundantly checks whether or not the constraint $X \geq 3$ holds.

In [8] we have introduced some *transformation rules* and semiautomatic *strategies* for contextual specialization. Here we address various issues concerning the full automation of our strategies. In particular, we consider the problems of: (i) when and how to unfold, (ii) when and how to generalize, and (iii) when and how to apply the contextual constraint replacement rule. Our automatic strategy for contextual specialization of $CLP(\mathcal{D})$ programs is based on concepts borrowed from the fields of constraint programming, partial evaluation, and abstract interpretation. In particular, we consider: (i) suitable *solvers* for simplifying constraints [12], (ii) *well-quasi-orders* for ensuring the termination of the unfolding process and for activating the clause generalization process [15,16,25], and (iii) *widening operators* [4] for ensuring the termination of that generalization process.

2 Rules for Contextual Specialization of CLP Programs

In this section we recall the transformation rules which we use for specializing $CLP(\mathcal{D})$ programs. Our rules are a slight modification of the unfold/fold rules considered in [1,7,19] and they are designed for performing contextual specialization.

Let us begin by presenting some preliminary notions and notational conventions we will use. For notions not defined here the reader may refer to [12]. Throughout the paper we will consider a fixed first-order language $\mathcal{L}$. Let *Vars* be the (possibly infinite) set of variables in $\mathcal{L}$. Given a formula φ, the set of variables and the set of free variables occurring in φ are denoted by $vars(\varphi)$ and $FV(\varphi)$, respectively. Given a term t, the set of variables occurring in t is denoted by $vars(t)$. Similar notation will be used for sequences of formulas or terms. We will write $\forall X_1 \ldots X_m \, \psi$ also as $\forall X \, \psi$, where X denotes the set $\{X_1, \ldots, X_m\}$. Analogously for $\exists$, instead of $\forall$. Similarly, we will write the atom $p(t_1, \ldots, t_m)$ also as $p(t)$, where t denotes the sequence $t_1, \ldots, t_m$ of terms.

Constraints over the domain $\mathcal{D}$ are denoted by the letters $c, d, \ldots$, possibly with subscripts. The set of all constraints over $\mathcal{D}$ is denoted by $\mathcal{C}$ and we assume that it contains a given set of *primitive constraints* including *true*, *false*, and all equality constraints between terms, that is, $t_1 = t_2$, for all terms t_1 and t_2 in $\mathcal{L}$. We assume that $\mathcal{C}$ is closed w.r.t. conjunction (which, as usual, we denote by comma) and existential quantification. *Atoms* are denoted by the letters $H, A, B, \ldots$, possibly with subscripts. We assume that every atom is *pure*, that is, it is of the form $p(X_1, \ldots, X_m)$, where $X_1, \ldots, X_m$ are distinct variables. A *constrained atom* is the conjunction of a constraint and an atom. *Goals* are (possibly empty) conjunctions of atoms, and they are denoted by G, possibly with subscripts. A *constrained goal* is the conjunction of a constraint and a goal, and it is denoted by K, possibly with subscripts. Conjunction is commutative and, thus, the order of constraints and atoms in the body of a clause is immaterial. The empty conjunction (of constraints or atoms) is *true*. *Clauses* are denoted by lower case Greek letters $\gamma, \delta, \ldots$ and they are of the form $H \leftarrow c, G$. No variable in H, G is quantified.

The assumption that all atoms are pure is not restrictive because, for instance, any clause γ with occurrences of non-pure atoms, can be transformed into a clause δ with occurrences of pure atoms only, such that δ is equivalent to γ w.r.t. the least $\mathcal{D}$-model semantics. This can be done by adding suitable equality constraints. For example, the clause: $p(X+1) \leftarrow X \leq 0, \, r(X-1)$ can be transformed into the equivalent clause: $p(Y) \leftarrow X \leq 0, \, r(Z), \, Y = X+1, \, Z = X-1$, where all atoms are pure.

A *variable renaming* is a bijective mapping from *Vars* to itself. The application of a variable renaming ρ to a syntactic expression e is denoted by $e\rho$, and $e\rho$ is obtained from e by replacing each (bound or free) variable X of e by the variable $X\rho$. The expression $e\rho$ is said to be a *variant* of e. A clause γ is said to be *renamed apart* iff all its (bound or free) variables do not occur elsewhere. Given a clause γ there exists a variable renaming ρ such that $\gamma\rho$ is renamed apart.

For a clause γ of the form: $H \leftarrow K$, we say that H is the head of γ, denoted by $hd(\gamma)$, and K is the body of γ, denoted by $bd(\gamma)$. Given the clause γ of the form: $H \leftarrow K_1, K_2$, where K_1 and K_2 are constrained goals, the set of the *linking variables* of K_1 in γ is $FV(K_1) \cap FV(H, K_2)$. Similarly, we define the set of the linking variables of a constraint or a constraint atom in a clause.

The semantics of a CLP($\mathcal{D}$) program P is defined as the *least $\mathcal{D}$-model* of P, denoted $lm(P, \mathcal{D})$ [13]. Let $\mathcal{P}_{fin}(Vars)$ denote the set of all finite subsets of $Vars$. We assume that there exists a computable total function *solve*: $\mathcal{C} \times \mathcal{P}_{fin}(Vars) \to \mathcal{C}$ which is *sound* w.r.t. constraint equivalence, in the sense that: for every constraint c_1 and every finite set X of variables, if $solve(c_1, X) = c_2$ then $\mathcal{D} \models \forall X((\exists Y\, c_1) \leftrightarrow c_2)$ where $Y = FV(c_1) - X$ and $FV(c_2) \subseteq FV(\exists Y\, c_1)$. Thus, $solve(c_1, X)$ is a constraint c_2 which is equivalent to the existential quantification of c_1 w.r.t. all variables not in X.

We also require that *solve* is *complete* w.r.t. satisfiability in the sense that, for any constraint c such that $Y = FV(c)$:

(i) $solve(c, \emptyset) = true$ if c is *satisfiable*, that is, $\mathcal{D} \models \exists Y\, c$, and

(ii) $solve(c, \emptyset) = false$ if c is *unsatisfiable*, that is, $\mathcal{D} \not\models \exists Y\, c$.

In (i) and (ii) 'if' can be replaced by 'iff' because *solve* is sound w.r.t. constraint equivalence. The soundness and the totality of the *solve* function are necessary to guarantee the correctness and the termination, respectively, of the specialization strategy presented in Section 4. The assumption that the *solve* function is complete w.r.t. satisfiability guarantees that constraint satisfiability tests, which are required by our technique, are decidable and they can indeed be performed by applying the *solve* function.

The process of *specializing* a given program P whereby deriving program P_s, can be formalized as a sequence $P_0, \ldots, P_n$ of programs, called a *transformation sequence*, where $P_0 = P$, $P_n = P_s$ and, for $k = 0, \ldots, n-1$, program P_{k+1} is obtained from program P_k by applying one of the following transformation rules: *constrained atomic definition, unfolding, constrained atomic folding, clause removal*, and *contextual constraint replacement*. We will also apply the *constraint replacement rule* (see rule R6) which is an instance of the contextual constraint replacement rule (see rule R5).

R1. Constrained Atomic Definition. By *constrained atomic definition* (or *definition*, for short), we introduce the new clause

$$\delta: \quad newp(X) \leftarrow c, A$$

which is said to be a *definition*, where: (i) $newp$ is a predicate symbol not occurring in $P_0, \ldots, P_k$, (ii) X is a sequence of distinct variables occurring in the constrained atom c, A, and (iii) the predicate symbol of A occurs in P_0. From program P_k we derive the new program P_{k+1} which is $P_k \cup \{\delta\}$.

For $i \geq 0$, $Defs_i$ is the set of definitions introduced during the transformation sequence $P_0, \ldots, P_i$. Obviously, $Defs_0 = \emptyset$.

R2. Unfolding. Let $\gamma: H \leftarrow c, G_1, A, G_2$ be a renamed apart clause of P_k and let $\{A_j \leftarrow c_j, G_j \mid j = 1, \ldots, m\}$ be the set of *all* clauses in P_k such that the atoms A and A_j have the same predicate symbol. For $j = 1, \ldots, m$, let us consider the clause

$$\gamma_j : \quad H \leftarrow c, A = A_j, c_j, G_1, G_j, G_2$$

where $A = A_j$ stands for the conjunction of the equalities between the corresponding arguments. Then, by *unfolding* clause γ w.r.t. atom A, from program P_k we derive the new program P_{k+1} which is $(P_k - \{\gamma\}) \cup \{\gamma_j \mid j = 1, \ldots, m\}$.

R3. Constrained Atomic Folding. Let $\gamma : \ A \leftarrow c, G_1, B, G_2$ be a clause of P_k. Let $\delta : \ newp(X) \leftarrow d, B$ be a variant of a clause in $Defs_k$. Suppose that: (i) $\mathcal{D} \models \forall Y \ (c \rightarrow d)$, where $Y = FV(c, d)$, and (ii) no variable in $FV(\delta) - X$ occurs in $FV(A, c, G_1, G_2)$. By *folding* clause γ w.r.t. atom B using δ, we derive the new clause

$$\gamma_f : \quad A \leftarrow c, G_1, newp(X), G_2$$

and from program P_k we derive the new program P_{k+1} which is $(P_k - \{\gamma\}) \cup \{\gamma_f\}$.

In this rule R3 condition (i) may be replaced by the following weaker, but more complex condition: (i*) $\mathcal{D} \models \forall Y \ (c \rightarrow \exists Z \ d)$, where $Z = FV(d) - (X \cup vars(B))$ and $Y = FV(c, d) - Z$. However, by a suitable application of the constraint replacement rule R6 below, from clause δ we can derive a clause η of the form: $newp(X) \leftarrow (\exists Z \ d), B$ such that condition (i*) holds for γ and δ iff condition (i) holds for γ and η.

R4. Clause Removal. Let $\gamma : \ A \leftarrow c, G$ be a clause of P_k. If the constraint c is *unsatisfiable*, that is, $solve(c, \emptyset) = false$, then from program P_k we derive the new program P_{k+1} which is $P_k - \{\gamma\}$.

R5. Contextual Constraint Replacement. Let $\mathbf{C}$ be a set of constrained atoms. Let γ be a renamed apart clause in P_k of the form: $p(U) \leftarrow c_1, G$. Suppose that for some constraint c_2, we have that for every constrained atom $c, p(V)$ in $\mathbf{C}$,

$$\mathcal{D} \models \forall X \left((c, U = V) \ \rightarrow \ (\exists Y \ c_1 \leftrightarrow \exists Z \ c_2) \right)$$

where: (i) $Y = FV(c_1) - vars(U, G)$, (ii) $Z = FV(c_2) - vars(U, G)$, and (iii) $X = FV(c, U = V, c_1, c_2) - (Y \cup Z)$. Then, we derive program P_{k+1} from program P_k by replacing clause γ by the clause: $p(U) \leftarrow c_2, G$. In this case we say that P_{k+1} has been derived from P_k by contextual constraint replacement w.r.t. $\mathbf{C}$.

The following rule is an instance of rule R5 for $\mathbf{C} = \{true, p(U)\}$.

R6. Constraint Replacement. Let $\gamma : \ A \leftarrow c_1, G$ be a renamed apart clause of P_k. Assume that $\mathcal{D} \models \forall X (\exists Y \ c_1 \leftrightarrow \exists Z \ c_2)$ where: (i) $Y = FV(c_1) - vars(A, G)$, (ii) $Z = FV(c_2) - vars(A, G)$, and (iii) $X = FV(c_1, c_2) - (Y \cup Z)$. Then from program P_k we derive the new program P_{k+1} which is $(P_k - \{\gamma\}) \cup \{A \leftarrow c_2, G\}$.

In the *contextual specialization strategy* of Section 4, we will make use of the above rule R6 for replacing a clause γ of the form $A \leftarrow c_1, G$ by the clause $A \leftarrow solve(c_1, X), G$, where X is the set of the linking variables of c_1 in γ.

3 Well-Quasi-Orders and Clause Generalization

In this section we introduce the notions of: (i) *well-quasi-orders* over constrained goals, and (ii) *clause generalization*, which we will use in our program specialization strategy. These notions are extensions to the case of CLP($\mathcal{D}$) programs of similar notions considered in the case of partial evaluation of functional and logic programs (see, for instance, [15,16,25]). Let $\mathbf{N}$ denote the set of natural numbers.

Definition 1. A *well-quasi-order* (*wqo*, for short) over the set of constrained goals is a reflexive, transitive, binary relation $\preceq$ such that for every infinite sequence $\{K_i \mid i \in \mathbf{N}\}$ of constrained goals there exist two natural numbers i and j such that $i < j$ and $K_i \preceq K_j$ [6]. Given two constrained goals K_1 and K_2, if $K_1 \preceq K_2$ we say that K_1 is *embedded in* K_2.

Various examples of wqo's that are used for ensuring the termination of the unfolding process during the partial evaluation of logic and functional programs, can be found in [15,25]. For our specialization example of Section 5 we will use the simple wqo $\preceq_L$ defined as follows: given two constrained goals K_1 and K_2, we have that $K_1 \preceq_L K_2$ iff the leftmost atom (in the textual order) in K_1 and the leftmost atom (in the textual order) in K_2 have the same predicate symbol.

Definition 2. [*Constraint Lattice and Widening*] Given the set $\mathcal{C}$ of constraints over $\mathcal{D}$, we consider the partial order $\langle \mathcal{C}, \sqsubseteq \rangle$ such that for any two constraints c_1 and c_2 in $\mathcal{C}$, $c_1 \sqsubseteq c_2$ iff $\mathcal{D} \models \forall X (c_1 \rightarrow c_2)$ where $X = FV(c_1, c_2)$. We assume that $\langle \mathcal{C}, \sqsubseteq \rangle$ is a lattice, where: (i) the least element is *false*, (ii) the greatest element is *true*, (iii) the *least upper bound* of two constraints c_1 and c_2 is denoted by $c_1 \sqcup c_2$, and (iv) the *greatest lower bound* of two constraints c_1 and c_2 is their conjunction c_1, c_2.
A *widening operator* (see also [4]) is a binary operator ∇ between constraints such that:
(W1) $(c_1 \sqcup c_2) \sqsubseteq (c_1 \nabla c_2)$, and
(W2) for every infinite sequence $\{c_i \mid i \in \mathbf{N}\}$ of constraints, the infinite sequence $\{d_i \mid i \in \mathbf{N}\}$ of constraints where $d_0 = c_0$ and, for any $i \in \mathbf{N}$, $d_{i+1} = d_i \nabla c_{i+1}$, *stabilizes*, that is, $\exists h \in \mathbf{N}\ \forall k \geq h\ \mathcal{D} \models \forall X (d_h \leftrightarrow d_k)$ where $X = FV(d_h, d_k)$. Notice that, in general, ∇ is not commutative.
We say that the widening operator ∇ *agrees with* the wqo $\preceq$ iff for every atom $q(X)$ and constraints c and d, we have that $c \nabla d, q(X) \preceq c, q(X)$.
    We have that any widening operator ∇ agrees with the wqo $\preceq_L$ defined above.

We now introduce the notion of *clause generalization*, which is based upon the widening operator ∇. It will be used in our strategy for contextual specialization to be presented in the next section, for deriving from two given atomic definitions a new, generalized atomic definition.

Definition 3. [*Clause Generalization*] Given two clauses α: $new1(U) \leftarrow c_1, q(X)$ and η: $new2(V) \leftarrow c_2, q(X)$, where each variable in $(U, FV(c_1), V, FV(c_2))$ is in X, we define the *generalization of α w.r.t. η*, denoted by $gen(\alpha, \eta)$, to be the clause: $genp(W) \leftarrow c_1 \nabla c_2, q(X)$, where *genp* is a new predicate symbol and W is the sequence of the distinct variables occurring in (U, V).

Example 1. [$\mathcal{R}_{lin}$: *Linear equations and inequations over the reals*] Let us consider the domain $\mathcal{R}_{lin}$ of conjunctions of linear equations ($=$) and inequations ($<, \leq, >, \geq$) over real numbers. In this domain we may replace any existentially quantified constraint by an equivalent constraint without occurrences of $\exists$. Thus, without loss of generality, we may assume that every constraint is a conjunction of primitive constraints of the form $t_1 \, op \, t_2$, where $op \in \{=, <, \leq, >, \geq\}$. $\mathcal{R}_{lin}$ is a lattice whose least upper bound operation is defined by the convex hull construction. Let us now introduce a widening operator for $\mathcal{R}_{lin}$ which we will use in our program specialization example of Section 5. Given a constraint c, let $ineq(c)$ be the constraint obtained by replacing every equation $t_1 = t_2$ in c by the conjunction of the two inequations $t_1 \geq t_2$, $t_1 \leq t_2$. Assume that $ineq(c)$ is the conjunction of primitive constraints $c_1, \ldots, c_n$. For any constraint d, we define the widening $c \nabla d$ to be the conjunction of all c_i's, with $0 \leq i \leq n$, such that $d \sqsubseteq c_i$.

This widening operator satisfies Condition W1 because, by construction, $c \sqsubseteq c \nabla d$ and $d \sqsubseteq c \nabla d$, that is, $c \nabla d$ is an upper bound of c, d. Thus, we have that: $(c \sqcup d) \sqsubseteq (c \nabla d)$. Also Condition W2 holds for ∇, because for every constraint c and d the number of primitive constraints in $ineq(c)$ is not smaller than the number of primitive constraints in $ineq(c \nabla d)$.

Here is an example of clause generalization. Given the following two clauses:

α. $mmod_s(I, J, M) \leftarrow I = 0, J \geq 0, mmod(I, J, M)$
η. $newp(I, J, M) \leftarrow I = 1, J > 0, mmod(I, J, M)$

$gen(\alpha, \eta)$ is $genp(I, J, M) \leftarrow I \geq 0, J \geq 0, mmod(I, J, M)$, because we have that:
(i) $ineq(I = 0, J \geq 0) = (I \geq 0, I \leq 0, J \geq 0)$ and (ii) $(ineq(I = 0, J \geq 0)) \, \nabla \, (I = 1, J > 0) = (I \geq 0, J \geq 0)$ because it is not the case that $(I = 1, J > 0) \sqsubseteq (I \leq 0)$. □

4   An Automated Strategy for Contextual Specialization

We now describe the contextual specialization strategy for deriving efficient CLP($\mathcal{D}$) programs by specialization. This strategy is a generalization of the strategies for the partial evaluation of definite logic programs presented in [10,22,24].

Our strategy is parameterized by: (i) the function *solve* which is used for the application of the constraint replacement rule, (ii) an *unfolding function* *Unfold* for guiding the unfolding process, (iii) a well-quasi-order $\preceq_u$ over constrained goals which tells us when to terminate the unfolding process, (iv) a clause generalization function *gen*, with its associated widening operator ∇, and (v) a well-quasi-order $\preceq_g$ over constrained atoms which tells us when to activate the clause generalization process. Once the choice of these parameters has been made, our strategy can be applied in a fully automatic way.

The contextual specialization strategy in divided into two phases. Phase 1 consists of the iteration of two procedures, called *Unfold-Replace* and *Define-Fold*, respectively. During the *Unfold-Replace* procedure we unfold the program to be specialized so to expose some initial portions of its computation, and we simplify the derived clauses by replacing inefficient constraints by some more efficient ones using the given function *solve*. The termination of this procedure is ensured by the use of the well-quasi-order $\preceq_u$. We then apply the *Define-Fold* procedure and we fold the simplified clauses by using already available definitions and, possibly, some new definitions. Phase 1 is terminated when no new definitions need to be introduced for performing the folding steps. The termination of Phase 1 is ensured by the properties of the generalization function and well-quasi-order $\preceq_g$ which guarantee that the set of generated definitions is finite.

Then during Phase 2, we apply the contextual constraint replacement rule and from each clause defining a predicate, say p, we remove the constraints which are known to hold when the clause is used. This information is obtained by computing the least upper bound of the set of constraints which occur in the clauses containing a call of p.

For the formal description of our contextual specialization strategy we need to introduce the following data structures. We introduce a tree *Defstree*, called *definition tree*, whose nodes are the clauses introduced by the definition rule during program specialization. Moreover, for each clause δ in *Defstree* we introduce a tree *Utree*(δ), called *unfolding tree*. The root of *Utree*(δ) is δ itself, and the nodes of *Utree*(δ) are the clauses derived from δ by applying the unfolding and constraint replacement rules. The usual relation of *ancestor* between nodes in a tree gives us the relation of ancestor between clauses in *Defstree* and also between clauses in *Utree*(δ).

4.1   The Unfold-Replace Procedure

Let us first introduce some notions which will be useful in the definition of the *Unfold-Replace* procedure. Let P be a CLP program and Γ be a set of clauses.

(a) A clause of the form $H \leftarrow c, A_1, \ldots, A_n$ has a *non-failing* body iff c is satisfiable, and for $i = 1, \ldots, n$, the predicate of A_i occurs in the head of at least one clause in P;

(b) an *unfolding function* is a partial function *Unfold*, which takes a clause λ and an unfolding tree T of which λ is a leaf, and returns the set *Unfold*(λ, T) of clauses obtained by unfolding the clause λ in P w.r.t. an atom A in its body. We assume that the unfolding function *Unfold* is associated with the wqo $\preceq_u$. *Unfold*(λ, T) is defined iff (i) λ is a leaf of T, (ii) the body of λ is non-failing and it contains at least one atom, and (iii) there exists no ancestor α of λ in T such that $bd(\alpha) \preceq_u bd(\lambda)$. Notice that if T consists of the root clause λ only, and λ has non-failing body, then *Unfold*(λ, T) is defined;

(c) *Replace*(Γ) denotes the set of clauses Γ' obtained by applying the constraint replacement rule to each clause γ in Γ as follows:
If γ is of the form $H \leftarrow c, G$ then the clause $H \leftarrow solve(c, X), G$ is in Γ', where X is the set of the linking variables of c in γ.

The *Unfold-Replace* procedure which we now describe, takes as input a set *NewDefs* of definition clauses and, by using the *Unfold* and *Replace* functions defined above, constructs a forest *UForest* of unfolding trees, one for each definition in *NewDefs*. The *Unfold-Replace* procedure is parametric w.r.t. the choice of the unfolding function *Unfold* and its associated well-quasi-order $\preceq_u$ on constrained goals.

The Procedure *Unfold-Replace(NewDefs, UForest)*.
Input: a set *NewDefs* of definition clauses.
Output: a forest *UForest* of unfolding trees.
for each clause $\delta \in$ *NewDefs* **do**
  Let *Utree*(δ) be the root clause δ;
  while *Unfold*(λ, *Utree*(δ)) is defined for some leaf clause λ of *Utree*(δ) **do**
    $\Gamma 1 :=$ *Unfold*(λ, *Utree*(δ));
    $\Gamma 2 :=$ *Replace*($\Gamma 1$);
    Expand *Utree*(δ) by making every clause in $\Gamma 2$ a son of λ
  end-while
end-for
UForest := { *Utree*(δ) | $\delta \in$ *NewDefs*}   □

Notice that, by the properties of the unfolding function *Unfold*, for each clause δ in *NewDefs* with non-failing body, the tree *Utree*(δ) is constructed by applying the unfolding rule at least once.

4.2 The Define-Fold Procedure

The *Define-Fold* procedure takes as input a forest *UForest* of unfolding trees, constructed by the *Unfold-Replace* procedure, and a definition tree *Defstree* and it produces as output: (i) a possibly empty set *NewDefs* of new definition clauses, and (ii) a set *FoldedCls* of clauses derived from the leaves of *UForest* which have non-failing bodies, by a (possibly empty) sequence of applications of the folding rule. The definition clauses in *NewDefs*, together with those in *Defstree*, make it possible to fold each leaf of *UForest* with non-failing body w.r.t. each atom occurring in that same leaf. The definition clauses in *NewDefs* are added to the tree *Defstree* as new leaves.

We now introduce the notion of *folding equivalence* between definition clauses. This notion is used to avoid the introduction of unnecessary new definition clauses.

Definition 4. Given two clauses, δ_1 of the form $H_1 \leftarrow c_1, A_1$ and δ_2 of the form $H_2 \leftarrow c_2, A_2$, we say that δ_1 and δ_2 are *folding equivalent* iff there exists a variable renaming ρ such that (i) $A_1\rho = A_2$, (ii) $\mathcal{D} \models \forall X(c_1\rho \leftrightarrow c_2)$ where $X = FV(c_1\rho, c_2)$, and (iii) $vars(H_1\rho) = vars(H_2)$.

For example, the clauses $new1(X, Y) \leftarrow X > Y, p(Y)$ and $new2(V, U) \leftarrow V < U$, $p(V)$ are folding equivalent. We have that, if δ_1 and δ_2 are folding equivalent clauses, then a clause can be folded using δ_1 iff it can be folded using δ_2.

Notice that as consequence of the definitions of the widening operator and the generalization function given in Section 3, we have the following property, which will be useful for proving the termination of the contextual specialization strategy.

Property FE: For any clause γ_0 and infinite sequence $\{\delta_i \mid i \in \mathbf{N}\}$ of clauses, if $\{\gamma_i \mid i \in \mathbf{N}\}$ is the infinite sequence of clauses such that, for all $i \in \mathbf{N}$, $\gamma_{i+1} = gen(\gamma_i, \delta_i)$, then there exists an index h such that $\forall k \geq h$, the clauses γ_h and γ_k are folding equivalent.

For our contextual specialization strategy we also need the following notion of *call patterns* of a clause or set of clauses. Call patterns will be used for introducing new definitions and also for applying the contextual constraint replacement rule R5.

Definition 5. Given a clause γ of the form $p(X) \leftarrow d, A_1, \dots, A_k$, with $k > 0$, the set of *call patterns* of γ, which is denoted by $CP(\gamma)$, is the set of triples $\langle solve(d, Y), A, Y \rangle$ such that: (i) A is A_j for some $j = 1, \dots, k$, and (ii) Y denotes the linking variables of A_j in γ. $\langle solve(d, Y), A, Y \rangle$ is said to be the call pattern of γ for A. The set of call patterns of a set Γ of clauses, denoted by $CP(\Gamma)$, is the union of the sets of call patterns of the clauses in Γ.

We now introduce a *definition function Define*, which takes as input a definition tree *Defstree*, a leaf clause δ of *Defstree*, and a call pattern $\langle c, A, Y \rangle$ of a leaf clause λ of $Utree(\delta)$, and produces as output a clause to be used for folding λ w.r.t. A. *Define* is parametric w.r.t. the choices of a wqo $\preceq_g$ and a clause generalization function *gen*.

The Definition Function $Define(Defstree, \delta, \langle c, A, Y \rangle)$.
Let η be the clause: $newp(Y) \leftarrow c, A$, where $newp$ is a new predicate symbol.
if η is folding equivalent to a clause ϑ in *Defstree*
then return ϑ
else Let π be the path from the root of *Defstree* to clause δ
   if in π there exists a clause of the form $H \leftarrow d, B$ with the following properties:
       (1) $(d, B) \preceq_g (c, A)$ and (2) A and B have the same predicate
   then let α be the last clause in π with properties (1) and (2)
      if $gen(\alpha, \eta)$ is folding equivalent to a clause ϑ in *Defstree*
      then return ϑ
      else return $gen(\alpha, \eta)$ (case G)
   else return η (case F).   □

Now we are ready to present the *Define-Fold* procedure.

The Procedure $Define\text{-}Fold(UForest, Defstree, NewDefs, FoldedCls)$.
Input: a forest *UForest* of unfolding trees and a definition tree *Defstree*. Each root of the trees in *UForest* is a leaf clause of *Defstree*.
Output: a set *NewDefs* of new definition clauses and a set *FoldedCls* of derived clauses.

$NewDefs := \emptyset;$ $FoldedCls := \emptyset;$
for each unfolding tree $Utree(\delta)$ in *UForest* **do**
  for each leaf clause λ of $Utree(\delta)$ with non-failing body **do**
    Let λ be of the form $A_0 \leftarrow d, A_1, \dots, A_k$, with $k \geq 0$.
    if $k = 0$ **then** $FoldedCls := FoldedCls \cup \{\lambda\}$

      else begin $\gamma_1 := \lambda$;
        for $i = 1, \ldots, k$ **do**
        Let cp_i be the call pattern of γ_i for A_i and let η be the clause
        Define(*Defstree*, δ, cp_i).
        if η is not in *Defstree* **then**
            begin expand *Defstree* by making η a son of δ;
                NewDefs := *NewDefs* $\cup \{\eta\}$ **end** ;
        Fold γ_i w.r.t. A_i by using η thereby deriving clause γ_{i+1};
        end-for ;
        FoldedCls := *FoldedCls* $\cup \{\gamma_{k+1}\}$
      end
    end-for
end-for   □

Notice that the clauses whose body consists of a satisfiable constraint only, are not folded, and they are added to *FoldedCls*. Moreover the clauses with failing body are not folded, and they are not added to the set *FoldedCls*. This treatment of the clauses with failing body can be viewed as an implicit application of the clause removal rule R4.

4.3   The Contextual Specialization Strategy

We now present our strategy for contextual specialization of CLP($\mathcal{D}$) programs. It consists of two phases. During Phase 1 we apply the unfolding, constraint replacement, constrained atomic definition, and constrained atomic folding rules, according to the *Unfold-Replace* and *Define-Fold* procedures. During Phase 2 we eliminate redundant constraints by a suitable application of the contextual constraint replacement rule.

The condition $FV(c) \subseteq X$ on the input to the contextual specialization strategy below, is not actually a restriction, because our constraints are closed w.r.t. existential quantification.

Contextual Specialization Strategy
Input: (i) A CLP($\mathcal{D}$) program P and
       (ii) a constrained atom $c, p(X)$ such that $FV(c) \subseteq X$.
Output: A CLP($\mathcal{D}$) program P_s and an atom $p_s(X)$.

Phase 1. By the definition rule introduce a clause δ_0 of the form $p_s(X) \leftarrow c, p(X)$. Let *Defstree* consist of clause δ_0 only.
$P_s := \emptyset$;   *NewDefs* := $\{\delta_0\}$;

while *NewDefs* $\neq \emptyset$ **do**
    Unfold-Replace(*NewDefs*, *UForest*);
    Define-Fold(*UForest*, *Defstree*, *NewDefs*, *FoldedCls*);
    $P_s := P_s \cup$ *FoldedCls*
end-while

Phase 2. [*Contextual Constraint Replacement*] Let $\mathbf{C} = \{(solve(c, X), p_s(X))\} \cup \{(d, A) \mid \langle d, A, Y \rangle \in CP(P_s)\}$.

For every predicate symbol, say q, in P_s
- take the set $\{(d_1, q(V_1)), \ldots, (d_k, q(V_k))\}$ of all constrained atoms in $\mathbf{C}$ with predicate symbol q, and
- compute the least upper bound $m = d_1\{V_1/V\} \sqcup \ldots \sqcup d_k\{V_k/V\}$, where V is a tuple of new variables.
Replace each clause $q(W) \leftarrow f_1, \ldots, f_n, G$ in P_s, where $f_1, \ldots, f_n$ are primitive constraints, by the clause $q(W) \leftarrow f, G$, where f is the conjunction of all f_j's, with $1 \leq j \leq n$, such that it is not the case that $m\{V/W\} \sqsubseteq f_j$. This replacement is performed by applying the contextual constraint replacement rule, and the use of this rule is justified by the fact that, for $i = 1, \ldots, k$, $\mathcal{D} \models \forall Z\,((d_i, V_i = W) \rightarrow ((f_1, \ldots, f_n) \leftrightarrow f))$, where $Z = FV(d_i, V_i, W, f_1, \ldots, f_n, f)$.   □

Theorem 1. [*Correctness of the Contextual Specialization Strategy*] Let P be a CLP($\mathcal{D}$) program and $c, p(X)$ be a constrained atom with $FV(c) \subseteq X$. Let P_s and $p_s(X)$ be the CLP($\mathcal{D}$) program and the atom obtained by the contextual specialization strategy. Then, for every variable assignment σ, we have that
$$lm(P, \mathcal{D}) \models_\sigma c, p(X) \qquad \text{iff} \qquad lm(P_s, \mathcal{D}) \models_\sigma c, p_s(X)$$

It is based on the correctness of the transformation rules [1,7]. In particular, during the application of the contextual specialization strategy, folding is applied only to clauses which have been derived by one or more applications of the unfolding rule, followed by applications of the constraint replacement rule. Thus, we may apply Theorem 4.10 of [7] which ensures the correctness of the transformation rules w.r.t. the least $\mathcal{D}$-model.   □

Theorem 2. [*Termination of the Contextual Specialization Strategy*] Let P be a CLP($\mathcal{D}$) program, and $c, p(X)$ be a constrained atom with $FV(c) \subseteq X$. If the widening operator ∇ used for clause generalization agrees with the well-quasi-order $\preceq_g$, then the contextual specialization strategy terminates.

See Appendix.   □

5   An Extended Example

Let us consider the following CLP($\mathcal{R}_{lin}$) program *Mmod*:
1. $mmod(I, J, M) \leftarrow I \geq J, M = 0$
2. $mmod(I, J, M) \leftarrow I < J, I1 = I+1, mod(I, L), mmod(I1, J, M1),$
     $\qquad\qquad\qquad M = M1+L$
3. $mod(X, M) \leftarrow X \geq 0, M = X$
4. $mod(X, M) \leftarrow X < 0, M = -X$

$Mmod(I, J, M)$ holds if and only if $M = |I| + |I+1| + \cdots + |I+k|$ and k is the largest integer such that $I+k$ is smaller than J (recall that I, J, and M are real numbers). Let us assume that we want to specialize the program *Mmod* w.r.t. the constrained atom $I = 0, J \geq 0, mmod(I, J, M)$.

Recall that in $\mathcal{R}_{lin}$ the least upper bound operation $\sqcup$ is defined by the convex hull construction (see Section 3). In this example we instantiate our contextual specialization strategy as follows. (i) The function *solve* is the simplifier of conjunctions of linear equations and inequations over the reals implemented in Holzbaur's clp($\mathcal{Q},\mathcal{R}$) solver [11], (ii) *Unfold*(γ, *Utree*(δ)) returns the set of clauses obtained by unfolding clause γ w.r.t. the *leftmost* (in the textual order) atom A in its body, (iii) the well-quasi-order $\preceq_u$ is the relation $\preceq_L$ over constrained goals (see Section 3), (iv) the function *gen* for clause generalization is the one introduced in Example 1 (see Section 3), and (v) the wqo $\preceq_g$ is the restriction of $\preceq_L$ to constrained atoms.

We apply the contextual specialization strategy as follows.

Phase 1. We start off from the tree *Defstree* which consists of the root clause 5 only, where:

5. $mmod_s(I, J, M) \leftarrow I=0, J\geq 0, mmod(I, J, M)$

We apply the *Unfold-Replace* procedure as follows. The input for the procedure consists of the set *NewDefs* = {clause 5}. Let *Utree*(clause 5) consist of the root clause 5. The only atom in the body of clause 5 is $mmod(I, J, M)$, and *Unfold*(clause 5, *Utree*(clause 5)) is the set {clause 6, clause 7} where:

6. $mmod_s(I, J, M) \leftarrow I=0, J\geq 0, I\geq J, M=0$
7. $mmod_s(I, J, M) \leftarrow I=0, J\geq 0, I<J, I1=I+1, mod(I, L),$
     $mmod(I1, J, M1), M = M1+L$

We apply the constraint replacement rule using *solve*, thereby obtaining *Replace*({clause 6, clause 7}) = {clause 8, clause 9} where:

8. $mmod_s(I, J, M) \leftarrow I=0, J=0, M=0$
9. $mmod_s(I, J, M) \leftarrow I=0, J>0, I1=1, mod(I, L), mmod(I1, J, M1),$
     $M = M1+L$

Now we expand *Utree*(clause 5) by making clauses 8 and 9 sons of clause 5.
Unfold(clause 8, *Utree*(clause 5)) is not defined, because the body of clause 8 contains no atom, and thus, clause 8 is not unfolded.
The construction of *Utree*(clause 5) proceeds by first unfolding clause 9 w.r.t. $mod(I, L)$ and then applying the constraint replacement rule. We get the following clauses:

10. $mmod_s(I, J, M) \leftarrow false, mmod(I1, J, M1), M = M1+L$
10.1 $mmod_s(I, J, M) \leftarrow I=0, J>0, I1=1, mmod(I1, J, M)$

We expand *Utree*(clause 5) by making clauses 10 and 10.1 sons of clause 9.
There is no leaf clause λ of *Utree*(clause 5) such that *Unfold*(λ, *Utree*(clause 5)) is defined. Indeed: (a) clause 10.1 is the only leaf of *Utree*(clause 5) whose body is non-failing and contains at least one atom, and (b) clause 5 is an ancestor of clause 10.1 such that bd(clause 5) $\preceq_L bd$(clause 10.1). Thus, the *Unfold-Replace* procedure terminates with output *UForest* = {*Utree*(clause 5)}. The leaves of *Utree*(clause 5) are the clauses 8, 10, and 10.1.

We now apply the *Define-Fold* procedure as follows. The input for the procedure consists of the forest {*Utree*(clause 5)} and the definition tree *Defstree* made out of the root clause 5 only. The leaves of *Utree*(clause 5) with non-failing body are clause 8 and clause 10.1.

The body of clause 8 contains no atom, and so we add clause 8 to *FoldedCls*.

The body of clause 10.1 contains one atom, and the only call pattern of clause 10.1 is $\langle c, A, Y \rangle$, where c is $(J > 0, I1 = 1)$, A is $mmod(I1, J, M)$, and Y is $\{I1, J, M\}$.

We now compute *Define*(*Defstree*, clause 5, $\langle c, A, Y \rangle$). We consider the following clause:

η. $newp(I1, J, M) \leftarrow J > 0, I1 = 1, mmod(I1, J, M)$

Since there is no clause in *Defstree* which is folding equivalent to η and $bd(\text{clause 5}) \preceq_L bd(\eta)$, we compute *gen*(clause 5, η), which is (see Example 1 at the end of Section 3):

11. $genp(I1, J, M) \leftarrow I1 \geq 0, J \geq 0, mmod(I1, J, M)$

Since there is no clause in *Defstree* which is folding equivalent to clause 11 we are in case G. We expand *Defstree* by making clause 11 a son of clause 5 and we add clause 11 to the set *NewDefs*. Then we fold clause 10.1 by using the definition clause 11 and we get:

12. $mmod_s(I, J, M) \leftarrow I = 0, J > 0, I1 = 1, genp(I1, J, M)$

The *Define-Fold* procedure terminates with output *FoldedCls* = {clause 8, clause 12} and *NewDefs* = {clause 11}. Since *NewDefs* is non-empty, we continue the execution of the while-loop of the contextual specialization strategy.

We apply the *Unfold-Replace* procedure as follows. The input for the procedure consists of the set *NewDefs* = {clause 11}. Initially, *Utree*(clause 11) consists of the root clause 11. The only atom in the body of clause 11 is $mmod(I1, J, M)$, and *Unfold*(clause 11, *Utree*(clause 11)) is the set {clause 13, clause 14} where:

13. $genp(I1, J, M) \leftarrow I1 \geq 0, J \geq 0, I1 \geq J, M = 0$
14. $genp(I1, J, M) \leftarrow I1 \geq 0, J \geq 0, I1 < J, I2 = I1 + 1, mod(I1, L),$
         $mmod(I2, J, M2), M = M2 + L$

We apply the constraint replacement rule using *solve*, and we get *Replace*({clause 13, clause 14}) = {clause 15, clause 15.1} where:

15. $genp(I1, J, M) \leftarrow I1 \geq J, J \geq 0, M = 0$
15.1 $genp(I1, J, M) \leftarrow I1 \geq 0, I1 < J, I2 = I1 + 1, mod(I1, L),$
         $mmod(I2, J, M2), M = M2 + L$

Now we expand *Utree*(clause 11)) by making clauses 15 and 15.1 sons of clause 11. *Unfold*(clause 15, *Utree*(clause 11)) is not defined, because the body of clause 15 contains no atom.

The construction of *Utree*(clause 11) proceeds by first unfolding clause 15.1 w.r.t. $mod(I1, L)$ and then applying the constraint replacement rule. We get, as the reader may verify, the following clauses:

16    $genp(I1, J, M) \leftarrow false, mmod(I2, J, M2)$
16.1 $genp(I1, J, M) \leftarrow I1 \geq 0, I1 < J, I2 = I1 + 1,$
         $mmod(I2, J, M2), M = M2 + I1$

We expand *Utree*(clause 11) by making clauses 16 and 16.1 sons of clause 15.1.

There is no leaf clause λ of $Utree$(clause 11) such that $Unfold(\lambda, Utree$(clause 11)) is defined. Indeed: (a) clause 16.1 is the only leaf of $Utree$(clause 11) whose body is non-failing and it contains at least one atom, and (b) clause 11 is an ancestor of clause 16.1 such that bd(clause 11) $\preceq_L bd$(clause 16.1). Thus, the $Unfold\text{-}Replace$ procedure terminates with output $UForest = \{Utree$(clause 11)$\}$.

We now apply the $Define\text{-}Fold$ procedure as follows. The input for the procedure consists of the forest $\{Utree$(clause 11)$\}$ and the definition tree $Defstree$ made out of the root clause 5 and its son clause 11. The leaves of $Utree$(clause 11) with non-failing body are clause 15 and clause 16.1.

The body of clause 15 contains no atom, and so we add clause 15 to $FoldedCls$. The body of clause 16.1 contains one atom and $\langle c', A', Y' \rangle$ is the only call pattern of clause 16.1 where c' is $(I2 \geq 1, J > I2-1)$, A' is $mmod(I2, J, M2)$, and Y' is $\{I2, J, M2\}$.

We now compute $Define(Defstree, $clause 11$, \langle c', A', Y' \rangle)$. Let us consider the clause:

$\eta 1$. $newq(I2, J, M2) \leftarrow I2 \geq 1, \ J > I2-1, \ mmod(I2, J, M2)$

Since there is no clause in $Defstree$ which is folding equivalent to $\eta 1$ and bd(clause 11) $\preceq_L bd(\eta 1)$, we compute clause $gen($clause 11$, \eta 1)$, which is clause 11 itself. Then we fold clause 16.1 by using the definition clause 11 and we get:

17. $genp(I1, J, M) \leftarrow I1 \geq 0, \ I1 < J, \ I2 = I1+1,$
$$genp(I2, J, M2), \ M = M2+I1$$

The $Define\text{-}Fold$ procedure terminates with output $FoldedCls = \{$clause 15, clause 17$\}$ and $NewDefs = \emptyset$.

Since during the last application of the $Define\text{-}Fold$ procedure we did not introduce any new definition, the while-loop of the contextual specialization strategy terminates and we get program P_s made out of clauses 8, 12, 15, and 17.

Phase 2. By computing the call patterns of P_s and performing a variable renaming we get:
$$\mathbf{C} = \{(I=0, \ J \geq 0, \ mmod_s(I, J, M)),$$
$$(I=1, \ J > 0, \ genp(I, J, M)),$$
$$(I \geq 1, \ J > I-1, \ genp(I, J, M))\}$$

Thus, the least upper bounds are:
for $mmod_s$: $m_1 = (I=0, J \geq 0)$ and for $genp$: $m_2 = (I \geq 1, J > I-1)$. We then process clauses 8, 12, 15, and 17 as indicated in Phase 2 of the contextual specialization strategy.

For clause 8, since $m_1 \sqsubseteq I=0$, we get:

8.c $mmod_s(I, J, M) \leftarrow J=0, \ M=0$

For clause 12, since $m_1 \sqsubseteq I=0$, we get:

12.c $mmod_s(I, J, M) \leftarrow J > 0, \ I1 = 1, \ genp(I1, J, M)$

For clause 15, since $m_2 \sqsubseteq J \geq 0$, after a variable renaming, we get:

15.c $genp(I, J, M) \leftarrow I \geq J, \ M=0$

For clause 17, since $m_2 \sqsubseteq I \geq 0$, after a variable renaming, we get:

17.c $genp(I, J, M) \leftarrow I < J,\ I2 = I+1,\ genp(I2, J, M2),\ M = M2+I$

The final program P_s we have derived, consists of clauses 8.c, 12.c, 15.c, and 17.c.

6   Experimental Results

The following table shows the speedups achieved by applying our constraint specialization strategy to some CLP programs. The speedups after Phase 1 and after Phase 2 are both computed w.r.t. the initial program. The Dynamic Input Size denotes the size of the constrained goal which is supplied to the specialized program. The experimental results were obtained by using SICStus Prolog 3.8.5 and the clp(Q,R) solver.

Program	Dynamic Input Size	Speedup after Phase 1	Speedup after Phase 2
Mmod	$\|J\| = 250$	3.26	3.78
Mmod	$\|J\| = 25000$	345	388
Summatch (†)	$\|S\| = 500$	451	915
Summatch (†)	$\|S\| = 1000$	881	1788
Summatch (††)	$\|S\| = 500$	818	2159
Summatch (††)	$\|S\| = 1000$	1594	4225
Cryptosum	—	1.27	1.27

- *Mmod* is the program described in Section 5 which defines the predicate $mmod(I,J,M)$. It has been specialized w.r.t. $I=0, J \geq 0$.
- *Summatch* is a program which defines a predicate $summatch(P,S)$ which holds iff there exists a substring G of S such that: (i) G and P have the same length, and (ii) the sum of the elements of G is equal to the sum of the elements of P. It has been specialized w.r.t. (†) a list P of 3 nonnegative integers whose sum is at most 5, and (††) a list P of 10 nonnegative integers whose sum is at most 5.
- *Cryptosum* is a program which solves a cryptoarithmetic puzzle over three lists $L1$, $L2$, and $L3$ of digits, such that $L1+L2=L3$. It has been specialized w.r.t. SEND+MORE=MONEY.

The specialized programs were derived semiautomatically by using the MAP transformation system, which is a tool for transforming constraint logic programs. MAP provides support both for interactive derivations and for semiautomatic specializations based on the parameterized strategy presented in Section 4. In the latter case, the choice of the parameters which are most suited to the problem at hand, is left to the user.

7   Related Work and Conclusions

There are various methods for specializing programs w.r.t. properties of their input data [2,3,20,21,23]. Contextual specialization can be viewed as one of these methods. In a previous paper [8] we have illustrated the basic ideas of the contextual specialization of CLP($\mathcal{D}$) programs and we have presented a set of transformation rules for this form of specialization. In this paper we build upon our previous work and we propose an automated strategy for the contextual specialization of constraint logic programs.

For our specialization strategy we have assumed the existence of a solver which simplifies constraints in a given domain $\mathcal{D}$. We abstractly represent that solver as a computable total function *solve* and we do not make any assumption on how this function is computed. The motivation for this choice comes from the observation that most of the available constraint solvers are based on the so called *black box* approach and they provide the user with very limited ways of interaction. In particular, in the black box approach, it is not possible to control the constraint solving process.

For this reason the efficiency improvements which can be achieved by our program specialization strategy are limited to the way the constraints are generated and interact with each other. Indeed, at specialization time we may simplify constraints by discovering inconsistencies, exploiting entailments, and applying the function *solve*. These opportunities for constraint simplification are triggered by applications of the unfolding rule and are realized by the constraint replacement rule. The unfolding rule, in fact, may gather in a single clause constraints which come from different clauses.

However, our specialization strategy cannot improve the efficiency of the constraint solving algorithms. To overcome this limitation we plan to apply our method to programs based on *glass box* solvers, for example by using Constraint Handling Rules [9], a high-level language designed for the purpose of building application-specific constraint solvers.

In our specialization strategy we have also assumed the existence of: (i) a function *Unfold* and a well-quasi-order $\preceq_u$ between constrained goals for guiding the unfolding process, (ii) a clause generalization function *gen* parameterized by a widening operator ∇, and (iii) a well-quasi-order $\preceq_g$ between constrained atoms, which activates the clause generalization process during program specialization. We have shown that our specialization strategy preserves the least $\mathcal{D}$-model and it terminates.

The hypothesis that the function *solve* is complete w.r.t. satisfiability, makes our approach different from the one in [2], where program specialization is based on some undecidable properties and thus, it cannot be easily automated.

Partial evaluation of logic programs [18], also called *partial deduction*, is the technique for program specialization which is most related to ours. However, we would like to mention the following differences which make our contextual specialization technique a proper extension of the traditional techniques for partial evaluation.

(1) The most apparent difference is that traditional techniques for partial evaluation do not handle constraints, so that our optimizations concerning constraint solving cannot be performed.

(2) Partial evaluation may require post processing methods, like Redundant Argument Filtering [5], to minimize the number of variables occurring in clauses, whereas we use the folding rule during program specialization to avoid redundant occurrences of variables.

(3) The use of our contextual constraint replacement rule R5 allows us to perform optimizations which cannot be performed by applying the techniques for partial evaluation of logic programs presented in [17,26]. Indeed, our contextual constraint replacement rule takes into account, for simplifying the clauses of a predicate, say p, a global constraint which is obtained by computing the least upper bound of the set of constraints which occur in the clauses containing a call of p. Nor can contextual constraint replacement be performed by using the transformation rules presented in [1,7,19].

(4) What it is usually done by automatic partial evaluation techniques (see, for instance, [16]) basically corresponds with Phase 1 of our contextual specialization strategy. Similarly to partial evaluation, in that phase we address *local control* and *global control* issues. In our approach local control refers to the termination of the *Unfold-Replace* procedure, while global control refers to the termination of Phase 1 of the contextual specialization strategy as a whole. In particular, global control refers to the policy of introducing new constrained atoms which generalize old constrained atoms. For these control issues we extend to the case of constrained logic programs the well-quasi-order techniques used for proving termination in the field of rewriting systems [6]. These techniques were also used for partial evaluation [15,16]. With regard to these control issues the main difference between partial evaluation and our approach is that generalization used in partial evaluation can be seen as a particular instance of our generalization by taking both the least upper bound operator and the widening operator to be the most specific generalization over finite terms.

Among the many techniques for simplifying and manipulating constraints to get more efficient specialized programs, here we want to mention the following methods which are related to ours.

In [23] the authors propose a method based on abstract interpretation, for the implementation of multiple specialization of logic programs. Particular emphasis is given to program parallelization. Similarly to their work, our specialization strategy may produce several specialized versions of the same predicate by introducing different definitions corresponding to different call patterns.

In [20] the authors present a methodology for compiling $CLP(\mathcal{D})$ languages so that the workload of the constraint solver is reduced. However, their methodology may generate *non-monotonic* $CLP(\mathcal{D})$ programs, whose execution requires the ability of removing constraints from the constraint store. In contrast, in our approach we generate monotonic $CLP(\mathcal{D})$ programs which at runtime do not remove constraints from the store. However, we require the solver to test for the satisfiability and entailment of constraints, and to compute the existential closure of constraints w.r.t. given sets of variables. These capabilities are indeed provided by most constraint solvers.

Finally, our work is related to the approach presented in [3] for a strict first-order functional language. As in that paper, we too specify the context of use w.r.t. which the programs should be specialized, by providing a property which may cover an infinite set of queries.

References

1. N. Bensaou and I. Guessarian. Transforming constraint logic programs. *Theoretical Computer Science*, 206:81–125, 1998.
2. A. Bossi, N. Cocco, and S. Dulli. A method for specializing logic programs. *ACM Transactions on Programming Languages and Systems*, 12(2):253–302, April 1990.
3. C. Consel and S. C. Khoo. Parameterized partial evaluation. *ACM Transactions on Programming Languages and Systems*, 15(3):463–493, 1993.
4. P. Cousot and R. Cousot. Abstract interpretation: A unified lattice model for static analysis of programs by construction of approximation of fixpoints. In *Proceedings 4th ACM-SIGPLAN Symposium on Principles of Programming Languages (POPL '77)*, pages 238–252. ACM Press, 1977.
5. D. De Schreye, R. Glück, J. Jørgensen, M. Leuschel, B. Martens, and M. H. Sørensen. Conjunctive partial deduction: Foundations, control, algorithms, and experiments. *Journal of Logic Programming*, 41(2–3):231–277, 1999.
6. N. Dershowitz and J.-P. Jouannaud. Rewrite systems. In J. van Leeuwen, editor, *Handbook of Theoretical Computer Science*, volume B, pages 243–320. Elsevier, 1990.
7. S. Etalle and M. Gabbrielli. Transformations of CLP modules. *Theoretical Computer Science*, 166:101–146, 1996.
8. F. Fioravanti, A. Pettorossi, and M. Proietti. Rules and strategies for contextual specialization of constraint logic programs. In M. Leuschel, editor, *Proceedings of the ICLP'99 Workshop on Optimization and Implementation of Declarative Programming Languages, WOID '99*, Las Cruces University, New Mexico, USA, pages 1–9, December 2–3, 1999.
9. T. Frühwirth. Theory and practice of Constraint Handling Rules. *Journal of Logic Programming, Special Issue on Constraint Logic Programming*, pages 95–138, October 1998.
10. T. J. Hickey and D. A. Smith. Towards the partial evaluation of CLP languages. In *Proceedings ACM Symposium on Partial Evaluation and Semantics Based Program Manipulation, PEPM '91, New Haven, CT, USA*, SIGPLAN Notices, 26, 9, pages 43–51. ACM Press, 1991.
11. C. Holzbaur. OFAI clp(q,r) manual, Edition 1.3.2. Technical Report TR-95-09, Austrian Research Institute for Artificial Intelligence, Vienna, 1995.
12. J. Jaffar and M. Maher. Constraint logic programming: A survey. *Journal of Logic Programming*, 19/20:503–581, 1994.
13. J. Jaffar, M. Maher, K. Marriott, and P. Stuckey. The semantics of constraint logic programming. *Journal of Logic Programming*, 37:1–46, 1998.
14. N. D. Jones, C. K. Gomard, and P. Sestoft. *Partial Evaluation and Automatic Program Generation*. Prentice Hall, 1993.
15. M. Leuschel. Improving homeomorphic embedding for online termination. In P. Flener, editor, *Proceedings of LOPSTR'98, Manchester, UK, June 1998*, Lecture Notes in Computer Science 1559, pages 199–218. Springer-Verlag, 1999.

16. M. Leuschel, B. Martens, and D. De Schreye. Controlling generalization and poly-variance in partial deduction of normal logic programs. *ACM Transactions on Programming Languages and Systems*, 20(1):208–258, 1998.

17. M. Leuschel and D. De Schreye. Constrained partial deduction. In F. Bry, B. Freitag, and D. Seipel, editors, *Proceedings of the 12th Workshop Logische Programmierung (WLP'97)*, pages 116–126, Munich, Germany, September 1997.

18. J. W. Lloyd and J. C. Shepherdson. Partial evaluation in logic programming. *Journal of Logic Programming*, 11:217–242, 1991.

19. M. J. Maher. A transformation system for deductive database modules with perfect model semantics. *Theoretical Computer Science*, 110:377–403, 1993.

20. K. Marriott and P. Stuckey. The 3 R's of optimizing constraint logic programs: Refinement, Removal and Reordering. In *POPL'93: Proceedings ACM SIGPLAN Symposium on Principles of Programming Languages*, pages 334–344, 1993.

21. A. Pettorossi and M. Proietti. A theory of logic program specialization and generalization for dealing with input data properties. In O. Danvy, R. Glück, and P. Thiemann, editors, *Proceedings of the Dagstuhl Seminar on Partial Evaluation*, Lecture Notes in Computer Science 1110, pages 386–408. Springer-Verlag, 1996.

22. S. Prestwich. Online partial deduction of large programs. In *Proceedings ACM Sigplan Symposium on Partial Evaluation and Semantics-Based Program Manipulation, PEPM '93, Copenhagen, Denmark*, pages 111–118. ACM Press, 1993.

23. G. Puebla and M. Hermenegildo. Abstract multiple specialization and its application to program parallelization. *J. of Logic Programming. Special Issue on Synthesis, Transformation and Analysis of Logic Programs*, 41(2&3):279–316, November 1999.

24. D. Sahlin. Mixtus: An automatic partial evaluator for full Prolog. *New Generation Computing*, 12:7–51, 1993.

25. M. H. Sørensen and R. Glück. An algorithm of generalization in positive super-compilation. In J. W. Lloyd, editor, *Proceedings of the 1995 International Logic Programming Symposium (ILPS '95)*, pages 465–479. MIT Press, 1995.

26. A. Wrzos-Kaminska. Partial evaluation in constraint logic programming. In Z. W. Ras and M. Michalewicz, editors, *Proceedings of the 9th International Symposium on Foundations of Intelligent Systems, Zakopane, Poland*, Lecture Notes in Computer Science 1079, pages 98–107. Springer-Verlag, 1996.

Appendix. Proof of Theorem 2.

Let us begin by showing the termination of the *Unfold-Replace* procedure. It follows from the properties of the wqo $\preceq_u$ and the hypothesis that for any leaf clause λ of an unfolding tree T, if there exists an ancestor α of λ such that $bd(\alpha) \preceq_u bd(\lambda)$, then $Unfold(\lambda, T)$ is not defined.

Also the *Define-Fold* procedure and Phase 2 of the contextual specialization strategy trivially terminate because of the absence of while-loop statements in their definitions.

To prove the termination of the contextual specialization strategy we have to show that the set *NewDefs* of new definitions introduced by the *Define-Fold* procedure will eventually be empty, that is, *Defstree* is a finite tree.

Every node of *Defstree* has finite branching. Indeed, (i) each clause δ occurring in *Defstree* has a number of sons which is not greater than the number of atoms in the bodies of the leaf clauses of $Utree(\delta)$ to be folded, and (ii) for all δ, the unfolding tree $Utree(\delta)$ constructed by the *Unfold-Replace* procedure is finite.

We now show that every path starting from the root of *Defstree* is finite. Consider a generic path π of *Defstree*, of the form $\delta_0 \ldots \delta_k \ldots$, where δ_0 is the root clause of *Defstree*. We can partition the clauses of π into two sets: the set *GenDefs* of clauses which have been introduced as generalizations of one of its ancestors in π (see Case G of the definition function *Define*) and the set *FreshDefs* of all other clauses in π (see Case F of the definition function *Define*). In particular, $\delta_0 \in$ *FreshDefs*.

Let us introduce the following binary relation $\preceq_{gp}$ over constrained atoms: $(c, A) \preceq_{gp} (d, B)$ iff (1) $(c, A) \preceq_g (d, B)$ and (2) A and B have the same predicate symbol. We have that $\preceq_{gp}$ is a wqo, because $\preceq_g$ is a wqo and the set of predicate symbols is finite (recall that the predicate symbols occurring in the bodies of the definitions also occur in the initial program). We also have that *gen* agrees with $\preceq_{gp}$ because *gen* agrees with $\preceq_g$.

We will show that for any path π, we can construct a tree $T(\pi)$ whose nodes are the clauses of π, such that:

(Property F*) for any $h > 0$, a clause δ_h is the left son of a clause δ_j iff $\delta_h \in$ *FreshDefs* and δ_j is the last clause in $\delta_0 \ldots \delta_{h-1}$ which is in *FreshDefs*. Thus, $bd(\delta_i) \npreceq_{gp} bd(\delta_h)$ for all $i = 0, \ldots, h - 1$.

(Property G*) for any $h > 0$, a clause δ_h is the right son of a clause δ_j iff $\delta_h \in$ *GenDefs* and δ_h has been introduced as a generalization of δ_j, that is, $\delta_h = gen(\delta_j, \eta)$ for some clause η (which does not belong to the set *Defstree*, and thus, it is not in π). Thus, (i) δ_j is the last clause in $\delta_0 \ldots \delta_{h-1}$ such that $bd(\delta_j) \preceq_{gp} bd(\eta)$, (ii) $bd(\delta_h) \preceq_{gp} bd(\delta_j)$, because *gen* agrees with $\preceq_{gp}$, and (iii) there is no clause in $\delta_0 \ldots \delta_{h-1}$ which is folding equivalent to δ_h.

We will show that for any path π we can construct the tree $T(\pi)$ by proving that, for all finite prefixes $\delta_0 \ldots \delta_k$ of π, there exists $T(\delta_0 \ldots \delta_k)$ satisfying Property F* and Property G* above. The proof proceeds by induction on k. The base case ($k = 0$) is trivial. For the inductive step, let us assume that Property F* and Property G* hold for $T(\delta_0 \ldots \delta_k)$ and let us show them for $T(\delta_0 \ldots \delta_{k+1})$.

(Case F) Let $\delta_{k+1} \in$ *FreshDefs* and (A) let δ_j be the last clause in $\delta_0 \ldots \delta_k$ such that $\delta_j \in$ *FreshDefs*. Let $T(\delta_0 \ldots \delta_{k+1})$ be the tree obtained from $T(\delta_0 \ldots \delta_k)$ by adding δ_{k+1} as left son of δ_j. Property F* holds for $T(\delta_0 \ldots \delta_{k+1})$: (if part) by construction; (only if part) δ_{k+1} is the only left son of δ_j in $T(\delta_0 \ldots \delta_{k+1})$. Indeed, if there exists a left son δ_h of δ_j, then by inductive hypothesis $\delta_h \in$ *FreshDefs* and $j < h \le k$, which contradicts the assumption (A). The validity of Property G* for $T(\delta_0 \ldots \delta_{k+1})$ follows immediately from the validity of Property G* for $T(\delta_0 \ldots \delta_k)$.

(Case G) Let $\delta_{k+1} \in$ *GenDefs*, that is, $\delta_{k+1} = gen(\delta_j, \eta)$ for some clause η, where: (B) δ_j is the last clause in $\delta_0 \ldots \delta_k$ such that $bd(\delta_j) \preceq_{gp} bd(\eta)$. Let $T(\delta_0 \ldots \delta_{k+1})$ be the tree obtained from $T(\delta_0 \ldots \delta_k)$ by adding δ_{k+1} as right son of δ_j. The validity of Property F* for $T(\delta_0 \ldots \delta_{k+1})$ follows immediately from the validity of Property F* for $T(\delta_0 \ldots \delta_k)$. Property G* holds for $T(\delta_0 \ldots \delta_{k+1})$ because: (if part) by construction; (only if part) δ_{k+1} is the only right son of δ_j in $T(\delta_0 \ldots \delta_{k+1})$. Indeed, if there exists a right son δ_h of δ_j in $T(\delta_0 \ldots \delta_k)$, then by inductive hypothesis $j < h$ and $bd(\delta_h) \preceq_{gp} bd(\delta_j)$. Thus, by transitivity of $\preceq_{gp}$ we have $bd(\delta_h) \preceq_{gp} bd(\eta)$ and $j < h$, which contradicts the assumption (B). We now show that a generic path π of $Defstree$ is finite by showing that $T(\pi)$ is finite, that is (a) $T(\pi)$ is finitely branching, and (b) each path in $T(\pi)$ is finite. (a) By Properties F* and G*, we have that each node of $T(\pi)$ has at most two sons and thus $T(\pi)$ has finite branching. (b) Consider a path τ from the root of $T(\pi)$ of the form: $\delta_0 \gamma_1 \ldots \gamma_k \ldots$ Let γ_h be a clause in τ such that $\gamma_h \in GenDefs$. If such a γ_h does not exist then all clauses in τ belong to $FreshDefs$, and thus, for all distinct $i, j \geq 0$ we have $\gamma_j \not\preceq_{gp} \gamma_i$. In this case τ cannot be infinite because $\preceq_{gp}$ is a wqo. If such a γ_h does exist, then by Properties F* and G* the suffix of τ of the form: $\gamma_h \gamma_{h+1} \ldots$ is such that for all $i \geq h$, $\gamma_{i+1} = gen(\gamma_i, \eta_i)$. By Point (iii) of Property G* we have that: for all $i \geq h$ and for all $j < i$, clause γ_j is not folding equivalent to γ_i. The path $\gamma_h \gamma_{h+1} \ldots$ is finite because, by Property FE of Section 4, if it were infinite, then there exist two folding equivalent clauses γ_s and γ_t, with $h \leq s < t$. Thus, τ is finite.   □

Measuring the Precision of Abstract Interpretations

Alessandra Di Pierro[1] and Herbert Wiklicky[2]

[1] Dipartimento di Informatica, Universitá di Pisa, Italy
`dipierro@di.unipi.it`
[2] Department of Computing, Imperial College, London, UK
`herbert@doc.ic.ac.uk`

Abstract. We develop a methodology for constructing semantics-based analyses of programs by approximating their probabilistic semantics. The framework we introduce resembles the one based on Galois connections used in abstract interpretation, the main difference being the choice of linear space structures instead of order-theoretic ones as semantical (concrete and abstract) domains. The intrinsic quantitative nature of linear spaces makes the method suitable for investigations on the problem of a numerical comparison of abstract interpretations with respect to their precision. After introducing the notion of probabilistic abstract interpretation, we define a measure of its precision by means of the norm of a linear operator which encodes the "incompleteness" of the abstraction. Finally we show the application of our results in a series of classical examples.

1 Introduction

The construction of semantics-based program analysis algorithms or in general the specification and validation of the analyses of programs finds a good support in the theory of Abstract Interpretation, which has become very popular since it was introduced in 1977 by Patrick and Radhia Cousot [5,6].

Despite its appeal and generality there are still some aspects of semantic approximation within the abstract interpretation framework which seem to be in need of further investigation. One of such aspects is the problem of "measuring" the precision of an abstraction, as remarked for example in [14, Section 3.4]:

> "One shortcoming of the development [...] is that a correct analysis may be so imprecise as to be practically useless. [...] The notion of correctness is topological in nature but we would ideally like something that was a bit more metric in nature so that we could express how imprecise a correct analysis is. Unfortunately no one has been able to develop an adequate metric for these purposes."

In this paper we propose and discuss a solution to this problem by means of a methodology for *probabilistic abstract interpretation*. The basic idea is that an appropriate re-formulation of the Cousot framework in a probabilistic setting

Kung-Kiu Lau (Ed.): LOPSTR 2000, LNCS 2042, pp. 147–164, 2001.

provides us with a means to give an exact estimate of the approximation error introduced by a certain abstraction α and its corresponding concretisation γ. This allows us to "quantify" somehow the imprecision of the various abstract interpretations, thus making the notion of precision more effective: for example, we could choose among the correct abstract interpretations for a given analysis the one which is "precise up to 35%".

The essential element of a probabilistic abstract interpretation is the definition of the abstraction function α as a linear operator between two vector spaces representing the concrete and abstract domains of the approximated function. The corresponding concretisation function γ is defined by using the notion of Moore-Penrose pseudo-inverse, which shows some important structural similarities with the Galois connection.

By interpreting in this setting the completeness conditions for classical abstract interpretation, we obtain a method which produces a numerical estimate of the (im-)precision of an abstraction. This method consists in the calculation of the norm of a linear operator comparing the two terms of the completeness conditions. We apply this method for calculating the precision of three abstract interpretations typical in the classical theory, namely the Rule of Signs for addition and multiplication and the Proof by Nine.

2   Probabilistic Abstract Interpretation

2.1   Probabilistic Semantics

Our approach towards a quantitative version of abstract interpretation has its origins in our investigation of the semantics of probabilistic languages. Although it can easily be applied also to conventional programs (e.g. the examples in Section 5) the need of introducing a quantitative semantics, in the form of a vector space based semantics, was first realised in that context.

Probabilistic programs are programs which are formulated by reference to a "coin flipping" device (e.g. random choice or assignment) which determines the flow of information. As a consequence, a probabilistic program execution will deliver results with a *probability* attached to them expressing their likelihood of actually being computed. A denotational semantics for such programs must therefore contemplate structures which are able to reflect both the qualitative and the quantitative aspects of the information flow. There exist several approaches towards the semantics of probabilistic programming languages, starting with the contributions of the fundamental papers by Saheb-Djahromi [20] and Kozen [15]. More recently, the authors have developed a probabilistic version of the concurrent constraint programming paradigm in [9,10], where other references to the literature on probabilistic semantics can be found.

For the purpose of this paper we will consider vector spaces as the prototypical semantic domain for probabilistic programs. Moreover, we will consider as a standard semantics a denotational semantics defined via a linear fixpoint operator $\Phi : \mathcal{V} \mapsto \mathcal{V}$, on a vector space $\mathcal{V}$ (for further details see e.g. [10,11]).

2.2   Abstract Interpretation

Classical abstract interpretation — as defined by Cousot and Cousot — is a method for designing *approximate* semantics of programs which can be used for analysis purposes [5,6]. In order to prove the correctness of an abstract interpretation (that is the fact that the approximation does not affect the reliability of the analysis although this might be imprecise), it is required the existence of a reference *standard* semantics. Both the approximate (or abstract) and the standard (or concrete) semantics are given by specifying domains which are usually complete partial orders (lattices), and the relation between them is defined in terms of a Galois connection between the two partially ordered domains.

For probabilistic programs the standard semantics refers to domains which are usually structurally different from cpo's as explained in Section 2.1. In the following we will show how a notion similar to Galois connection can be defined for probabilistic domains (vector spaces). One advantage in doing so is that we can now use the real numbers expressing the probabilities to give a quantitative estimate of the precision of a (correct) abstract interpretation.

We will concentrate on the case of finite-dimensional vector spaces, where we can represent all involved maps by matrices. Nevertheless, it is possible to generalise our approach to the infinite-dimensional case — i.e. Banach and Hilbert spaces, cf. Section 3.4. For the finite-dimensional case we exploit the fact that any n-dimensional vector space, with $n < \infty$, is isomorphic to $\mathbb{R}^n$ [19]. Therefore we can take, without loss of generality, the spaces $\mathbb{R}^n$ as a concrete domain and $\mathbb{R}^m$ as an abstract domain, for some positive integers n, m. An abstraction function will then be a linear map $\alpha : \mathbb{R}^n \mapsto \mathbb{R}^m$.

2.3   Galois Connections and Moore-Penrose Pseudo-Inverse

In the classical Cousot framework the relation between the abstraction function α and the concretisation function γ is that of a Galois connection:

Definition 1. *Let $C = (\mathcal{C}, \leq)$ and $\mathcal{D} = (\mathcal{D}, \sqsubseteq)$ be two partially ordered set. If there are two functions $\alpha : C \mapsto \mathcal{D}$ and $\gamma : \mathcal{D} \mapsto C$ such that for all $c \in C$ and all $d \in \mathcal{D}$:*

$$c \leq_{\mathcal{C}} \gamma(d) \text{ iff } \alpha(c) \sqsubseteq d,$$

then $(\mathcal{C}, \alpha, \gamma, \mathcal{D})$ forms a Galois connection.

An equivalent definition is as follows:

Definition 2. *Let $C = (\mathcal{C}, \leq)$ and $\mathcal{D} = (\mathcal{D}, \sqsubseteq)$ be two partially ordered set together with two order preserving functions $\alpha : C \mapsto \mathcal{D}$ and $\gamma : \mathcal{D} \mapsto C$. Then $(\mathcal{C}, \alpha, \gamma, \mathcal{D})$ form a Galois connection iff*

1. *$\alpha \circ \gamma$ is reductive, and*
2. *$\gamma \circ \alpha$ is extensive.*

The first condition means that for all $d \in D$, $\alpha \circ \gamma(d) \sqsubseteq d$. Analogously, the second condition means that for all $c \in C$, $c \leq \gamma \circ \alpha(c)$.

In a linear setting the condition of order preservation of the functions forming a Galois connection becomes linearity (i.e. general structure preservation). Thus, we will define our probabilistic abstraction and concretisation functions as linear maps between the concrete and the abstract vector spaces. Conditions 1. and 2. find their linear analogues in two similar conditions which are expressed in terms of *projections*. Intuitively, a projection gives for each vector its "shadow" (on a screen represented by the image space of the projection). According to this intuition, the projection of a vector can be seen as an approximation of that vector. Formally, projections are defined as idempotent linear operators:

Definition 3. *Given a finite-dimensional (complex) vector space V, a linear map $\pi : V \mapsto V$ is called a* projection *if $\pi^2 = \pi \circ \pi = \pi$. A projection is* orthogonal *if it coincides with its adjoint.*

For finite-dimensional vector spaces one can think of the adjoint of a linear map as the *transpose* of the matrix representing the map, i.e. the matrix where rows and columns are exchanged [19].

Given two finite-dimensional vector spaces V and W, and a linear map $\rho : V \mapsto W$, the image of ρ, $\rho(V) \subseteq W$, is a sub-space of W. Associated to such a sub-space there is a unique orthogonal projection $\pi_{\rho(V)} : W \mapsto W$ mapping each vector in W into the sub-space $\rho(V)$. By using this notion of orthogonal projection, properties 1. and 2. of Galois connection can be transferred into a vector space setting as follows. The condition $\alpha \circ \gamma(d) \sqsubseteq d$ becomes the condition that $\alpha \circ \gamma$ is the orthogonal projection in the image of α, that is $\alpha \circ \gamma = \pi_\alpha$, and $\gamma \circ \alpha(c) \geq c$ turns into $\gamma \circ \alpha = \pi_\gamma$. These new conditions exactly define the so-called *Moore-Penrose pseudo-inverse*:

Definition 4. *Let C and D be two finite-dimensional (complex) vector spaces and $\alpha : C \mapsto D$ a linear map between them. A linear map $\alpha^\dagger = \gamma : D \mapsto C$ is the (unique)* Moore-Penrose pseudo-inverse *of α iff*

1. $\alpha \circ \gamma = \pi_\alpha$, and
2. $\gamma \circ \alpha = \pi_\gamma$.

An alternative characterisation of the Moore-Penrose pseudo-inverse is given by:

Theorem 1. *Let C and D be two finite-dimensional vector spaces. For a linear map $\alpha : C \mapsto D$ the Moore-Penrose pseudo-inverse $\gamma : D \mapsto C$ is uniquely characterised by the following conditions:*

1. $\alpha \circ \gamma \circ \alpha = \alpha$,
2. $\gamma \circ \alpha \circ \gamma = \gamma$,
3. $(\alpha \circ \gamma)^* = \alpha \circ \gamma$,
4. $(\gamma \circ \alpha)^* = \gamma \circ \alpha$.

This theorem provides further evidence of the similarity between Galois connections and Moore-Penrose pseudo-inverse, since the following proposition holds for Galois connections:

Proposition 1. *Let $(\mathcal{C}, \alpha, \gamma, \mathcal{D})$ be a Galois connection. Then α and γ are* quasi-inverse, *i.e.*

1. $\alpha \circ \gamma \circ \alpha = \alpha$, *and*
2. $\gamma \circ \alpha \circ \gamma = \gamma$.

It would be interesting to investigate the properties of Galois connections which correspond to conditions 3. and 4. in Theorem 1. We believe that an appropriate setting for these investigations is category theory, and we plan to develop such studies in a future work.

By using the notion Moore-Penrose pseudo-inverse, we can now define a *probabilistic abstract interpretation* as follows:

Definition 5. *Let $\mathcal{C}$ an $\mathcal{D}$ be two probabilistic domains. A* probabilistic abstract interpretation *is a pair of linear maps, $\alpha : \mathcal{C} \mapsto \mathcal{D}$ and $\gamma : \mathcal{D} \mapsto \mathcal{C}$, between (the concrete domain) $\mathcal{C}$ and (the abstract domain) $\mathcal{D}$, such that γ is the Moore-Penrose pseudo-inverse of α, and vice versa.*

Example 1. Consider $\mathcal{C} = \mathbb{R}^3$ as a concrete probabilistic domain. We can define an abstraction function $\alpha : \mathbb{R}^3 \mapsto \mathbb{R}^2$ by $\alpha(c_1, c_2, c_3) = (c_1, c_3)$, i.e. we abstract in as far as we ignore the second component of a concrete (distribution) vector. The linear operator α and its Moore-Penrose pseudo-inverse $\gamma = \alpha^\dagger$ can be represented by the following matrices:

$$A = \begin{pmatrix} 1 & 0 & 0 \\ 0 & 0 & 1 \end{pmatrix} \text{ and } \Gamma = \begin{pmatrix} 1 & 0 \\ 0 & 0 \\ 0 & 1 \end{pmatrix}$$

The image of $\mathcal{D} = \mathbb{R}^2$ under γ in $\mathcal{C} = \mathbb{R}^3$ is therefore the c_1-c_3-plane (i.e. the two-dimensional sub-space generated by c_1 and c_3). Thus we get the following matrix, which indeed is a projection into the c_1-c_3-plane:

$$\Gamma \cdot A = \begin{pmatrix} 1 & 0 & 0 \\ 0 & 0 & 0 \\ 0 & 0 & 1 \end{pmatrix}$$

In a probabilistic abstract interpretation the notion of projection operators is essentially used to replace the notion of partial order in classical abstract interpretation. The orthogonality property of such projections allows us furthermore to conclude that the probabilistic abstract interpretation we define in Definition 5 are the *best* in the sense that the pair (α, γ) is among all the other pairs (α, γ') (which we could possibly define) the one mapping the abstraction $\alpha(d)$ to the concrete vector closest to d. This is justified by the fact that $\gamma \circ \alpha$ is an orthogonal projection and by the following proposition [2, Corr 2.1.1], [18, 44.2.10]:

Proposition 2. *Let $\pi_\mathcal{W}$ be the orthogonal projection on a finite-dimensional vector space $\mathcal{V}$ associated to the sub-space $\mathcal{W} \subseteq \mathcal{V}$. Then for every vector $x \in \mathcal{V}$ its image $\pi_\mathcal{W}(x)$ is the unique vector in $\mathcal{W}$ such that $\|x - \pi_\mathcal{W}(x)\|_2$ is minimal.*

There are various possible measures for the length, i.e. *norm* of a vector, and different norms would correspond to different metrics on $\mathcal{V}$. In general, a whole family of *p-norms* can be defined by:

$$\|x\|_p = \|(x_c)_{c \in \mathcal{C}}\|_p = \left(\sum_{c \in \mathcal{C}} |x_c|^p \right)^{1/p}$$

Although in Proposition 2 we refer to a particular norm, namely the Euclidean norm or 2-norm, $\|x\|_2 = (|x_1|^2 + \ldots + |x_n|^2)^{(1/2)}$, in a finite-dimensional space the choice of one norm or another is not relevant for topological considerations, as they all induce the same topology [19].

3   Construction of Probabilistic Abstract Interpretations

We discuss here a method for constructing probabilistic abstract interpretations, which represents a first step towards a more complete and structured study of construction and combination methods similar to the catalogues in the classical case, e.g. [17,7].

3.1   Probabilistic Induced Analysis

The construction we discuss first is that of a fixpoint abstraction using Moore-Penrose pseudo-inverses (for further details see [11]). The same construction using Galois connections gives in the classical case so called *induced analysis*.

We assume that we have a probabilistic semantics in terms of a (concrete) fixpoint operator Φ on some vector space $\mathcal{V}$, as mentioned in Section 2.1. Furthermore, assume that there is a linear abstraction function $\alpha : \mathcal{V} \mapsto \mathcal{W}$ from the concrete domain into an abstract domain $\mathcal{W}$.

In order to construct a probabilistic abstract interpretation we now compute the (unique) Moore-Penrose pseudo-inverse $\gamma = \alpha^\dagger$ of α. The abstract semantics can then be defined as a linear fixpoint operator on the abstract domain $\mathcal{W}$, obtained by a formal computation starting from the concrete linear fixpoint operator $\Phi : \mathcal{V} \mapsto \mathcal{V}$ as follows:

$$\Psi = \alpha \circ \Phi \circ \gamma.$$

Since α and γ are linear (thus continuous) it is immediate that:

$$\gamma \circ (\lim \Psi) = \gamma \circ (\lim \alpha \circ \Phi \circ \gamma) = \gamma \circ \alpha \circ (\lim \Phi) \circ \gamma.$$

Thus, the operator $\gamma \circ \alpha$ exactly describes the "gap" between the concretisation of the abstract semantics and the concrete semantics.

3.2   Vector Space Lifting

In order to apply our probabilistic abstract interpretation methodology we may need to recast a cpo based semantics in a vector space setting. A straightforward method to *lift* a cpo to a vector space — similar to lifting a semantics to a power space setting in the classical framework — is based on a free vector space construction.

Given a classical semantic domain (cpo) $\mathcal{C}$, we define the *free real vector space* $\mathcal{V}(\mathcal{C})$ on $\mathcal{C}$ as the set of all formal linear combinations:

$$\mathcal{V}(\mathcal{C}) = \left\{ \sum x_c c \mid x_c \in \mathbb{R},\ c \in \mathcal{C} \right\}.$$

An *extraction* function $\alpha : \mathcal{C} \mapsto \mathcal{D}$ of $\mathcal{C}$ into an abstract domain $\mathcal{D}$ (e.g. [17, 4.3]), can be then *lifted* to a linear map $\alpha : \mathcal{V}(\mathcal{C}) \mapsto \mathcal{V}(\mathcal{D})$ as follows:

$$\alpha(p_1 \cdot c_1 + p_2 \cdot c_2 + \ldots) = p_1 \cdot \alpha(c_1) + p_2 \cdot \alpha(c_2) \ldots$$

Remark Note that the probabilistic version of an induced fixpoint semantics in Section 3.1 can also be seen as arising from a lifting construction. In fact, the domains $\mathcal{V}$ and $\mathcal{W}$ we investigated in [11] are indeed constructed as free vector spaces on the underlying abstract and and concrete lattices of constraints.

3.3   General Construction

In the construction of Section 3.1 we examined the special case of a fixpoint abstraction, which represents a typical framework for the analyses of programming languages. The same construction applies also to the the general case of semantical functions $f : \mathcal{A} \mapsto \mathcal{B}$. In this case, a classical abstract interpretation is given by two abstraction functions, α and α', mapping the input domain $\mathcal{A}$ and the output domain $\mathcal{B}$ into an abstract input domain $\mathcal{A}^{\#}$ and an abstract output domain $\mathcal{B}^{\#}$ respectively, and by an abstract semantical functions $f^{\#} : \mathcal{A}^{\#} \mapsto \mathcal{B}^{\#}$. The following diagram illustrates this case in the classical cpo-based framework.

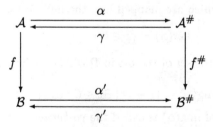

In the general scenario described above (which includes fixpoint abstractions as particular cases) an abstract function $f^{\#} : \mathcal{A}^{\#} \mapsto \mathcal{B}^{\#}$ is a *correct* approximation of a concrete function $f : \mathcal{A} \mapsto \mathcal{B}$ if

$$\alpha' \circ f \leq_{\mathcal{B}^{\#}} f^{\#} \circ \alpha,$$

where $\leq_{\mathcal{B}^{\#}}$ is the order relation on the abstract domain $\mathcal{B}^{\#}$.

Given two abstract domains $\mathcal{A}^{\#}$ and $\mathcal{B}^{\#}$, there always exists a *best correct approximation* of a concrete function $f : \mathcal{A} \mapsto \mathcal{B}$. This is defined by $f^{\#} = \alpha' \circ f \circ \gamma$.

However, the choice of the best correct approximation of a function does not guarantee in general that the results of an abstract computation are best approximations of the corresponding concrete ones. Whenever this happens then the abstract interpretation is complete. Formally, an abstract function $f^{\#} : \mathcal{A}^{\#} \mapsto \mathcal{B}^{\#}$ is a *complete* approximation of a concrete function $f : \mathcal{A} \mapsto \mathcal{B}$ if

$$\alpha' \circ f = f^{\#} \circ \alpha.$$

Unlike the correctness condition, completeness is not an essential requirement, but rather an ideal situation which does not occur very often in practice. In the literature it is often also referred to as *exactness* [4] or *optimality* [8].

By applying the same lifting technique described in Section 3.2 to both abstract domains $\mathcal{A}^{\#}$ and $\mathcal{B}^{\#}$ we can construct a probabilistic abstract interpretation in this general case too. Obviously, we will have now to compute two Moore-Penrose pseudo-inverses, namely $\gamma = \alpha^{\dagger}$ for α, and $\gamma' = \alpha'^{\dagger}$ for α'. In the following we will denote a probabilistic abstract interpretation of a function f by specifying the abstract domains and function, $(\mathcal{A}^{\#}, \mathcal{B}^{\#}, f^{\#})$.

3.4   Infinite-Dimensional Abstractions

The construction of the Moore-Penrose pseudo-inverse, as presented here, is essentially based on *finite-dimensional* vector spaces. Although this gives an elegant quantitative analysis for finite domains, one is more than often confronted with an infinite concrete domain. For example a simple parity analysis starts with the set of all natural numbers for which we therefore have to construct an infinite-dimensional vector space like $\mathcal{V}(\mathbb{N})$.

In this case we can still guarantee the existence of a pseudo-inverse by defining our abstractions as *Fredholm operators* [1]. We just sketch here the basic argument and definitions.

The *kernel* of a map α between two vector spaces $\mathcal{C}$ and $\mathcal{D}$ is the set of all those elements of $\mathcal{C}$ which are mapped into the null vector in $\mathcal{D}$, i.e.

$$\ker(\alpha) = \{x \in \mathcal{C} \mid \alpha(x) = o\}.$$

The *image* of α is the set of vectors in $\mathcal{D}$ which are images under α of vectors in $\mathcal{C}$:

$$\text{img}(\alpha) = \{y \in \mathcal{D} \mid \exists x \in \mathcal{C} : \alpha(x) = y\}.$$

The complement of $\text{img}(\alpha)$ is called the *co-kernel* $\text{coker}(\alpha)$.

Definition 6. *[16, p23] A bounded linear operator α between two Banach spaces $\mathcal{C}$ and $\mathcal{D}$ is* Fredholm *iff the dimensions of kernel and co-kernel are finite.*

For Fredholm operators the following theorem holds [16, Thm 1.4.15]:

Theorem 2. *Let α be a Fredholm operator α between two Banach spaces $\mathcal{C}$ and $\mathcal{D}$, then α admits a pseudo-inverse.*

It is relatively easy to guarantee that a lifted abstraction $\alpha : \mathcal{V}(C) \mapsto \mathcal{V}(D)$ stemming from an extraction function $\alpha : C \mapsto D$ (see Section 3) is a Fredholm operator and thus possesses a pseudo-inverse. If the original extraction function α is defined for all elements in C, i.e. if α is a total function, then the kernel is always the empty set, as no element in $\mathcal{V}(C)$ will be mapped to the null vector. If this is not the case, a partial α can be made total in the usual way, namely by adding an "undefined" element $\perp$ to D. On the other hand, if α is a surjective function on D then the co-kernel of α is empty. Otherwise, we can replace D by the image of C, $D' = \alpha(D) \subseteq D$. In other words, for lifted abstractions it is always possible to define α such that $\text{img}(\alpha) = \emptyset$ and $\text{coker}(\alpha) = \emptyset$.

A common case is when only one of the two domains is infinite-dimensional, namely the concrete one. One example is the parity test, where we abstract from an infinite domain to a finite one containing just two representatives for the even and the odd numbers respectively, and the undefined element. This situation is especially simple. Since the abstract domain is finite-dimensional the co-kernel condition is trivially fulfilled. On the other hand, the extraction function is total — e.g. every natural number has a well-defined parity, either even or odd — and thus the kernel is empty.

4 Measuring Probabilistic Abstract Interpretations

As already mentioned, in our probabilistic setting we have the possibility of measuring the precision of a probabilistic abstract interpretation in numerical terms. For abstract interpretations constructed as in Section 3.1, the difference between $\gamma \circ (\lim \Psi)(d)$ and $(\lim \Phi) \circ \gamma(d)$ describes the approximation error and is obviously determined by the "size" of the map (or matrix) $\gamma \circ \alpha$. This size can be measured by means of an *operator norm*, which allows us to estimate the worst approximation error made. This norm is defined for an operator β as:

$$\|\beta\| = \sup_{\|x\|=1} \|\beta(x)\|$$

i.e. as the length of the "longest" vector a unit vector may be mapped to. The meaning of an operator norm for a linear map $\beta : V \mapsto W$ is thus the largest value by which β stretches an element of V. Depending on the application we could choose a particular vector norm $\|x\|$. In the examples below we will use $\|x\|_1$ for calculating some numerical results, as it corresponds to a kind of simple average.

As already pointed out, the assumption of a finite-dimensional vector space makes it not relevant the choice of a particular vector norm $\|x\|$. In the examples below we will use $\|x\|_1$ for calculating some numerical results, but the choice of any other p-norm would lead us essentially to the same conclusions.

In the general case of a generic semantic function $f : \mathcal{A} \mapsto \mathcal{B}$ described in Section 3.3, it seems reasonable to measure the precision of a probabilistic abstract interpretation defined by $(\mathcal{A}^{\#}, \mathcal{B}^{\#}, f^{\#})$ by means of the norm of the "pseudo-quotient":

$$\Delta = (\alpha' \circ f) \circ (f^{\#} \circ \alpha)^{\dagger}.$$

An estimate of the precision of the abstraction is then given by calculating the norm $\|\Delta\|$ of the linear operator Δ.

The operator $\Delta : \mathcal{B}^\# \mapsto \mathcal{B}^\#$ is an operator on $\mathcal{B}^\#$, mapping an abstract vector $b_1 \in \mathcal{B}^\#$ into another abstract vector b_2 resulting from abstracting the result of $f(a)$, where a is the concrete vector such that $f^\# \circ \alpha(a) = b_1$. Therefore, the norm $\|\Delta\|$ gives us a measure of the approximation introduced by (α, γ) in the form of an expansion factor expressing how much the abstraction b_1 can be bigger than b_2.

According to this notion of precision we can define correctness and completeness of probabilistic abstract interpretations as follows:

Definition 7. *Let $(\mathcal{A}^\#, \mathcal{B}^\#, f^\#)$ be a probabilistic abstract interpretation, and let Δ be the associated pseudo-quotient operator. Then*

Correctness: $(\mathcal{A}^\#, \mathcal{B}^\#, f^\#)$ *is* correct *iff* $\|\Delta\| \geq 1$;
Completeness: $(\mathcal{A}^\#, \mathcal{B}^\#, f^\#)$ *is* complete *iff* $\|\Delta\| = 1$.

This definition is intuitively justified by re-interpreting the correctness and completeness conditions of the classical theory in the probabilistic setting.

As mentioned at the beginning of this section, for the fixpoint abstraction the approximation error is measured by $\|\gamma \circ \alpha\|$, and we would expect that such an abstract interpretation is complete when $\|\gamma \circ \alpha\| = 1$ The following proposition shows that this is coherent with Definition 7.

Proposition 3. *Let $(\mathcal{A}^\#, \Psi)$ be a probabilistic abstract interpretation as in Section 3.1. Then,*

$$\|\gamma \circ \alpha\| = 1 \text{ iff } \|\Delta\| = 1,$$

where Δ is the pseudo-quotient $(\alpha' \circ f) \circ (f^\# \circ \alpha)^\dagger$.

5 Examples

In this section we illustrate our approach by means of some examples, which are well understood in the classical case, namely the "Rule of Sign for Multiplications" (Example 5.1), the "Rule of Sign for Additions" (Example 5.2), and the "Proof by Nine" or "Cast out of Nine" (Example 5.3). We refer to [7] for the classical counterpart of these examples.

5.1 Rule of Sign: Multiplication

The Setting The problem of multiplying two integers a and b is abstracted to the problem of determining the sign of $a \times b$, given the sign of its factors.

The abstract domain of signs is given by Sign $= \{\bot, -, 0, +, \top\}$, where $\bot$ can be read as "undefined" and $\top$ as "any sign". The abstract multiplication $\times^\# :$ Sign $\mapsto$ Sign is defined in Figure 2.

The problem is therefore to relate the concrete multiplication $\times$ with the abstract multiplication $\times^\#$, where the abstraction function $\alpha : \mathbb{Z} \mapsto$ Sign is simply the sign of an integer.

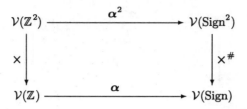

Fig. 1. Lifting and Abstracting Multiplication

$\times^{\#}$	$\perp$	$-$	0	$+$	$\top$
$\perp$	$\perp$	$\perp$	$\perp$	$\perp$	$\perp$
$-$	$\perp$	$+$	0	$-$	$\top$
0	$\perp$	0	0	0	$\top$
$+$	$\perp$	$-$	0	$+$	$\top$
$\top$	$\perp$	$\top$	$\top$	$\top$	$\top$

$+^{\#}$	$\perp$	$-$	0	$+$	$\top$
$\perp$	$\perp$	$\perp$	$\perp$	$\perp$	$\perp$
$-$	$\perp$	$-$	$-$	$\top$	$\top$
0	$\perp$	$-$	0	$+$	$\top$
$+$	$\perp$	$\top$	$+$	$+$	$\top$
$\top$	$\perp$	$\top$	$\top$	$\top$	$\top$

Fig. 2. Abstract Multiplication and Addition

Numerical Results The situation — lifted to the vector space level — is depicted in Figure 1. As $\perp$ and $\top$ are largely irrelevant for our considerations we will ignore them in the following and identify $\mathcal{V}(\text{Sign})$ with $\mathbb{R}^3$. The basis vectors for the vector space $\mathcal{V}(\text{Sign}) = \mathbb{R}^3$ are identified with the signs $-, 0, +$:

$$- \longrightarrow (1,0,0)$$
$$0 \longrightarrow (0,1,0)$$
$$+ \longrightarrow (0,0,1)$$

Analogously, pairs of signs form a basis for the vector space $\mathcal{V}(\text{Sign}^2) = \mathbb{R}^6$:

$$- \times - \longrightarrow (1,0,0,0,0,0)$$
$$- \times 0 \longrightarrow (0,1,0,0,0,0)$$
$$- \times + \longrightarrow (0,0,1,0,0,0)$$
$$0 \times 0 \longrightarrow (0,0,0,1,0,0)$$
$$0 \times + \longrightarrow (0,0,0,0,1,0)$$
$$+ \times + \longrightarrow (0,0,0,0,0,1).$$

Given the concrete representation of the vector spaces, we can construct the matrices representing α, γ, etc. The problem is that we actually had to consider infinite-dimensional vector spaces $\mathcal{V}(\mathbb{Z})$ and $\mathcal{V}(\mathbb{Z}^2)$, but one can easily see that any "truncation", i.e. replacing $\mathcal{V}(\mathbb{Z})$ by $\mathcal{V}(\{-n, -n+1 \ldots, 0, \ldots, n-1, n\}) = \mathbb{R}^{(2n+1)}$ and $\mathcal{V}(\mathbb{Z}^2)$ by $\mathbb{R}^{(2n+1)^2}$, will lead to the same pseudo-quotient of $\alpha \circ \times$ and $\times^{\#} \circ \alpha^2$, namely:

$$(\alpha \circ \times) \circ (\times^{\#} \circ \alpha^2)^{\dagger} = \begin{pmatrix} 1.00 & 0.00 & 0.00 \\ 0.00 & 1.00 & 0.00 \\ 0.00 & 0.00 & 1.00 \end{pmatrix}$$

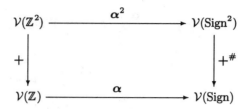

Fig. 3. Lifting and Abstracting Addition

According to the fact that the rule of sign, i.e. $\times^{\#}$, is a **complete** approximation of the multiplication $\times$, we obtain as a measure of precision:

$$\|(\alpha \circ \times) \circ (\times^{\#} \circ \alpha^2)^{\dagger}\|_1 = 1$$

5.2   Rule of Sign: Addition

The Setting The problem is very similar to the one above, the difference being that now our interest is in determining the sign of the addition of two integers instead of their multiplication. Again we have the abstract domain: Sign = $\{\perp, -, 0, +, \top\}$.

Contrary to the previous example, we now do not have a complete abstraction: It is not possible to know the sign of a sum just by looking at the signs of the factors. Therefore, we get an abstract addition function $+^{\#}$ where we eventually have to leave it open which sign the sum will have, indicating this by using the abstract "sign" $\top$ in Figure 2. The undefined "sign" $\perp$ is irrelevant as we consider only well-defined concrete additions. The basis vectors for the vector space $\mathcal{V}(\text{Sign}) = \mathbb{R}^4$ are identified with the signs $-, 0, +, \top$:

$$- \longrightarrow (1, 0, 0, 0)$$
$$0 \longrightarrow (0, 1, 0, 0)$$
$$+ \longrightarrow (0, 0, 1, 0)$$
$$\top \longrightarrow (0, 0, 0, 1).$$

Numerical Results Figure 3 again depicts the overall situation. In this case, considering a truncation instead of the actual infinite-dimensional vector spaces, $\mathcal{V}(\mathbb{Z})$ and $\mathcal{V}(\mathbb{Z}^2)$, does not lead to the same result. In fact, the "truncations" $\mathcal{V}([-n, n])$ and $\mathcal{V}([-n, n]^2)$ for different n lead to different pseudo-quotients. Therefore, we need to consider all of them and look at their limit. Some of these truncated pseudo-quotients Q_n for $n = 2$, $n = 5$, $n = 10$, $n = 20$, $n = 30$ are depicted in Figure 4. The sequence of the pseudo-quotients $Q_n = (\alpha \circ +) \circ (+^{\#} \circ \alpha^2)^{\dagger}$, where we consider only pairs in $[-n, n]$, converges to:

$$Q_2 = \begin{pmatrix} 1.00000 & 0.00000 & 0.00000 & 0.00000 \\ 0.00000 & 1.00000 & 0.00000 & 0.00000 \\ 0.00000 & 0.00000 & 1.00000 & 0.00000 \\ 0.25000 & 0.50000 & 0.25000 & 0.00000 \end{pmatrix}$$

$$Q_5 = \begin{pmatrix} 1.00000 & 0.00000 & 0.00000 & 0.00000 \\ 0.00000 & 1.00000 & 0.00000 & 0.00000 \\ 0.00000 & 0.00000 & 1.00000 & 0.00000 \\ 0.40000 & 0.20000 & 0.40000 & 0.00000 \end{pmatrix}$$

$$Q_{10} = \begin{pmatrix} 1.00000 & 0.00000 & 0.00000 & 0.00000 \\ 0.00000 & 1.00000 & 0.00000 & 0.00000 \\ 0.00000 & 0.00000 & 1.00000 & 0.00000 \\ 0.45000 & 0.10000 & 0.45000 & 0.00000 \end{pmatrix}$$

$$Q_{20} = \begin{pmatrix} 1.00000 & 0.00000 & 0.00000 & 0.00000 \\ 0.00000 & 1.00000 & 0.00000 & 0.00000 \\ 0.00000 & 0.00000 & 1.00000 & 0.00000 \\ 0.47500 & 0.05000 & 0.47500 & 0.00000 \end{pmatrix}$$

$$Q_{30} = \begin{pmatrix} 1.00000 & 0.00000 & 0.00000 & 0.00000 \\ 0.00000 & 1.00000 & 0.00000 & 0.00000 \\ 0.00000 & 0.00000 & 1.00000 & 0.00000 \\ 0.48333 & 0.03333 & 0.48333 & 0.00000 \end{pmatrix}$$

Fig. 4. The pseudo-quotients Q_n for $n = 2$, $n = 5$, $n = 10$, $n = 20$, $n = 30$

$$\lim_{n \to \infty} Q_n = \begin{pmatrix} 1.00 & 0.00 & 0.00 & 0.00 \\ 0.00 & 1.00 & 0.00 & 0.00 \\ 0.00 & 0.00 & 1.00 & 0.00 \\ 0.50 & 0.00 & 0.50 & 0.00 \end{pmatrix}$$

The 1-norm this time is larger than 1, namely:

$$\| \lim_{n \to \infty} Q_n \|_1 = 1.50 = 1\frac{1}{2},$$

which is indicating the fact that the rule of sign for the addition i.e. $+^{\#}$, is a (correct) non-complete abstraction of the concrete addition, i.e. $+$.

5.3   Cast Out of Nine

As another example — actually a whole set of examples — we now investigate a probabilistic version of the so called "Proof by Nine" or "Cast out of Nine". The idea behind such a proof is to check the plausibility of the result of a multiplication by comparing it with the corresponding multiplication of the 'check-sums' modulo some digit d; in the classical case d is the digit 9. The question we want to address in our quantitative setting is: Why is $d = 9$ "better" than for example $d = 2$?

A complete formal presentation of this classical plausibility check was given in [7]. For our purposes we will need only a simplified and slightly changed presentation.

The Setting The problem is to look at a multiplication of two natural numbers, i.e. an expression of the form "$a \times b = c$" and check if it is "correct". We can identify the set of all expressions of this form with $\mathbb{N} \times \mathbb{N} \to \mathbb{N} \equiv \mathbb{N}^3$.

Not all possible (syntactically well-formed) expressions of this type are (semantically) correct, i.e. indeed represent a valid multiplication. For example "$2 \times 2 = 4$" is correct but "$2 \times 2 = 5$" is not. We will express the correctness of an expression by a map $eval : \mathbb{N}^3 \mapsto \mathbb{B}$, where $\mathbb{B} = \{\bot = true, false = \top\}$ defined as:

$$eval(\text{"}a \cdot b = c\text{"}) = eval((a, b, c)) = \begin{cases} true & \text{if } c = a \cdot b \\ false & \text{if } c \neq a \cdot b \end{cases}$$

We implement the plausibility check by mapping each (concrete) multiplication into a multiplication expression involving the 'check sums' modulo some d, i.e. we introduce an abstraction map $\alpha : \mathbb{N}^3 \mapsto \mathbb{D}^3$ defined by $\alpha((a, b, c)) = (\bar{a}, \bar{b}, \bar{c})$ where $\bar{x} = x \bmod d$.

Again we can check the correctness of an abstract multiplication expression modulo d by a mapping $eval^\# : \mathbb{D}^3 \mapsto \mathbb{B}$ defined by:

$$eval^\#(\text{"}\bar{a} \cdot \bar{b} = \bar{c}\text{"}) = eval^\#((\bar{a}, \bar{b}, \bar{c})) = \begin{cases} true & \text{if } \bar{c} = \bar{a} \cdot \bar{b} \bmod d \\ false & \text{if } \bar{c} \neq \bar{a} \cdot \bar{b} \bmod d \end{cases}$$

The relevant observation is that the correctness of the simplified multiplication expression (over $\mathbb{D}$) is a plausibility test for the correctness of the multiplication expression over $\mathbb{N}$: If the expression over $\mathbb{D}$ is incorrect then the original expression *is* incorrect too, but if $eval^\# \circ \alpha$ maps an expression into *true* we can only conclude that it *may* be correct (in other words, some expressions which are mapped into *false* under $eval$ may be mapped into *true* under $eval^\# \circ \alpha$).

In this sense the abstraction is conservative: We can detect incorrect expressions, but we cannot be sure about the expressions which pass this plausibility test. However, we can try to estimate the proportion of incorrect expressions which pass the test. This would give us a measure of the precision of the abstraction. To this purpose we look at the lifting of the situation above to the free vector space setting. The measure of precision is again the pseudo-quotient S_d between $id \circ eval = eval$ and $eval^\# \circ \alpha$. This situation is depicted in Figure 5.

Some Numerical Experiments For truncated — i.e. finite-dimensional — versions of the functions involved we can compute the matrices involved explic-

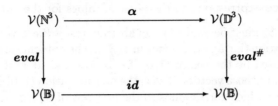

Fig. 5. Abstraction and Concretisation of "Cast by d"

itly. Therefore we again have to overcome the problem that $\mathcal{V}(\mathbb{N})$ is infinite-dimensional. This time we do this by an experimental method, in the spirit of various Monte-Carlo techniques. Concretely, we have checked 3333 randomly chosen triples $a * b = c$ with $a, b, c \in [0, 10]$. This was implemented using the interactive numerical computation system octave [12].

The results show that the percentage of incorrect concrete multiplications which pass the test decreases when d becomes larger. That means that the precision of "Proof by d" increases as d gets larger. Each of the following matrices $S_d = (id \circ eval) \circ (eval^{\#} \circ \alpha)^{\dagger}$ for the cases $d = 2, 3, 5, 7, 9$ respectively, shows the results of our experiments.

$$\|S_2\|_1 = \left\| \begin{pmatrix} 0.06392 \ 0.93607 \\ 0.00000 \ 1.00000 \end{pmatrix} \right\|_1 = 1.93$$

$$\|S_3\|_1 = \left\| \begin{pmatrix} 0.10072 \ 0.89928 \\ 0.00000 \ 1.00000 \end{pmatrix} \right\|_1 = 1.89$$

$$\|S_5\|_1 = \left\| \begin{pmatrix} 0.15156 \ 0.84844 \\ 0.00000 \ 1.00000 \end{pmatrix} \right\|_1 = 1.84$$

$$\|S_7\|_1 = \left\| \begin{pmatrix} 0.22178 \ 0.77822 \\ 0.00000 \ 1.00000 \end{pmatrix} \right\|_1 = 1.78$$

$$\|S_9\|_1 = \left\| \begin{pmatrix} 0.27792 \ 0.72208 \\ 0.00000 \ 1.00000 \end{pmatrix} \right\|_1 = 1.72$$

The maps $S_d : \mathcal{V}(\mathbb{B}) \mapsto \mathcal{V}(\mathbb{B})$, are represented with respect to the following basis vectors for $\mathcal{V}(\mathbb{B})$:

$$true \longrightarrow (1, 0)$$
$$false \longrightarrow (0, 1)$$

and with the following convention concerning the rows and columns of these matrices:

Row Indices correspond to the boolean values for the **abstract** results, and **Columns Indices** correspond to the boolean values for the **concrete** results.

Each matrix S_d must be applied to an abstract result (i.e. a vector in $\mathcal{V}(\mathbb{B})$) to get its concretisation (i.e. again a vector in $\mathcal{V}(\mathbb{B})$). The outcome of the plausibility check is represented by the vector $(1,0)$ if it is *true* and $(0,1)$ if it is *false*. The application of S_d to these vectors, that is the multiplication $(1,0)\cdot S_d$ or $(0,1)\cdot S_d$, results in a vector which corresponds to the first row of S_d if the abstract vector is $(1,0)$, and to the second row of S_d if the abstract vector is $(0,1)$. It is then easy to see that for all d, if the outcome of the plausibility test is *false*, then it indeed corresponds (with probability 1) to an incorrect concrete multiplication; however, if a multiplication passes the plausibility test — i.e. the result is *true* — the original multiplication still might be incorrect; in the particular case $d = 2$ there is a 93% chance of such an incorrect classification.

We see furthermore, that casting out of nine is "better" than casting out of two, as only 72% of the incorrect expressions pass undetected, compared to 89% for $d = 3$, 84% for $d = 5$ and 77% for $d = 7$.

6   Conclusions and Related Work

We presented a quantitative version of the classical Cousot and Cousot framework for abstract interpretation in which the notion of a Galois connection (based on order-theoretic concepts) is replaced by the notion of Moore-Penrose pseudo-inverse (of a linear map between vector spaces). This framework not only allows for the analysis of probabilistic programs [11], but additionally introduces the possibility of measuring the precision of an abstract interpretation.

Various authors have investigated the problem of comparing abstract interpretations with respect to their precision, starting from Cousot and Cousot, who in [5] introduce a partial ordering relation to encode the levels of abstraction of the interpretations. Successive work has concentrated on the study of abstract domains as representatives of their corresponding abstract interpretations, and operators on domains have been defined which allow for combining domains in order to enhance their precision (see [13] and references there in). Also in this case the comparison is expressed by means of a partial ordering (in fact a complete lattice) on the set of the domains. A slightly different approach is the one in [3] where domains are compared by means of a notion of *quotient* with respect to the property which is to be analysed. This approach seems to be closer to ours in as far as it is also based on the idea that the level of precision of an abstract interpretation can be estimated by measuring the "gap" missing for completeness. Contrary to our pseudo-quotient, their notion is still only qualitative and cannot give a numerical estimate as a result of such a measuring.

The possibility of deciding which of various available abstract interpretations is most appropriate for a given problem is of course an important advantage for those who have to analyse the problem. This explains the reason why so much work has been devoted to the study of the comparison of abstract interpretations. A common feature of all these previous approaches is the characterisation of the precision of an abstract interpretation or (equivalently) an abstract domain from a purely qualitative viewpoint. The significance of our work in this framework is in the consideration of a *quantitative* estimate of the precision of an abstract interpretation as opposed to the qualitative one considered up to now. This numerical quantification of the precision is an additional information which the user can effectively exploit in the choice of the appropriate abstract interpretation in order to optimise the balance accuracy/cost of an analysis. For example, if an analysis which requires a considerable implementational cost is just 0.02% more precise than another which is easier or less expensive then she/he could opt for the latter. Note that in a classical qualitative framework the first analysis would be regarded as "just" more precise than the other ignoring "how much" more precise it is. This could force the choice of the more expensive one when accuracy is a primary issue even thought the actual loss of precision is insignificant.

More work needs to be devoted to the construction and combination of probabilistic abstract interpretations along the lines of [17,7], in particular in the infinite-dimensional case. Not the least reason for this is that a direct computation of the Moore-Penrose pseudo-inverse can be numerically very expensive.

References

1. Frederick J. Beutler. The operator theory of the pseudo-inverse. *Journal of Mathematical Analysis and Applications*, 10:451–470,471–493, 1965.
2. Stephen L. Campbell and D. Meyer. *Generalized Inverse of Linear Transformations*. Constable and Company, London, 1979.
3. A. Cortesi, G. File', and W. Winsborough. The Quotient of an Abstract Interpretation. *Theoretical Computer Science*, 202(1–2):163–192, 1998.
4. Patrick Cousot. Constructive design of a Hierarchy of Semantics of a Transition System by Abstract Interpretation. In S. Brooks and M. Mislove, editors, *13th International Symposium on Mathematical Foundations of Programming Semantics (MFPS97)*, volume 6 of *Electronic Notes in Theoretical Computer Science*, Amsterdam, 1997. Elsevier.
5. Patrick Cousot and Radhia Cousot. Abstract Interpretation: A Unified Lattice Model for Static Analysis of Programs by Construction or Approximation of Fixpoints. In *Symposium on Principles of Programming Languages (POPL)*, pages 238–252, Los Angeles, 1977.
6. Patrick Cousot and Radhia Cousot. Systematic Design of Program Analysis Frameworks. In *Symposium on Principles of Programming Languages (POPL)*, pages 269–282, San Antonio, Texas, 1979.
7. Patrick Cousot and Radhia Cousot. Abstract Interpretation and Applications to Logic Programs. *Journal of Logic Programming*, 13(2-3):103–180, July 1992.
8. D. Dams, R. Gerth, and O. Grumberg. Abstract Interpretations of Reactive Systems. *ACM Trans. Program. Lang. Syst.*, 19(2):253–291, 1997.
9. Alessandra Di Pierro and Herbert Wiklicky. An operational semantics for Probabilistic Concurrent Constraint Programming. In P. Iyer, Y. Choo, and D. Schmidt, editors, *ICCL'98 – International Conference on Computer Languages*, pages 174–183. IEEE Computer Society Press, 1998.

10. Alessandra Di Pierro and Herbert Wiklicky. Probabilistic Concurrent Constraint Programming: Towards a fully abstract model. In L. Brim, J. Gruska, and J. Zlatuska, editors, *MFCS'98 – Mathematical Foundations of Computer Science*, volume 1450 of *Lecture Notes in Computer Science*, pages 446–455, Berlin – New York, August 1998. Springer Verlag.
11. Alessandra Di Pierro and Herbert Wiklicky. Concurrent Constraint Programming: Towards Probabilistic Abstract Interpretation. In M. Gabbrielli and F. Pfenning, editors, *Proceedings of PPDP'00 – Priciples and Practice of Declarative Programming*, pages 127–138, Monteéal, Canada, September 2000. ACM SIGPLAN, Association of Computing Machinery.
12. John W. Eaton. *Octave*. Boston, MA, 1997.
13. R. Giacobazzi and F. Ranzato. Completeness in abstract interpretation: A domain perspective. In M. Johnson, editor, *Proc. of the 6th International Conference on Algebraic Methodology and Software Technology (AMAST'97)*, volume 1349 of *Lecture Notes in Computer Science*, pages 231–245. Springer-Verlag, Berlin, 1997.
14. Neil D. Jones and Flemming Nielson. Abstract interpretation: A semantic-based tool for program analysis. In S.Abramsky, D. M. Gabbay, and T. S. E. Maibaum, editors, *Semantic Modelling*, volume 4 of *Handbook of Logic in Computer Science*, pages 527–636. Clarendon Press, Oxford, 1995.
15. Dexter Kozen. Semantics for probabilistic programs. *Journal of Computer and System Sciences*, 22:328–350, 1981.
16. Gerard J. Murphy. C^*-*Algebras and Operator Theory*. Academic Press, San Diego, 1990.
17. Flemming Nielson, Hanne Riis Nielson, and Chris Hankin. *Principles of Program Aanalysis*. Springer Verlag, Berlin – Heidelberg, 1999.
18. Viktor V. Prasolov. *Problems and Theorems in Linear Algebra*, volume 134 of *Translation of Mathematical Monographs*. American Mathematical Society, Providence, Rhode Island, 1994.
19. Walter Rudin. *Functional Analysis*. International Series in Pure and Applied Mathematics. McGraw-Hill, 1991. Second Edition.
20. N. Saheb-Djahromi. CPO's of measures for nondeterminism. *Theoretical Computer Science*, 12:19–37, 1980.

Specifying Prolog Trace Models with a Continuation Semantics

Erwan Jahier, Mireille Ducassé, and Olivier Ridoux

IRISA-INSA-IFSIC, Campus Universitaire de Beaulieu,
F-35042 RENNES Cedex - France
{jahier,ducasse,ridoux}@irisa.fr

Abstract. Byrd's box model is a fine-grained Prolog execution model that can be the basis of high-level debugging tools. In this article, we provide a formal specification of Byrd's box model, based on an already existing operational and denotational continuation semantics for Prolog with cut. We show how this specification can be extended to specify richer Prolog trace models. To be able to experiment with trace models, we translate these specifications into λProlog. This translation leads to a Prolog interpreter that performs execution traces. We have hence a formal framework to specify, prototype, and validate Prolog trace models.

1   Introduction

The most popular trace model for Prolog is Byrd's box model [9], a fine-grained Prolog execution model that provides a precise image of program executions. It is sometimes stated that it is too verbose to be used in debuggers. Whether Byrd's trace is a proper output format for an end-user may indeed be discussed. The Byrd trace however can, as we have shown for debugging [13] and monitoring [16], be the basis of higher level tools. In general, automated dynamic analysis needs an execution model to be based upon, and Byrd's box model is a good candidate for logic programming languages.

As detailed by Tobermann and Beckstein [30], many Prolog debugging systems [9,15,22,28] have quite different interpretations of what Byrd's box model is. It is not always clear whether these differences come from a misinterpretation of the original model or from a will to improve it. In this article we propose a formal specification of Byrd's box model. One can conjecture that a formal specification would avoid misinterpretations. Indeed, people would have the formal framework to prove that their model conforms to the specification. Furthermore, people enhancing the model would then be able to state precisely what the enhancements are. We also show how our specification can be extended to specify richer trace models, and how those specifications can be animated to give experimental insights about the specified models.

An operational semantics formally specifies the way a program is executed. Since a trace reflects the program execution, relying on an existing formal operational semantics to specify a trace is natural. Our formal specification of Byrd's

Kung-Kiu Lau (Ed.): LOPSTR 2000, LNCS 2042, pp. 165–181, 2001.

box model is based on the Prolog operational semantics given by Nicholson and Foo [24]. De Bruin and De Vink proposed a very similar semantics [11] at the same time. This semantics is simple, concise, and it captures very elegantly the cut predicate ('!') behavior. Moreover, this semantics is compositional. This is an important property to allow program properties proofs to be carried more easily; proofs are local and can be carried by case on the syntactic structure of the semantics.

We instrument this semantics in such a way that it specifies how to compute query answers as well as Byrd's execution traces associated to them. Another advantage of this semantics is that it can be directly translated into a λProlog program which leads to a Prolog interpreter. Whereas this interpreter is not an efficient implementation of a trace generator, it is a convenient way to validate the formal specification on a pragmatic basis. One can test the specification on simple Prolog programs to convince oneself that the generated trace is indeed what one would expect.

The contribution of this article is to give a formal specification of Byrd's box model, to show how this model can be extended, and thus to give a formal framework to specify trace models. We also show how to translate the specification into λProlog, which lets one easily prototype trace models.

In Section 2 we present the operational semantics for Prolog that we use in Section 3 to formally specify Byrd's box model. We also show how it can be translated into a λProlog program. We define several extensions of the model in Section 4. We discuss related work in Section 5 and conclude in Section 6.

2   An Operational Continuation Semantics for Prolog

Nicholson and Foo [24] define a continuation passing style (CPS) operational semantics for Prolog which captures very elegantly the cut behavior. In order to define an operational semantics for λProlog, Brisset and Ridoux [7] reformulate it by abstracting away the data flow to concentrate on the control flow. Since Byrd's box model is related to the control flow, the Prolog subset of this reformulation is a very good candidate to be the basis of Prolog trace model specifications. In the following, we briefly describe this semantics; more detailed descriptions can be found in [7] and [24].

Pettorossi and Proietti [25,27] also propose an operational semantics for Prolog, but it does not handle the cut. The direct style semantics proposed by Jones and Mycroft [17] as well as the one of Debray and Mishra [12] do handle the cut. But we believe that the semantics of Nicholson and Foo is more elegant because the search stack and the resolvent are not handled by explicit data-structures. This leaves open all kinds of actual representations of the search-stack and the resolvent.

2.1   Description of the Operational CPS Semantics

Figure 1 defines the Nicholson and Foo operational semantics for Prolog. We suppose that all the predicates are of arity 1; this is not a restriction as Prolog

$$unify \stackrel{1}{\equiv} \lambda t_1 t_2 \kappa \zeta \begin{cases} (\kappa \ \zeta) & \text{if } t_1 \text{ unifies with } t_2 \\ (\zeta) & \text{otherwise} \end{cases}$$

$$\mathcal{S}_{query} \stackrel{2}{\equiv} \lambda p X (\mathcal{S}_g[\![p(X)]\!] \ \lambda \zeta(\text{yes}.\zeta) \ \text{no.nil no.nil}) \quad \text{(top-level query)}$$

$$\mathcal{S}_c[\![C_1.C_2]\!] \stackrel{3}{\equiv} \lambda \varepsilon \kappa \xi \zeta (\mathcal{S}_c[\![C_1]\!] \ \varepsilon \ \kappa \ \xi \ (\mathcal{S}_c[\![C_2]\!] \ \varepsilon \ \kappa \ \xi \ \zeta)) \qquad \text{(sequence of clauses)}$$

$$\mathcal{S}_c[\![p(X)]\!] \stackrel{4}{\equiv} \lambda \varepsilon \kappa \xi \zeta (unify \ [\![X]\!] \ \varepsilon \ \kappa \ \zeta) \qquad \text{(clause without body)}$$

$$\mathcal{S}_c[\![p(X) \text{ :- } G]\!] \stackrel{5}{\equiv} \lambda \varepsilon \kappa \xi \zeta (unify \ [\![X]\!] \ \varepsilon \ \lambda \zeta'(\mathcal{S}_g[\![G]\!] \ \kappa \ \xi \ \zeta') \ \zeta) \qquad \text{(clause with body)}$$

$$\mathcal{S}_g[\![G_1, G_2]\!] \stackrel{6}{\equiv} \lambda \kappa \xi \zeta (\mathcal{S}_g[\![G_1]\!] \ \lambda \zeta'(\mathcal{S}_g[\![G_2]\!] \ \kappa \ \xi \ \zeta') \ \xi \ \zeta) \qquad \text{(conjunction of goals)}$$

$$\mathcal{S}_g[\![q(X)]\!] \stackrel{7}{\equiv} \lambda \kappa \xi \zeta (\mathcal{S}_c[\![cl(q)]\!] \ [\![X]\!] \ \kappa \ \zeta \ \zeta) \qquad \text{(atomic goal } (\neq \text{cut))}$$

$$\mathcal{S}_g[\![\ ! \ ]\!] \stackrel{8}{\equiv} \lambda \kappa \xi \zeta (\kappa \ \xi) \qquad \text{(cut)}$$

Fig. 1. An Operational Continuation Passing Style Semantics for Prolog

constructs can be used to deal with greater arities. We note $cl(p)$ the set of clauses defining the predicate p. Abstractions are written $\lambda x_1...x_n(E)$ where $x_1, ..., x_n$ are λ-variables and E is a λ-expression. The application of the λ-term t_1 to the λ-term t_2 is written $(t_1 \ t_2)$. Nested applications $((t_1 \ t_2) \ t_3)$ are written $(t_1 \ t_2 \ t_3)$. The semantic function $\lambda x(\mathcal{S}_c[\![x]\!])$ gives the semantics of a sequence of clauses; $\lambda x(\mathcal{S}_g[\![x]\!])$ gives the semantics of a goal; $\lambda x([\![x]\!])$ gives the semantics of a Prolog term. $\lambda x([\![x]\!])$ is not defined in this semantics (see [24] for such a definition), but it can be regarded as the identity function; this is the reason why we have given it no name (we could have called it $\lambda x(\mathcal{S}_t[\![x]\!])$).

Continuations denote code that remains to be executed. The success continuation, κ, is the code to be executed after a success; it controls the formation of proofs and can be thought of as the resolvent. The failure continuation, ζ, is the code to be executed after a failure and it can be thought of as the search stack. The cut failure continuation, ξ, is the code to be executed after a failure in a goal that occurs to the rigth of a cut. Actually, the cut failure continuation is initially simply a copy of the failure continuation (see the two ζ's in Equation 1.7[1]). The types of semantic functions of Figure 1 are given in Figure 2; f is the type of failure continuations, s is the type of success continuations, term is the type of Prolog terms, and pred denotes the type of predicate symbols.

Combinator $unify$ (Equation 1.1) takes two terms, as well as a success and a failure continuation. If the terms are unifiable, it outputs the success continuation. It is applied to the failure continuation so that the solutions contained in the failure continuation can be found if other solutions for the current goal are requested on backtracking. If the terms are not unifiable, $unify$ outputs the failure continuation.

Equation 1.2 tells how to translate a top level query (e.g., ?- p(X).). This equation excepted, the type of continuations is very general. The only constraints

---

[1] The convention we use is that Equation n.m refers to the mth equation of Figure n.

```
f = yes* no.            (a list of atoms yes and then an atom no)
s = (f → f).
unify: term → term → s → f → f.
S_query: pred → term → f.
S_c[[C]]: term → s → f → f → f.
S_g[[G]]: s → f → f → f.
```

Fig. 2. The types of semantic functions of Figure 1

are: (1) the cut failure and failure continuations should have the same type, since the former is a copy of the latter (see Equation 1.7); (2) success continuations are functions from failure continuations to failure continuations (see the definition of *unify*). Equation 1.2 further constrains failure continuations to be lists of yes and no. For example, according to the semantics of Figure 1, a query '$(S_{query}\ p\ X)$' that leads to two solutions produce the list 'yes.yes.no.nil'.

Equation 1.3 inductively gives the semantics of a sequence of clauses $C_1.C_2$ (coding the disjunction). The translation of the first part of the clause sequence, C_1, takes as arguments a term ε (the argument of the selected goal), the success continuation κ, and the cut failure continuation ξ of the whole conjunction. Its failure continuation is the translation of the second part of the sequence of clauses C_2. Indeed, if a solution is requested after the resolution of the first part of the clause sequence, the second one must be tried. Note that how a sequence of clauses is split un 2 subsequences C_1 and C_2 does not matter ; the result will be the same.

Equation 1.4 gives the semantics of a clause with an empty body. The argument of the clause head, $[[X]]$, is unified with the argument of the selected goal ε. Equation 1.5 gives the semantics of a clause with a non empty body. The argument of the clause head, $[[X]]$, is unified with the selected goal argument ε. The code to be executed if this unification succeeds is the translation of the body of the clause: $\lambda\zeta'(S_g[[G]]\ \kappa\ \xi\ \zeta')$. Otherwise, the failure continuation ζ is executed.

Equation 1.6 gives the semantics of non atomic goals. The left-hand part of the conjunction of goals takes as arguments the failure continuation ζ and the cut failure continuation ξ of the whole conjunction as second and third argument respectively. Its first argument (i.e., its success continuation) is the evaluation of the right-hand part of the conjunction of goals. Indeed, once the first conjunction has succeeded, the second one needs to be tried. As for sequenses of clauses, a clause body can be split into two subgoals arbitrarily. Equation 1.7 gives the semantics of an atomic goal. It is called the selected goal. Its semantics is obtained by applying the semantic function of the sequence of clauses that defines the predicate q (produced by S_c) to the argument of the goal $[[X]]$, and to both the success and the failure continuations. The cut failure continuation is initialized with the failure continuation for the current predicate; it will replace the failure continuation when a cut is encountered, removing in this way all the choice points that might have been created in Equation 1.5. Note that ξ is not used here, since the scope of a cut is local to a predicate. Equation 1.8 gives the semantic of the cut goal. When a cut is encountered, the failure continuation is replaced by the cut failure continuation; this is done by applying the success continuation to the cut failure one.

Contrary to usage, we write all λ-terms in their η-expanded form, for example, $\lambda\zeta'(\mathcal{S}_g[\![G]\!]\ \kappa\ \xi\ \zeta')$ instead of $(\mathcal{S}_g[\![G]\!]\ \kappa\ \xi)$. The reasons are multiple: using η-reduced form worries beginners who could believe that an argument is missing; the feasibility of η-reduction depends too much on a smart choice of parameter ordering; the different variants of the semantics that we propose are not equally η-reducible; and finally, adopting an η-expanded form makes the presentation more homogeneous. The only exception where we do not write λ-terms in their η-expanded form is when there is no application at all; for example, we write the success continuation κ, whereas its η-expanded form is $\lambda\zeta(\kappa\ \zeta)$.

2.2   Examples

We can derive from the semantic functions of Figure 1 the translation of predicates such as `true/1`, `false/1`, and `=/1` (which unifies two elements):

$$\mathcal{S}_g[\![true(arg())]\!] \equiv \lambda\kappa\xi\zeta(\kappa\ \zeta)$$
$$\mathcal{S}_g[\![false(arg())]\!] \equiv \lambda\kappa\xi\zeta(\zeta)$$
$$\mathcal{S}_g[\![\ =(arg(t_1,t_2))]\!] \equiv \lambda\kappa\xi\zeta(unify\ [\![t_1]\!]\ [\![t_2]\!]\ \kappa\ \zeta)$$

We use the term constructors `arg/0` and `arg/2` to deal with predicates of which arity is different from 1. These definitions directly result from the definition of *unify*. Another example is the clause '`p(f(X,Y)) :- X = Y.`' which is translated as follows:

$$\mathcal{S}_c[\![p(f(X,Y)) :- = (arg(X,Y))]\!] \equiv \lambda\epsilon\kappa\xi\zeta(unify\ [\![f(X,Y)]\!]\ \epsilon\ (unify\ [\![X]\!]\ [\![Y]\!]\ \kappa\ \zeta)\ \zeta)$$

3   A Formal Specification of Byrd's Box Model

In Byrd's box model, boxes model the program predicates, and arrows relate the different boxes through ports. The `call` port corresponds to the initial invocation of the predicate. The `exit` port corresponds to a successful return of the predicate. The `redo` port indicates that a subsequent goal has failed and that the system is backtracking to search for other solutions to the predicate. The `fail` port corresponds to an unsuccessful return of the predicate. *Events* are program points that correspond to those ports. In the rest of this section, we give a formal specification of this model. Then, we show how it is possible to animate the specification by a direct translation into λProlog.

3.1   A Formal Specification of Byrd's Box Model

The equations presented in the previous section specify the operational semantics for any query. In particular, they specify how the control flows from one predicate

$$unify \stackrel{1}{\equiv} \lambda t_1 t_2 \kappa \zeta \begin{cases} (\kappa\ \zeta) & \text{if } t_1 \text{ unifies with } t_2 \\ (\zeta) & \text{otherwise} \end{cases}$$

$$\mathcal{B}yrd_{query} \stackrel{2}{\equiv} \lambda pX(\mathcal{B}yrd_g[\![p(X)]\!]\ \lambda\zeta(\texttt{yes}.\zeta)\ \texttt{no.nil}\ \texttt{no.nil})$$

$$\mathcal{B}yrd_c[\![C_1.C_2]\!] \stackrel{3}{\equiv} \lambda\varepsilon\kappa\xi\zeta(\mathcal{B}yrd_c[\![C_1]\!]\ \varepsilon\ \kappa\ \xi\ (\mathcal{B}yrd_c[\![C_2]\!]\ \varepsilon\ \kappa\ \xi\ \zeta))$$
$$\mathcal{B}yrd_c[\![p(X)]\!] \stackrel{4}{\equiv} \lambda\varepsilon\kappa\xi\zeta(unify\ [\![X]\!]\ \varepsilon\ \kappa\ \zeta)$$
$$\mathcal{B}yrd_c[\![p(X) :\text{-} G]\!] \stackrel{5}{\equiv} \lambda\varepsilon\kappa\xi\zeta(unify\ [\![X]\!]\ \varepsilon\ \lambda\zeta'(\mathcal{B}yrd_g[\![G]\!]\ \kappa\ \xi\ \zeta')\ \zeta)$$

$$\mathcal{B}yrd_g[\![G_1, G_2]\!] \stackrel{6}{\equiv} \lambda\kappa\xi\zeta(\mathcal{B}yrd_g[\![G_1]\!]\ \lambda\zeta'(\mathcal{B}yrd_g[\![G_2]\!]\ \kappa\ \xi\ \zeta')\ \xi\ \zeta)$$
$$\mathcal{B}yrd_g[\![q(X)]\!] \stackrel{7}{\equiv} \lambda\kappa\xi\zeta(\texttt{<call},q(X)\texttt{>}.(\mathcal{B}yrd_c[\![cl(q)]\!]\ [\![X]\!]$$
$$\lambda\zeta'(\texttt{<exit},q(X)\texttt{>}.(\kappa\ \texttt{<redo},q(X)\texttt{>}.\zeta'))$$
$$\texttt{<fail},q(X)\texttt{>}.\zeta\ \texttt{<fail},q(X)\texttt{>}.\zeta))$$
$$\mathcal{B}yrd_g[\![!]\!] \stackrel{8}{\equiv} \lambda\kappa\xi\zeta(\texttt{<call,!>}.\texttt{<exit,!>}.(\kappa\ \texttt{<redo,!>}.\texttt{<fail,!>}.\xi))$$

Fig. 3. A CPS semantics that specifies the Byrd trace (Eq. 7 and 8 have been extended)

---

to another. In order to specify Byrd's box model, we extend this semantics in such a way that it does not only compute answers to queries, but also the Byrd's trace corresponding to their resolutions. We extend Figure 1 into Figure 3; Equations 1.7 and 1.8, which give the semantics of atomic goals, are extended with *execution events*. Events are pair of event attributes represented with the term constructor <_,_>; the first element of the pair is a port symbol, and the second one is a term containing the current goal. Note that events can (and will, in the next section) have more attributes.

The new semantics produces a sequence of events and query answers. The only type that changes in the equations is the type of the failure continuation that becomes: 'f = {<port,term>|yes}* no'. We insert a call event before each goal invocation. If the goal succeeds, its success continuation κ will be executed; therefore we insert an exit event just before κ. If another solution for that goal is requested on backtracking, the execution will search for another solution in the failure continuation ζ'; therefore we insert a redo event just before the continuation to which the success continuation is applied, i.e., just before ζ'. If the goal fails, its failure continuation ζ will be executed; hence we insert a fail event just before ζ.

Equation 1.8 specifies the semantics of the cut. Since the way the cut should be traced is not described in Byrd's original article [9], we handle it the same way as any other atomic goals, and we instrument Equation 1.8 in the same manner as Equation 1.7 to get Equation 3.8; we insert a call event before the goal invocation, an exit event before the goal success continuation κ, a fail event before the failure continuation ξ, and a redo event before the continuation to which the success continuation is applied.

3.2 Skipped and Traced Predicates

When tracing an execution, there are predicates, such as built-in and library predicates, that do not need to be traced. We call them *skipped predicates*. To handle them, we only need to replace in Equation 3.7 the function call $\mathcal{B}yrd_c$ by $\mathcal{S}_c$; then, events related to the detail of the resolution of such predicates do not appear in the trace.

3.3 Animation of the Specification by a Translation into λ Prolog

One of the advantages of the semantics of Figure 3 is that the language used to write it can be easily coded into any language that manipulates λ-terms. Hence, we can animate this formal specification and check that it corresponds to the informal specification of Byrd [9].

We translate the specification into λProlog [3,23]. λProlog is able to manipulate λ-terms and is well suited for meta-programming, as demonstrated by Miller and Nadathur [21]. In the following, we show how this semantics directly derives into a λProlog program which is a Prolog interpreter that produces the specified trace. The translation from Figure 1 or 3 to λProlog is purely syntactical. In order to transform functions into relations, we pass the result of each semantic function as an argument of its corresponding λProlog predicate. For example, Equation 3.2 '$\mathcal{B}yrd_{query} \equiv \lambda pX(\mathcal{B}yrd_g[\![p(X)]\!]\,\lambda\zeta(\text{yes}.\zeta)\,\text{no.nil no.nil})$' is translated into:

```
byrd_query Program Predicate X Result :-
    byrd_goal Program (app Predicate X) SemGoal,
    Result = (SemGoal (Z~[yes|Z]) [no] [no]).
```

The semantic function $\mathcal{B}yrd_{query}$ is translated by the predicate byrd_query/4. The principal syntactic difference between Prolog and λProlog is in the way terms and predicates are represented; the Prolog equivalent of 'app Predicate X' is 'app(Predicate, X)', where app is a term constructor, and Predicate as well as X are logical variables. The abstraction λx is translated by x\. Predicate byrd_query/4 takes a program name, a predicate name, and a term (the Prolog predicate argument) respectively as first, second and third argument. It outputs the result of the function in its fourth argument; this result is obtained by applying a success continuation (Z~[yes|Z]), a cut failure [no], and a failure continuation [no] to the result of byrd_goal/4, the λProlog version of $\lambda x(\mathcal{B}yrd_g[\![x]\!])$.

We give below the translation of semantic functions of Equation 1.7 and then the one of Equation 3.7 in order to illustrate how the event instrumentation is done in λProlog. '$\mathcal{S}_g[\![q(X)]\!] \equiv \lambda\kappa\xi\zeta(\mathcal{S}_c[\![cl(q)]\!]\,[\![X]\!]\,\kappa\,\zeta\,\zeta)$', which gives the Prolog semantics of an atomic goal different from cut, is translated as follows:

```
semprolog_goal Program (app Q X) Result :-
    \+(Q = cut),
    semprolog_term X SemX,
    clause Program Q ClauseQ,
    semprolog_clause Program ClauseQ SemQ,
    Result = K\XI\Z~(SemQ SemX K Z Z).
```

The predicates `semprolog_goal/3`, `semprolog_term/3`, and `semprolog_cl-ause/2` implement respectively the functions $\lambda x.(\mathcal{S}_g[\![x]\!])$, $\lambda x.([\![x]\!])$, and $\lambda x.(\mathcal{S}_c[\![x]\!])$. The predicate `clause/3` extracts from a Prolog program the sequence of clauses that defines a predicate. The higher-order term (`app Q X`) is a representation of a goal whose functor is `Q` and whose argument is `X`. The predicate `cut/0` is the cut of Prolog. Now we give the translation of the instrumented version of Equation 1.7, i.e., the translation of Equation 3.7. In order to instrument the semantics more easily, we make use of the macro facilities of Prolog/MALI [6] to define combinators:

```
#define CALL (p\e~ [(port_call p)|e])
```

This '`#define`' directive tells the Prolog/MALI pre-processor to replace in the program all the occurrences of 'CALL' by the λ-term $\lambda pe([(\texttt{port\_call } p)|e])$. (`port_call p`) is the λProlog representation of the event <`call`,p>. In the same way, we define combinators that ease the instrumentation of `exit`, `fail`, and `redo` ports. Then, we translate Equation 3.7 as follows:

```
byrd_goal Program (app Q X) Result :-
    \+(Q = cut),
    semprolog_term X SemX,
    clause Program Q ClauseQ,
    byrd_clause Program ClauseQ SemQ,
    Result = K\XI\Z~(CALL Q (SemQ SemX (Z2~(EXIT Q (K (REDO Q Z2))))
        (FAIL Q Z) (FAIL Q Z))).
```

```
p :- q, r.              q :- s.                q :- t.
r :- a, b.              a.                     s.
```
Fig. 4. The Prolog program example given by Byrd [9]

```
[<call,p>, <call,q>, <call,s>, <exit,s>, <exit,q>, <call,r>, <call,a>,
<exit,a>, <call,b>, <fail,b>, <redo,a>, <fail,a>, <fail,r>, <redo,q>,
<redo,s>, <fail,s>, <call,t>, <fail,t>, <fail,q>, <fail,p>, no]
```
Fig. 5. The trace produced by the program of Fig. 4 and the query '?- p.'

Figure 4 contains the Prolog program example given in the original article of Byrd [9]. This program and the query '$\mathcal{B}yrd_{query}\ p\ arg()$', once evaluated by the interpreter that results from the λProlog translation of Figure 2, produce the trace of Figure 5. We can observe that it is the same trace as in [9].

4   Extending Byrd's Box Model

In this section, we describe a few possible extensions of Byrd's box model. They are useful for understanding the control and data-flow of Prolog program executions, and they show the flexibility of the specification technique. For didactic purposes, each extension is described as an extension of the basic model of Figure 3. The extensions are then all combined in Figure 7.

4.1   Special Treatment for Deterministic Predicates

Byrd's original article is not explicit about the way the cut predicate should be traced. In Equation 3.8, we conservatively chose to treat the cut as any other predicate. However, since the cut always succeeds exactly once, the event sequence '<redo,!>.<fail,!>' is redundant; we can therefore remove it from the trace by replacing Equation 3.8 by: $\mathcal{B}yrd_g[\![!]\!] \equiv \lambda\kappa\xi\zeta(\texttt{<call,!>.<exit,!>}.(\kappa\ \xi))$.

Hence, the trace produced by the evaluation of a cut only consists of the event sequence: '<call,!>.<exit,!>'. We could do the same for all deterministic predicates, i.e., predicates that have exactly one solution.

4.2   A unify port

The unify port corresponds to events generated when the execution finds a clause whose head unifies with the current goal. This port gives the result of the unification of the current goal with the matching clause head. This port is very useful to understand the control and data flow of Prolog executions. For example, when the execution backtracks from a very deep branch of the SLD-tree, what one sees is a long sequence of redo events. A unify event means that a choice point leads to a successful unification between the current goal and a clause head. Therefore, we insert a unify event before the success continuation of Equations 3.4 and 3.5 which explicitly handle unification:

$$\mathcal{B}yrd_c[\![p(X)]\!] \stackrel{4}{\equiv} \lambda\varepsilon\kappa\xi\zeta(unify\ [\![X]\!]\ \varepsilon\ \lambda\zeta'(\texttt{<unify},p(X)\texttt{>}.(\kappa\ \zeta'))\ \zeta)$$
$$\mathcal{B}yrd_c[\![p(X)\text{:-}G]\!] \stackrel{5}{\equiv} \lambda\varepsilon\kappa\xi\zeta(unify\ [\![X]\!]\ \varepsilon\ \lambda\zeta'(\texttt{<unify},p(X)\texttt{>}.(\mathcal{B}yrd_g[\![G]\!]\ \kappa\ \xi\ \zeta')\ \zeta))$$

4.3   Clause Number in unify Events

We call *clause number of a predicate* p the rank of a clause in the definition of p. This information is useful at unify ports because it tells which clause successfully unifies with the current goal. This is particularly important in order to combine static and dynamic analyzes. To implement the clause number, we add a counter ι that we pass as argument of the failure continuation of $\mathcal{B}yrd_c$. We modify this continuation because it is through the failure continuation that the clause number is incremented; indeed, new clauses are tried when the current one fails to produce a solution. The type of the latter semantic function therefore becomes:

$$\mathcal{B}yrd_c[\![C]\!]: \texttt{term}\ \rightarrow\ \texttt{s}\ \rightarrow\ \texttt{f}\ \rightarrow\ \texttt{f'}\ \rightarrow\ \texttt{int}\ \rightarrow\ \texttt{f}.$$

where $\texttt{s} = (\texttt{f -> f})$, $\texttt{f} = \{\texttt{<port,term,int>}|\texttt{yes}\}^*$ no and $\texttt{f'} = \{\texttt{int}\ \rightarrow \{\texttt{<port,term,int>}|\texttt{yes}\}^*$ no. Note that we do not need to change the type of the cut failure continuation since when a cut is encountered, the remaining clauses (in the search stack) are not tried; thus the value of this counter is useless in that case. We do not change the types of the other semantic functions either, as the scope of this counter does not need to be larger than the sequence of clauses. The clause counter ι is initialized to 1 when $\mathcal{B}yrd_c[\![cl(q)]\!]$ is called (in Equation 3.7). We increment this counter every time another clause is tried, in the failure continuations of Equations 3.4 and 3.5. The new Equations 3.3, 3.4, 3.5 and 3.7 are given below. We have underlined what has changed; the other equations remain unchanged.

$$\mathcal{B}yrd_c[\![C_1.C_2]\!] \overset{3}{\equiv} \lambda\varepsilon\kappa\xi\zeta\underline{\iota}(\mathcal{B}yrd_c[\![C_1]\!] \ \varepsilon \ \kappa \ \xi \ \underline{(\lambda\iota'.(\mathcal{B}yrd_c[\![C_2]\!] \ \varepsilon \ \kappa \ \xi \ \zeta \ \iota'))\ \underline{\iota})}$$

$$\mathcal{B}yrd_c[\![p(X)]\!] \overset{4}{\equiv} \lambda\varepsilon\kappa\xi\zeta\underline{\iota}(unify \ [\![X]\!] \ \varepsilon \ \lambda\zeta'(\texttt{<unify},p(X),\underline{\iota}\texttt{>}.(\kappa \ \zeta')) \ (\zeta \ \underline{\iota+1}))$$

$$\mathcal{B}yrd_c[\![p(X)\text{:-}G]\!] \overset{5}{\equiv} \lambda\varepsilon\kappa\xi\zeta\underline{\iota}(unify \ [\![X]\!] \ \varepsilon$$
$$\lambda\zeta'(\texttt{<unify},p(X),\underline{\iota}\texttt{>}.(\mathcal{B}yrd_g[\![G]\!] \ \kappa \ \xi \ \zeta')) \ (\zeta \ \underline{\iota+1}))$$

$$\mathcal{B}yrd_g[\![q(X)]\!] \overset{7}{\equiv} \lambda\kappa\xi\zeta(\texttt{<call},q(X)\texttt{>}.(\mathcal{B}yrd_c[\![cl(q)]\!] \ [\![X]\!]$$
$$\lambda\zeta'(\texttt{<exit},q(X)\texttt{>}.(\kappa \ \texttt{<redo},q(X)\texttt{>}.\zeta'))$$
$$\texttt{<fail},q(X)\texttt{>}.\zeta \ (\lambda\iota \ \texttt{<fail},q(X)\texttt{>}.\zeta) \ \underline{1}))$$

Adding counters in continuations might seems difficult when one is not used to manipulate pure λ-terms. In order to get an intuition, it might help to think in terms of functions. For example, if x and y are 2 unbound variables, adding the argument y to a function $f(x)$ requires to replace all occurrences of $f(x)$ by $f(x,y)$; in λ-terms settings, it means to replace $\lambda x(f \ x)$ by $\lambda xy(f \ x \ y)$ (both are η-equivalent to f). When one applies the function to a bound value, e.g. $f(x,1)$, the corresponding λ-term version is $(\lambda xy(f \ x \ y) \ 1)$. E.g., in Equation 3, the value of the clause number ι is not known while splitting a conjunction of clauses because nothing says where the partition is made. Therefore, the clause number ι is not applied in Equation 3 $(\lambda\iota'(... \ \iota'))$, but in Equations 4 and 5, where the actual clause number is available; there, we apply the failure continuation to the incremented clause number, $(\zeta \ \iota + 1)$.

```
f = {<port,term,int>|yes}* no.
f' = (int → f).
s' = (f' → f').
unify: term → term → s' → f' → int → f.
Byrd_query: pred → term → int → f.
Byrd_c[[C]]: term → s' → f' → f' → int → f.
Byrd_g[[G]]: s' → f' → f' → int → f.
```

Fig. 6. The types of semantic functions of Figure 3 extended to handle the depth

4.4 Execution Depth

The *execution depth* of a goal is its number of ancestors plus 1 (i.e., the size of the call stack). The depth is important to be able to build proof trees or SLD-trees from the trace. In order to compute it within our semantics, we add a counter, δ, as argument of all the failure continuations. The types of the new semantic functions are given in Figure 6. The equations of Figure 2 are almost unchanged; the counter δ is simply added as argument of Equations 3.3 to 3.8. For example, Equations 3.3 and 3.6 become:

$$\mathcal{B}yrd_c[\![C_1.C_2]\!] \overset{3}{\equiv} \lambda\varepsilon\kappa\xi\zeta\underline{\delta}.(\mathcal{B}yrd_c[\![C_1]\!] \ \varepsilon \ \kappa \ \xi \ \underline{\lambda\delta'}(\mathcal{B}yrd_c[\![C_2]\!] \ \varepsilon \ \kappa \ \xi \ \zeta \ \underline{\delta}) \ \underline{\delta})$$
$$\mathcal{B}yrd_g[\![G_1,G_2]\!] \overset{6}{\equiv} \lambda\kappa\xi\zeta\underline{\delta}(\mathcal{B}yrd_g[\![G_1]\!] \ \lambda\zeta'\underline{\delta'}(\mathcal{B}yrd_g[\![G_2]\!] \ \kappa \ \xi \ \zeta' \ \underline{\delta}) \ \xi \ \zeta \ \underline{\delta})$$

The two parts of a clause sequence and the two parts of a goal sequence are passed the same depth. The only semantic functions that really change are Equations 3.2 and 3.7:

$$\mathcal{B}yrd_{query} \overset{2}{\equiv} \lambda pX(\mathcal{B}yrd_g[\![p(X)]\!] \ \lambda\zeta(\texttt{yes}.\zeta) \ \ \texttt{no.nil no.nil} \ \underline{1})$$
$$\mathcal{B}yrd_g[\![q(X)]\!] \overset{7}{\equiv} \lambda\kappa\xi\zeta\underline{\delta}(\texttt{<call},q(X),\delta\texttt{>}.(\mathcal{B}yrd_c[\![cl(q)]\!] \ [\![X]\!]$$
$$\lambda\zeta'(\texttt{<exit},q(X),\delta\texttt{>}.(\kappa \ \texttt{<redo},q(X),\delta\texttt{>}.\zeta'))$$
$$\texttt{<fail},q(X),\delta\texttt{>}.\zeta \ \ \texttt{<fail},q(X),\delta\texttt{>}.\zeta \ \ \underline{(\delta+1)}))$$

The depth counter is initialized to 1 in the top level function, namely, the function defined by Equation 3.2. This counter is incremented every time a call is made, i.e., in Equation 3.7.

4.5 Goal Invocation Number

We call *goal invocation number* or *call number* a counter that is incremented every time a goal is invoked. Unlike the depth, the goal invocation number always grows. This number is very useful to be able to distinguish different recursive calls. Contrary to the depth, the goal invocation number always grows.

To implement it, we do the same transformation as for the execution depth; we add a counter (ν) as argument of Equations 3.3 to 3.8. This counter is initialized in Equation 3.2 and incremented in Equations 3.7 and 3.8, where each atomic goal translation is made. The only difference with the depth is in Equations 3.3 and 3.6 because the value of the call number of the second sequence of clauses and of the second conjunction of goals respectively, is not known at that point. Therefore the goal number is not applied in Equations 3.3 and 3.6, but in Equation 3.7. Equation 3.7 is transformed in exactly the same way as for the execution depth. Equation 3.3 and 3.6 become:

$$\mathcal{B}yrd_c[\![C_1.C_2]\!] \overset{3}{\equiv} \lambda\varepsilon\kappa\xi\zeta\underline{\nu}(\mathcal{B}yrd_c[\![C_1]\!] \ \varepsilon \ \kappa \ \xi \ \underline{\lambda\nu'}.(\mathcal{B}yrd_c[\![C_2]\!] \ \varepsilon \ \kappa \ \xi \ \zeta \ \underline{\nu'}) \ \underline{\nu})$$
$$\mathcal{B}yrd_g[\![G_1,G_2]\!] \overset{6}{\equiv} \lambda\kappa\xi\zeta\underline{\nu}(\mathcal{B}yrd_g[\![G_1]\!] \ \lambda\zeta'\underline{\nu'}(\mathcal{B}yrd_g[\![G_2]\!] \ \kappa \ \xi \ \zeta' \ \underline{\nu'}) \ \xi \ \zeta \ \underline{\nu})$$

4.6   Chronological Event Number

The *chronological event number* is the rank of an event in the trace. It is different from the call number since it is is incremented for each event, and each goal generates several events. To implement this event counter, again we add an integer (γ) as argument of the failure continuation, and we increment it whenever an event is generated. The previous counters were incremented when applied to a continuation. This time, we want to increment a counter at program points where no application is made. The general method to modify the value of an argument of a λ-term is first to make the argument explicit by η-expansion, and then to apply the abstraction to the modified argument. For example, $\lambda\gamma(\zeta\ \gamma + 1)$ increments the first argument of failure continuation ζ. Thus, to increment γ each time an event is generated, we transform events such as <fail,$p(X)$,γ>.ζ into $\lambda\gamma'$(<fail,$p(X)$,γ>.(ζ ($\gamma' + 1$))). Equation 3.7 becomes:

$$\mathcal{B}yrd_g[\![q(X)]\!] \stackrel{7}{\equiv} \lambda\kappa\xi\zeta\underline{\gamma}(\text{CALL } q\ X\ \underline{\gamma}\ (\mathcal{B}yrd_c[\![cl(q)]\!]\ [\![X]\!]$$
$$\lambda\zeta'(\text{EXIT } q\ X\ \underline{\gamma}\ (\kappa\ (\text{REDO } q\ X\ \underline{\gamma}\ \zeta')))\ (\text{FAIL } q\ X\ \underline{\gamma}\ \zeta)\ (\text{FAIL } q\ X\ \underline{\gamma}\ \zeta)\ \underline{(\gamma + 1)}))$$

$$\text{CALL } \equiv\ \lambda t\gamma\zeta(\text{<call},t,\gamma\text{>}.\zeta)$$
$$\text{PORT } \equiv\ \lambda t\gamma\zeta\gamma'(\text{<port},t,\gamma'\text{>}.(\zeta\ (\gamma' + 1)))$$

where PORT is in {EXIT, FAIL, REDO}, and where port is in {exit, fail, redo}. The combinators CALL, EXIT, FAIL and REDO have been introduced to instrument the semantics in the λProlog program. We also use them here to reduce the opportunities of inconsistencies between the equations and their λProlog translations (which produce the intended traces).

4.7   Merging All the Extensions

The result of merging the previously described extensions is given in Figure 7. In the previous sections, we have described two kinds of extensions to the basic Byrd's box model; (1) an extension that adds a new event type (unify) and (2) extensions that add event attributes to the Byrd events. Merging all these extensions is systematic; one simply needs to apply the extensions in sequence. The only thing that remains to be done is to handle the new event attributes for the new event type unify. As a matter of fact, for the depth and goal numbers, we just need to use the depth and goal counters that were added in Equations 7.4 and 7.5 for the Byrd ports. The call number, however, requires a little extra work. Indeed, the value of ν, that is passed down in argument of $\lambda x(\mathcal{B}yrd_c[\![x]\!])$ in Equation 7.7, will change before we want to use it to generate the unify event in Equations 7.4 and 7.5. In order to get the right value for this counter, we need to make a copy, μ, of ν, and add it as an argument of $\lambda x(\mathcal{B}yrd_c[\![x]\!])$ (Equations 7.3, 7.4, 7.5). This new counter is initialized with the current value of ν in Equation 7.7.

Figure 8 gives an example of what those semantic functions output; it displays on two columns the output of the program of Figure 4 with the query '?- p.'. For each trace line, the first integer is the chronological event number, the second

$$unify \stackrel{1}{\equiv} \lambda t_1 t_2 \kappa \zeta \begin{cases} (\kappa \ \zeta) & \text{if } t_1 \text{ unifies with } t_2 \\ (\zeta) & \text{otherwise} \end{cases}$$

$$\mathcal{B}yrd_{query} \stackrel{2}{\equiv} \lambda p X (\mathcal{B}yrd_g[\![p(X)]\!] \ \lambda \zeta \nu \delta \gamma(\text{yes}.(\zeta \ \nu \ \delta \ \gamma)) \\ \lambda \nu \delta \gamma(\text{no.nil}) \ \lambda \nu \delta \gamma(\text{no.nil}) \ 1 \ 1 \ 1)$$

$$\mathcal{B}yrd_c[\![C_1.C_2]\!] \stackrel{3}{\equiv} \lambda \varepsilon \kappa \xi \zeta \iota \nu \mu \delta \gamma (\mathcal{B}yrd_c[\![C_1]\!] \ \varepsilon \ \kappa \ \xi \\ \lambda \iota' \nu' \delta' \gamma' (\mathcal{B}yrd_c[\![C_2]\!] \ \varepsilon \ \kappa \ \xi \ \zeta \ \iota' \ \nu' \ \mu \ \delta \ \gamma') \ \iota \ \nu \ \mu \ \delta \ \gamma)$$

$$\mathcal{B}yrd_c[\![p(X)]\!] \stackrel{4}{\equiv} \lambda \varepsilon \kappa \xi \zeta \iota \nu \mu \delta \gamma (unify \ [\![X]\!] \ \varepsilon \\ \lambda \zeta' (\text{UNIFY } p(X) \ \mu \ \delta \ \gamma \ \iota \ (\kappa \ \zeta'))) \ (\zeta \ \iota + 1) \ \nu \ \delta \ \gamma)$$

$$\mathcal{B}yrd_c[\![p(X) :\!\text{-} \ G]\!] \stackrel{5}{\equiv} \lambda \varepsilon \kappa \xi \zeta \iota \nu \mu \delta \gamma (unify \ [\![X]\!] \ \varepsilon \ \lambda \zeta' \nu' \delta' \gamma' (\text{UNIFY } p(X) \ \mu \ \delta \ \gamma \ \iota \\ (\mathcal{B}yrd_g[\![G]\!] \ \kappa \ \xi \ \zeta') \ \nu' \ \delta' \ \gamma') \ (\zeta \ \iota + 1) \ \nu \ \delta \ \gamma)$$

$$\mathcal{B}yrd_g[\![G_1, G_2]\!] \stackrel{6}{\equiv} \lambda \kappa \xi \zeta \nu \delta \gamma (\mathcal{B}yrd_g[\![G_1]\!] \\ \lambda \zeta' \nu' \delta' \gamma' (\mathcal{B}yrd_g[\![G_2]\!] \ \kappa \ \xi \ \zeta' \ \nu' \ \delta' \ \gamma') \ \xi \ \zeta \ \nu \ \delta \ \gamma)$$

$$\mathcal{B}yrd_g[\![q(X)]\!] \stackrel{7}{\equiv} \lambda \kappa \xi \zeta \nu \delta \gamma (\text{CALL } q(X) \ \gamma \ (\mathcal{B}yrd_c[\![cl(q)]\!] \ [\![X]\!] \\ \lambda \zeta' (\text{EXIT } q(X) \ \nu \ \delta \ \gamma \ (\kappa \ (\text{REDO } q(X) \ \nu \ \delta \ \gamma \ \zeta'))) \\ (\text{FAIL } q(X) \ \nu \ \delta \ \gamma \ \zeta) \ (\lambda \iota \ (\text{FAIL } q(X) \ \nu \ \delta \ \gamma \ \zeta)) \\ 1 \ (\nu + 1) \ \nu \ (\delta + 1) \ (\gamma + 1))$$

$$\mathcal{B}yrd_g[\![\ ! \ ]\!] \stackrel{8}{\equiv} \lambda \kappa \xi \zeta \nu \delta \gamma (\text{CALL } ! \ \nu \ \delta \ \gamma \ ((\text{EXIT } ! \ \nu \ \delta \ \gamma \ (\kappa \ \xi)) \ (\nu + 1) \ \delta \ (\gamma + 1)))$$

$\text{CALL} \equiv \lambda t \nu \delta \gamma \zeta (\text{<call}, t, \nu, \delta, \gamma \text{>}.\zeta)$

$\text{UNIFY} \equiv \lambda t \nu \delta \gamma \iota \zeta \nu' \delta' \gamma' (\text{<unify}, t, \nu, \delta - 1, \gamma', \iota \text{>}.(\zeta \ \nu' \ \delta' \ (\gamma' + 1)))$

$\text{PORT} \equiv \lambda t \nu \delta \gamma \zeta \nu' \delta' \gamma' (\text{<port}, t, \nu, \delta, \gamma' \text{>}.(\zeta \ \nu' \ \delta' \ (\gamma' + 1))),$

where $\text{PORT} = \text{EXIT}, \text{FAIL}, \text{REDO}; \text{port} = \text{exit}, \text{fail}, \text{redo}.$

Fig. 7. A CPS semantics that specifies an extended Byrd trace. κ = success continuation, $\{\zeta, \ \xi\}$ = failure continuations, ι = clause number, $\{\nu, \ \mu\}$ = goal invocation number, δ = execution depth, γ = chronological event number

one is the call number, and the last one is the execution depth; then come the port and the goal (γ: ν [δ] port goal).

5 Related Work

5.1 Using Natural Semantics and Structured Operational Semantics

Structured operational semantics (SOS) [26] describe in terms of a transition system the way expressions are evaluated. Bernstein and Stark [4] propose to base the definition of debuggers on such semantics. They define a simple functional programming language with a SOS. The transition rules are extended to specify the behavior of the debugger. Actually, these new rules are copies of the semantics rules extended with a debugging context. This debugging context

```
 1:  1 [1] call  p              14: 6 [3] call  b
 2:  1 [1] unify p (clause 1)   15: 6 [3] fail  b
 3:  2 [2] call  q              16: 5 [3] redo  a
 4:  2 [2] unify q (clause 1)   17: 5 [3] fail  a
 5:  3 [3] call  s              18: 4 [2] fail  r
 6:  3 [3] unify s (clause 1)   19: 2 [2] redo  q
 7:  3 [3] exit  s              20: 3 [3] redo  s
 8:  2 [2] exit  q              21: 3 [3] fail  s
 9:  4 [2] call  r              22: 2 [2] unify q (clause 2)
10:  4 [2] unify r (clause 1)   23: 7 [3] call  t
11:  5 [3] call  a              24: 7 [3] fail  t
12:  5 [3] unify a (clause 1)   25: 2 [2] fail  q
13:  5 [3] exit  a              26: 1 [1] fail  p
                               no (more) solution.
```

Fig. 8. Output of the semantics of Fig. 7 with the program of Fig. 4 and the query '?-p.'

contains the information that lets the user see (or not) the details of the evaluation for every sub-expression of an expression. Berry [5] and Da Silva [29] have a similar approach using natural semantics [18]. Natural semantics is similar to SOS, except that it abstracts away operational details that SOS describe. With natural semantics, each program statement is described in one step, whereas it can be defined by several steps with a SOS.

5.2   Deriving Programming Environments

PSG [2] is a tool that aims at automating the development of language-dependent programming environments. Bahlke and al. [1] show how to derive instrumented interpreters which PSG. These interpreters can then be used as debuggers. This automation is based on a denotational semantics. PSG also uses a grammar for the language that allows PSG to manipulate the language expressions as syntax trees. The nodes of the syntax tree are the potential event sites of the debugger. The denotational semantics is used to navigate in the tree to simulate the program execution.

5.3   Other Debugging Systems Based on Denotational Semantics

Kishon et al. [19,20] use a denotational CPS semantics to formally define monitors for functional programming languages. The kind of monitors they define are profilers, debuggers, and statistic collectors. From the operational semantics, a formal description of the monitor, and a program, they derive an instrumented executable file that performs the specified monitoring activity. Then, they use partial evaluation to make their monitors reasonably efficient. Their approach is similar to the one of Consel and Khoo [10], that use the same kind of semantics together with partial evaluation to derive Prolog compilers.

5.4 How Do We Compare with Those Systems

In the systems described above, even if the semantics style and the target language are different, the use of a formal operational semantics is similar to what we do. The focus, however, is not the same. They all aim at implementing real debuggers whereas we, more modestly, only try to formally specify them. Then, we provide means to help people to check experimentally that their implementation is correct w.r.t. to the specification. It should even be possible to prove the correction of the implementation formally, for example, when the implementation of the tracer is done by a source program transformation. We plan to do that with the Prolog tracer implementation described in [14]. Once the tracer is validated, we can safely base dynamic analyzes on it, as we have done for debugging [13] or monitoring [16].

There is no evidence we are aware of that deriving compilers from an operational semantics results in effective and performant systems. The consequence is that in general, users need to use a compiler together with the debugger which has been derived automatically. Dealing with two distinct systems to debug and to compile is not desirable. Indeed, as noted by Brooks et al. [8], firstly, some errors only occur (or do not occur) in presence of optimizations. Some programs can only be executed in their optimized form because of time and memory constraints; when searching for "hot spots", it is better to do it with the optimized program as lots of instructions can be optimized away. And finally, sometimes, the error comes from the optimizations themselves.

6 Conclusion

In this article, we have given a formal specification of Byrd's box model based on an existing denotational and operational semantics for Prolog with cut. We have shown how this specification can be extended to describe richer trace models. We have also shown how these specifications can be executed by a direct translation into λProlog, leading to a Prolog interpreter that generates execution traces. This interpreter can be used to experiment with various trace models and therefore to validate experimentally the different event specifications. Hence, we have a formal framework to specify and prototype trace models. This interpreter can also be used to experimentally check that a given tracer is correct w.r.t. a specification. This work therefore also constitutes a framework to validate tracers implementation with respect to a trace model specification.

Acknowledgments

We thank the anonymous referees for their fruitful comments.

References

1. R. Bahlke, B. Moritz, and G. Snelting. A generator for language-specific debugging systems. *ACM SIGPLAN Notices*, 22(7):92–101, 1987.

2. R. Bahlke and G. Snelting. The PSG system: From formal language definition to interactive programming environments. *ACM Transactions on Programming Languages and Systems*, 8(4):547–576, 1986.

3. C. Belleannée, P. Brisset, and O. Ridoux. A pragmatic reconstruction of λProlog. *Journal of Logic Programming*, 41(1):67–102, 1999.

4. K. L. Bernstein and E. W. Stark. Operational semantics of a focusing debugger. In ENCS, editor, *11th Conf. on the Mathematical Foundations of Programming Semantics*, 1995.

5. D. Berry. *Generating program animators from programming language semantics.* PhD thesis, University of Edinburgh, 1991.

6. P. Brisset and O. Ridoux. The compilation of λProlog and its execution with MALI. PI 687, IRISA, 1992.

7. P. Brisset and O. Ridoux. Continuations in λProlog. In David S. Warren, editor, *Tenth Int. Conf. Logic Programming*, pages 27–43. The MIT Press, 1993.

8. G. Brooks, G. J. Hansen, and S. Simmons. A new approach to debugging optimized code. In *SIGPLAN '92 Conf. on Programming Language Design and Implementation*, pages 1–11, 1992.

9. L. Byrd. Understanding the control flow of Prolog programs. In S.-A. Tärnlund, editor, *Logic Programming Workshop*, 1980.

10. C. Consel and S. C. Khoo. Semantics-directed generation of a Prolog compiler. In J. Maluszynski and M. Wirsing, editors, *3rd Int. Symp. on Programming Language Implementation and Logic Programming*, volume 528 of *LNCS*, pages 135–146. Springer-Verlag, 1991.

11. A. de Bruin and E. P. de Vink. Continuation semantics for Prolog with cut. In *TAPSOFT'89: Int. Joint Conf. on Theory and Practice of Software Development*, LNCS. Springer-Verlag, 1989.

12. S. K. Debray and P. Mishra. Denotational and operational semantics for Prolog. *Journal of Logic Programming*, 5:61–91, 1988.

13. M. Ducassé. Opium: An extendable trace analyser for Prolog. *Journal of Logic programming*, 39:177–223, 1999. Special issue on Synthesis, Transformation and Analysis of Logic Programs, A. Bossi and Y. Deville (eds).

14. M. Ducassé and J. Noyé. Tracing Prolog programs by source instrumentation is efficient enough. *Journal of Logic Programming*, 43(2), 2000. Tech. Notes.

15. M. Eisenstadt. A powerful Prolog trace package. In *6th European Conf. on Artificial Intelligence*. North-Holland, 1984.

16. E. Jahier and M. Ducassé. A generic approach to monitor program executions. In D. De Schreye, editor, *Int. Conf. on Logic Programming*, pages 139–153. MIT Press, 1999.

17. N. D. Jones and A. Mycroft. Stepwise development of operational and denotational semantics for Prolog. In *Int. Symp. Logic Programming*, pages 281–288. IEEE, Computer Society Press, 1984.

18. G. Kahn. Natural semantics. In *Symp. on Theoretical Aspects of Computer Science*, volume 247 of *LNCS*. Springer-Verlag, 1987. The paper is also available as INRIA Report 601, February, 1987.

19. A. Kishon and P. Hudak. Semantics directed program execution monitoring. *Journal of Functional Programming*, 5(4):501–547, 1995.

20. A. Kishon, P. Hudak, and C. Consel. Monitoring semantics: a formal framework for specifying, implementing and reasoning about execution monitors. *ACM Sigplan Notices*, 26(6):338–352, 1991.

21. D. Miller and G. Nadathur. A logic programming approach to manipulating formulas and programs. In *Fifth Int. Conf. and Symp. Logic Programming*. IEEE, Computer Society Press, 1987.

22. S. Moroshita and M. Numao. Prolog computation model BPM and its debugger PROEDIT2. In *5th Int. Conf. Logic Programming*, pages 147–158. Springer-Verlag, 1986.

23. G. Nadathur and D. A. Miller. An overview of λProlog. In R. A. Kowalski and K. A. Bowen, editors, *Joint Int. Conf. and Symp. Logic Programming*, pages 810–827. MIT Press, 1988.

24. T. Nicholson and N. Foo. A denotational semantics for Prolog. *ACM Transactions on Programming Languages and Systems*, 11(4):650–665, 1989.

25. A. Pettorossi and M. Proietti. Transformation of logic programs: Foundations and techniques. *Journal of Logic Programming*, 19 & 20:261–320, 1994.

26. G. D. Plotkin. A structural approach to operational semantics. Technical Report DAIMI FN-19, Computer Science Department, Aarhus University, 1981.

27. M. Proietti and A. Pettorossi. Semantics preserving transformation rules for Prolog. In *Symp. on Partial Evaluation and Semantics-Based Program Manipulation*, pages 274–284. ACM Press, 1991. Sigplan Notices 26:9.

28. A. Schleiermacher and J. F. H. Winkler. The implementation of ProTest, a Prolog Debugger for a refined box model. *Software Practice and Experience*, 20, 1990.

29. F. Q. B. Da Silva. *Correctness Proofs of Compilers and Debuggers: an Approach Based on Structural Operational Semantics*. PhD thesis, Univ. of Edinburgh, 1991.

30. G. Tobermann and C. Beckstein. What's in a trace: The box model revisited. In Peter Fritzon, editor, *AADEBUG*, volume 749 of *LNCS*. Springer-Verlag, 1993.

Author Index

Lecture Notes in Computer Science